COLONIALISM, DEVELOPMENT AND INDEPENDENCE

COLONIALISM, DEVELOPMENT AND INDEPENDENCE

The case of the Melanesian islands in the South Pacific

H. C. BROOKFIELD

Professor of Geography, and Research Associate in the Centre for Developing-Area Studies, McGill University, Montreal, Quebec

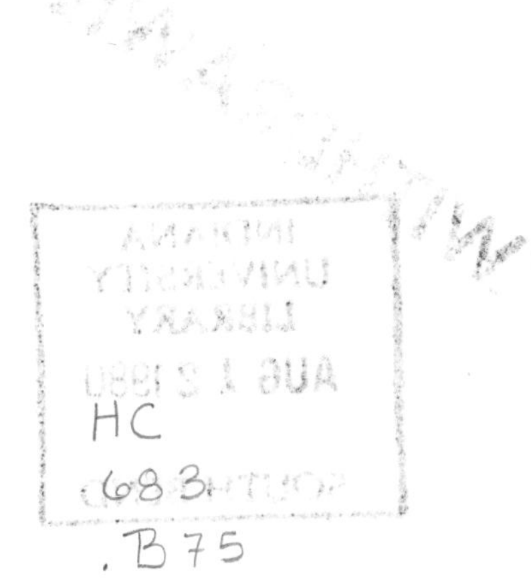

CAMBRIDGE

AT THE UNIVERSITY PRESS 1972

Published by the Syndics of the Cambridge University Press
Bentley House, 200 Euston Road, London NW1 2DB
American Branch: 32 East 57th Street, New York, N.Y. 10022

Library of Congress Catalogue Card Number: 72-75305

ISBN: 0 521 08590 X

Printed in Great Britain
at the University Printing House, Cambridge
(Brooke Crutchley, University Printer)

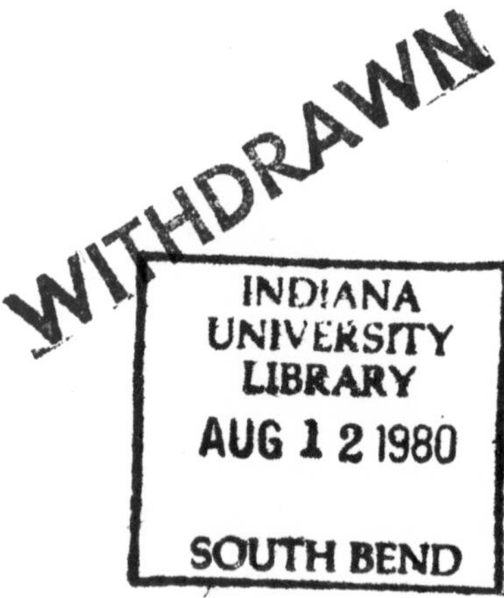

CONTENTS

List of figures *page* vii

Preface ix

Note on conventions xv

1 ON COLONIALISM AND DEVELOPMENT 1

The nature of 'colonialism' and 'independence'; society and economy under colonialism; production for use; the supply of effort and risk-taking in peasant societies; behaviour in the invading system; structure and behaviour in a mixed economy; the stages of colonialism; references and sources

2 COLONIAL BEGINNINGS 20

The invading system and the residentiary complex at contact; fatal impact?; the entry of the invading colonial system; the miners; references and sources

3 DIFFUSION AND ESTABLISHMENT 30

The labour trade; islanders, convicts and Asians in New Caledonia; the West Indian model in Fiji; land at a shilling an acre; the rôle of capital in the establishment period; the burden of white man's government; on being colonized; references and sources

4 HIGH NOON: MELANESIA IN A WHITE MAN'S WORLD 48

Firm establishment of export staples in Fiji and New Caledonia; the reluctant hegemony of copra; government, infrastructure and the growth of towns; references and sources

5 TREMORS FROM FARAWAY CONVULSIONS – 1905–1920 58

Termination of the Fiji contract labour supply; the entry of Australia and Japan; Lenin, Wilson and anti-colonialism; the beginnings of economic disaster; references and sources

6 THE ILLS OF MERCANTILISM *page* 65

The ascendancy of Sydney; a French national economy in the New Hebrides; backwash of mercantilism; references and sources

7 HARD TIMES AND NEW BEGINNINGS 77

Readjustment in the colonial commercial system; the growth of government intervention in the economy; some consequences of the collapse of currencies; discovery and penetration of a new colonial frontier; references and sources

8 TRAUMA – 1940–1946 88

Detachment from the metropoles; the Japanese irruption; the reconquest of Melanesia; the Melanesian experience of war; the legacy of the armies; references and sources

9 THE HASLUCK PERIOD AND THE NEW COLONIALISM 98

Uniform development in Australian New Guinea; equity vs. efficiency elsewhere in Melanesia; the strategy of post-war development; the end of gradualism; references and sources

10 THE ADVANCE TOWARD POLITICAL INDEPENDENCE 110

The colonial administrative systems compared; grass-roots democracy; the advances in national constitutions; regionalism; the sanctity of colonial boundaries; references and sources

11 THE DEEPENING COMMERCIAL COLONIZATION OF MELANESIA 127

A set of small, open, satellite economies; a comparison of investment by fields of enterprise; investment, growth and development; size and dependency; references and sources

12 THE FACE OF PLURALISM IN MELANESIA 146

Masters, exploiters, newcomers, civilized men – the Europeans; Indo-Fijians and Asians; Melanesians in a pluralistic relation; pluralism in the towns; pluralism in politics; references and sources

13 MELANESIAN REACTION 159

The 'cargo cults'; Melanesian economic activity and motivation; economic protest and political protest; unwillingly to independence?; references and sources

14 A VIEW OF THE THIRD WORLD *page* 178

The economic dimension; radical economic solutions; the political dimension; the strategic dimension; references and sources

15 PERILS AND PROSPECTS 192

Education and the manpower problem; the channels of public information; how to run a country; an island is not a world; toward the night of the generals?; references and sources

Epilogue TOWARD AN UNDERSTANDING OF COLONIALISM 202

References and sources

Statistical appendix 207

List of references 209

Index 219

FIGURES

1 Melanesia *page* 2

2 The region about 1905, with detail of German New Guinea 59

3 Variation of average price of smoke-dried copra 78

4 The impact of war, 1942–5 92

5 Colonial administrative systems 112

To those who were
friends in need

PREFACE

On my first day in the Third World, in Nairobi in 1952, I bought a small and insightful book entitled *Attitude to Africa* (Lewis *et al.*, 1951). The book was aimed at a British public whose government at that time had responsibility for a huge African population, and it had the object of presenting a contemporary view of African problems and of outlining a policy for development leading to decolonization. Since that far-off day the British flag has been pulled down all over Africa, yet the problems of arriving at an understanding relationship between metropole and former colony remain alive, and much of what was written in 1951 remains surprisingly valid and relevant in 1971. This is because the 'metropole–periphery' relationship is not extinguished by the lowering of a flag; the same basic problems have continued beyond political independence, with changes, but none the less recognizable. It is the rules of the game that have changed, but the game itself continues.

I stayed only three years in Africa. Most of my experience of the Third World has been in the islands of the southwest Pacific, where I spent much time during the years from 1957 to 1969. I worked there from the Australian National University as a geographer, at first on detailed studies of land evaluation, allocation and use in a small area of inland New Guinea, later also on questions of resource use and development over a wider sweep from West Irian to Fiji. Recently I published an attempt, within my own discipline, to generalize over this region (Brookfield with Hart, 1971). But few social scientists who live and work in the Third World find it possible to accept disciplinary bounds to their interests. For one thing, something like the old nineteenth-century pattern of free cross-fertilization between disciplines studying closely related problems persists among workers in these countries, and more than this the transformations, conflicts and reorientations taking place are part of the environment within which they work, whether or not they adopt firm 'attitudes' toward the problems inherent in a colonial relationship. And if they are foreigners, as so many are, both the logistic and ethical problems of social science research are sharpened in such a way as almost to enforce consideration of the wider issues.

The expatriate social scientist in the Third World faces a problem of personal ethics more clearly defined than that which confronts academics who research within their own society or culture. Few would question the value of an outside view, but many would and do demand some demonstrable feedback to the people studied, and charge that the conduct of research is but an academic dimension of colonialism. Academics are a privileged breed. We demand, and need, the rights of independent choice of inquiry, and free expression. Such privileges should carry responsibilities, and among these the duty to inform of our findings is paramount. Some would argue that there are duties beyond the research, and that the necessity to disseminate information should be accompanied by an option to persuade. This is a tricky question, one that each individual must resolve according to his own conscience and motivation. My own view is that no one who is not asked his opinion should offer it on the basis of only a limited experience, but that the right and duty to express views on public issues grow with time, and after a decade or more become compelling.

The genesis of the present book lay in historical chapters written for the earlier work, and excised following a major change in the plan of writing. The chapters lay untouched for almost two years, and when I turned to them again I found the need to express much that has been on my mind for a long time, sharpened by distance and by newer experiences in the Caribbean. The historical material no longer has a central place and is greatly reduced in scope and content. Basically, I still write as a geographer who is seeking to interpret the temporal processes that have created and transformed spatial patterns. The spatial patterns themselves are hardly discussed at all, however, and I range – dangerously – over a number of disciplines in a manner that is certain to earn me criticism. But generalization over so wide a disciplinary span is unavoidable if an explanation of the colonial process and its converse are to be attained.

I must then apologize in advance to my colleagues in other fields, many of whom I quote, but of whose work I reveal an imperfect knowledge. I write not so much as a geographer, but rather as a social scientist who is also an observer of contemporary trends. The method is to interpret the colonial experience of one area of the world against the background of wider events that have impinged on this region as on others, and then to analyse present problems and prospects from within, but in the same wider context. But I cannot pretend that the analysis is always objective, or 'scientific': in important measure, this book is the personal interpretation of one who has lived through the years of late colonialism, independence and neo-colonialism from close to, and sometimes within, the action.

The theme of this book is set out in the first chapter, where it is argued that the terms 'colonialism' and 'independence' have meanings much deeper and wider than the narrow political sense with which they are usually endowed. I see them as opposing drives which persist throughout the whole period of interaction between local forces and invading forces from without. Both are revolutionary in intent, if not always in achievement. Western colonialism has been revolutionary in that it has sought, and still seeks, to transform indigenous or 'residentiary' societies and economies so as to link them to a world-wide system dominated from without. It may not be fashionable to describe the agents of Western colonialism as revolutionaries, but this is what they were and are in terms of their designs. Independence, taken as a continuing movement, is revolutionary in a more recognizable sense: it is a drive to retain or take local control of the management of society and economy, and hence to reverse the trend toward a dependent condition inherent in colonialism. Neither force can be defined solely by political status; the conflict persists from the initial penetration by colonial forces until a true independence, political, economic and cultural, is achieved.

This use of terms may cause some difficulty, and it requires me to distinguish 'political colonialism' and 'political independence' wherever the more normal meaning of these terms is intended. But because conceptualization of the colonial experience in these terms is alien to metropolitan thought in Western countries, the languages lack suitable expressions to cover my meaning. Westerners like to think of colonialism as past, and independence as achieved by the lowering of the metropolitan flag. I suspect that readers in the Third World may understand my meaning more readily: they often speak in this sense of their relationship with the metropoles, and use these terms on occasion in the way that I do here.

I draw my case material from a group of islands in the tropical southwest Pacific having a combined land area about equal to that of Pakistan, but with a population slightly under four millions. Following current as well as historical practice, I call this group of islands Melanesia, and include within it all of New Guinea, east and west, the Solomon Islands and New Hebrides, and also New Caledonia and Fiji. Even though I adhere to tradition going back to 1830, some would disagree with me in gathering Fiji within this ethnic collective, maintaining that Polynesian influence and a different contact history should separate this group from its western neighbours. I would argue that on the basis of its modern history, New Caledonia is more clearly to be separated, but essentially the region is for me one of convenience. Inclusion of New Caledonia and Fiji greatly widens the available variations in colonial experience, for both these territories have undergone massive alien immigration which has been absent elsewhere. I sought a group of territories which would include in its history as much of the world range of types of colonialism as I could muster, while remaining small enough to study and compare in depth. I lack some important elements, including the presence of indigenous states that were overwhelmed from without, and also slavery – though not indenture. My whole region has no colonial experience earlier than the beginning of the nineteenth century. Also there are some unusual features in modern times in that what I call 'late colonialism' was unusually prolonged in this area. Yet much of what has happened in these islands, and is now happening, has taken place also in other parts of the colonial world, and reactions too have been similar. Although no part of the Third World can stand simply as exemplar for all others, the common elements are many and it has been my object to emphasize them.

My aim has been to extract the meaning of the story, rather than present it in exhaustive detail. Removal from Melanesia by half a world has made this easier, for Simon Bolivar is reputed to have said that if one is to understand men and revolutions one must observe them from close at hand, but judge them only from far away. Even so, I still find myself mentally in these varied and beautiful islands as I write, and a sense of continuing involvement colours interpretation. Detachment is never wholly attainable, however desirable it might be. Yet I do not regret this, for a measure of dual loyalty is perhaps essential if outsiders are to participate effectively in the study of the Third World. But there is a corollary which I hope I have also observed: loyalty must remain dual if any sort of balance is to be approached, and undue partisanship avoided.

ACKNOWLEDGEMENTS

Though I have a debt to many people, a full list of acknowledgements would hardly be in order in a book of this nature. More than on my library research, I rest heavily on many years of close contact with Melanesians, with Europeans at work in Melanesia, with colleagues and students in the Australian National University and more recently at McGill, and with a range of others in public and private life in many lands. However, none of them bears any responsibility for what I have done here with their work, ideas and conversation. With the exception of my brief return visits in 1970 and 1971, which were incidental to other business, all field work was supported directly by the Australian National University, and a particular debt is due to Sir John Crawford and O. H. K. Spate who, as my immediate superiors, gave me unstinted encouragement to follow my own bent during many years of active work. O. H. K. Spate and J. W. Davidson also offered valuable criticism of lengthy first drafts of some of the earlier chapters. An especial word of gratitude is due to my research assistant in Canberra from 1964 to 1969, Mrs Doreen Hart, who collected and interpreted much of the historical data, especially on economic matters, and will be sorry to see it so lightly used. In Montreal, I am very appreciative of the unrestrictive support of McGill University and especially its Centre for Developing-Area Studies, where the final draft of the book was written, and patiently typed by Miss Caroline Stephens. And last, but by no means least, thanks are due to my most constant support and critic, Muriel, who is first among the treasured band to whom this book is dedicated.

Montreal, Quebec
September 1971

H. C. BROOKFIELD

NOTE ON CONVENTIONS

The territories of Melanesia have been under the control of six metropolitan governments, and two other powers – Japan and the United States – intruded during a brief but critical period in the 1940s. Where island groups are concerned I use the normally accepted geographical names without attempt at precise definition. The western half of New Guinea was part of the Nederlands Indië until 1949, then Nederlands Nieuw-Guinea, later Papua Barat, until 1962. It is now the Indonesian Province (Daerah) of Irian Barat. I call it West New Guinea to 1962, thereafter West Irian. The eastern part was initially divided between Britain and Germany in 1883, then administered by Australia in part as a direct colony (legally a Territory of the Commonwealth of Australia, as Australians insist), in part as a mandated territory under the League of Nations, and is now under unified administration as the Territory of Papua and New Guinea. The whole was renamed Papua New Guinea in 1971, but this may be only an interim change. I call the whole Australian New Guinea throughout this book, using the name Papua for the south-eastern portion, while the northeastern portion is termed German New Guinea to 1919, thereafter the mandated territory of New Guinea, or the trust territory. The British Solomon Islands Protectorate is usually the Solomon Islands, and the Anglo-French Condominium of the New Hebrides usually the New Hebrides. The French Overseas Territory of La Nouvelle-Calédonie et Dépendances is usually simply New Caledonia. The Colony of Fiji became the Dominion of Fiji in 1970; usually it is simply Fiji here, but sometimes 'the colony', being in strict constitutional terms the only such in the region. District and place names are given in the normal anglicized form, except within New Caledonia. Further changes in territorial and place names are likely to occur within the next few years.

All quotations are given in English, translations being by the writer except where otherwise stated.

Comparability demands standardization of measures, and the metric system is adopted except where the context would create absurdities. Currencies are given in Australian dollars for all dates since the mid-1930s; before this date they are given in pounds sterling (presented in decimalized form). Values during the inter-war period are commonly given in both currencies. The change in the basis of exchange rates in the region in the early 1930s is explained in Chapter 7, p. 83. Changes in exchange rates in 1967 hardly impinge on this book, and the 1971 changes are subsequent to any of the data presented.

In an effort to simplify presentation, I have shed a large part of the heavy referencing beloved of academics, and normal in my own writing. Most of my documentation has already been presented elsewhere, by myself or by others whose works are cited. Except in areas where documentation is particularly necessary, or has not been published elsewhere, only principal sources are given, grouped together in sections at the end of each chapter which are, in essence, bibliographic footnotes. I have also offered a rather large number of generalizations without the full supporting evidence, presentation of which would have made this a very different sort of book.

CHAPTER 1

ON COLONIALISM AND DEVELOPMENT

The greater part of Melanesia is now approaching the end of its period under direct political control from abroad. Fiji became an independent Dominion in October 1970, and a series of rapid steps toward greater internal autonomy in Australian New Guinea seems likely to lead to full internal self-government at a date between 1974 and 1976. A similar date for at least limited political independence is forecast for the Solomon Islands. The complex situation in the Anglo-French New Hebrides Condominium continues to defy the wit of man, but it seems improbable that the present form of direct double-colonial rule can much outlast the effective political independence of most neighbouring countries. Only in New Caledonia and West Irian are there contrary trends. Massive growth of the New Caledonian nickel industry has enhanced the value to France of this fragment of its former empire, and pressures for more internal self-rule continue to be resisted. In West Irian, the 1969 Act of Free Choice – or 'act of no choice' as it was described by cynics even in Djakarta – has confirmed the status of the region as an integral part of the Republic of Indonesia: whether this is to be described as 'independence' or as 'continued colonialism' is a matter of individual viewpoint.

But the departure of foreign rule marks the end of 'colonialism' only if we adopt a rather narrow definition of the term. It is certainly the popular usage, and in the main the usage of political scientists. But it can obscure the presence of other and more pervasive forms of colonial relationship, which may both precede and outlast the phase of direct political control.

THE NATURE OF 'COLONIALISM' AND 'INDEPENDENCE'

The theme of this book has been briefly foreshadowed in the Preface. It requires definitions of 'colonialism' and especially 'independence' that are somewhat at variance with normal use, and which extend far beyond the political context. The term 'colonialism' means many things to many people, and a survey of its use in the literature would be of little service. As here interpreted, 'colonialism' is a thoroughgoing, comprehensive and deliberate penetration of a local or 'residentiary' system by the agents of an external system, who aim to restructure the patterns of organization, resource use,

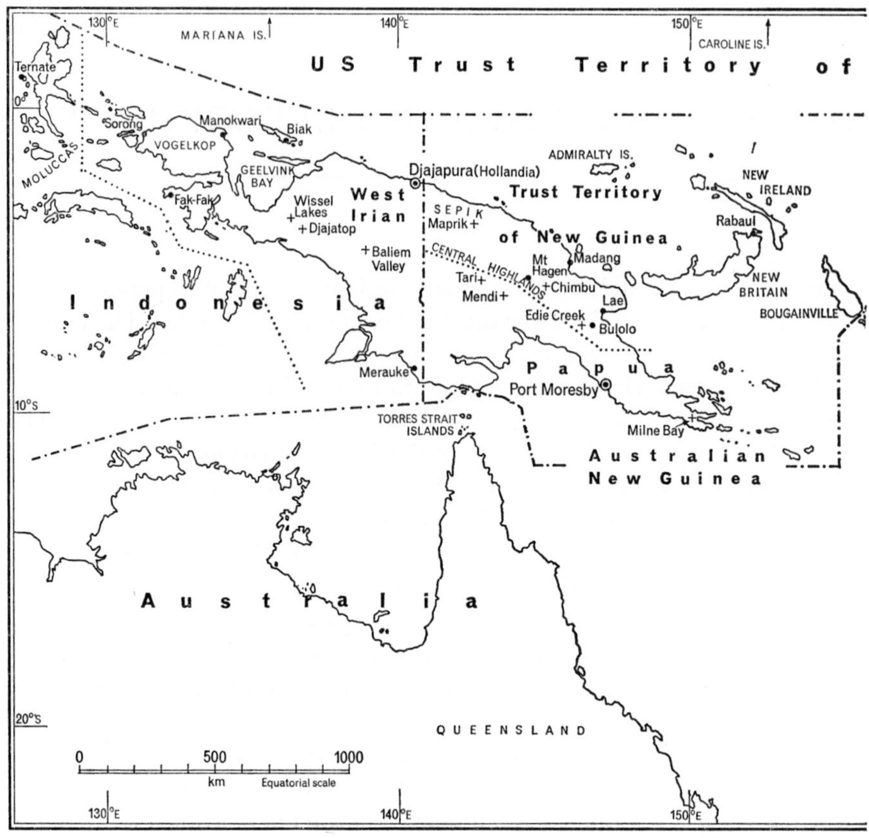

Figure 1. Melanesia, showing modern territorial boundaries and principal places named in the text

circulation and outlook so as to bring these into a linked relationship with their own system. The objective is an externally wrought or guided transformation of the residentiary system, revolutionary in the sense that it involves termination or diversion of former evolutionary trends.

'Independence' is here taken as the converse of this process, as the whole reaction of the residentiary system with the object of either retaining or regaining control both of its own evolution and of its relationships with other systems. The defence or acquisition of political independence is the most obvious expression of this process, hence the use of the term in this context. However, independence may be sought in both economic and cultural fields as well, and vigorous conflict between 'colonial' and 'independent' forces may take place in these areas within a context of complete political independence, as we are now seeing in many parts of the Third World. The two forces

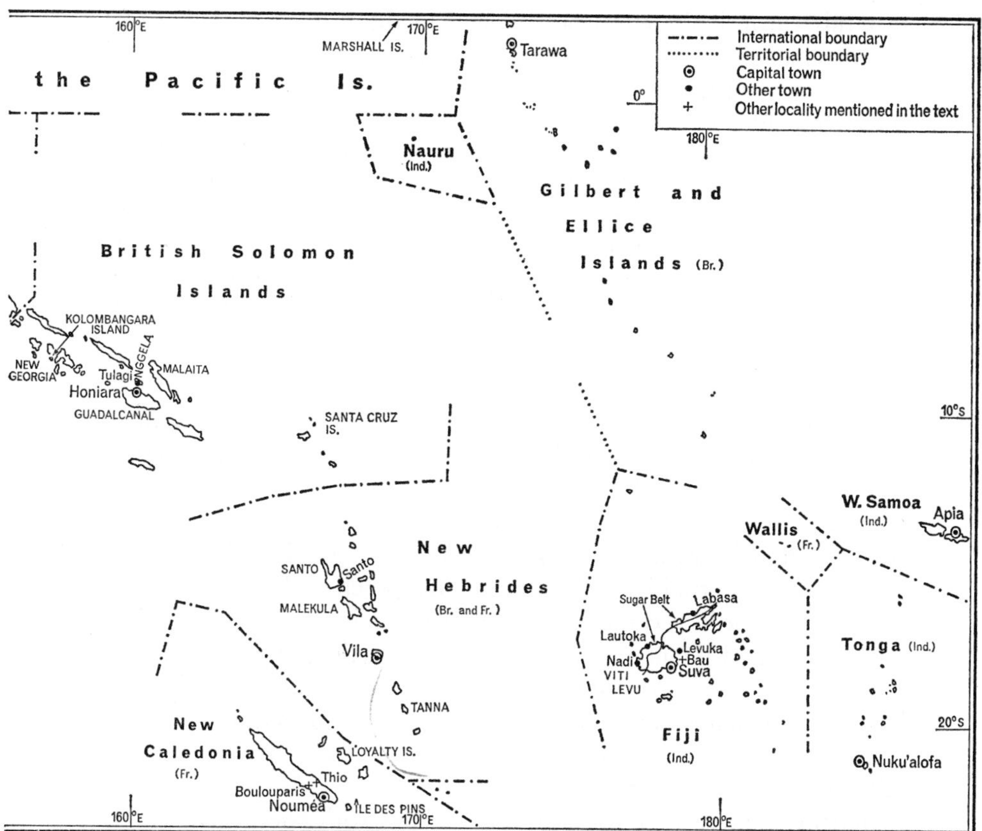

interact, and it is the fact of interaction that is stressed, especially in the later chapters of the book. This is not simply an analogy with the physical law that every action generates a reaction: the reaction to colonialism will almost never be equal and may not even be opposite. But it is important to realize that there is a reaction at all times and in all places: it is an error to conceive of the colonized residentiary system as simply the passive recipient of external innovation.

Within this conception, the initiation and continuation of colonial interaction demand inequality between the residentiary and invading forces. This inequality may be in terms of wealth, military strength, organization or simply ethos. There is usually inequality in all these respects, but the last two named are the most significant operationally. Contrasts in wealth and power create a potential for colonialism; exercise of this potential is facilitated by organizational contrasts, but the driving force is an expansionist or proselytizing ethos among the external agents and their backers. It is not necessary that this expansionist ethos be common to the whole population of the metropolitan country. It perhaps was so in the middle period of 'high colonialism', but was not at the beginning, and is not at the end. Currently, the metropolitan ethos is more commonly contractionist than expansionist, and this has facilitated the widespread withdrawal of political control. Yet as we shall see, the economic colonialism of organized business has achieved greater strength than ever before during this very period of 'decolonization'. Paradoxically, the essentially altruistic desire to 'develop' or 'modernize' the Third World that has evolved since World War II has even helped to achieve this result.

It may be useful to think of the process we are discussing in abstract terms, and to employ in a very simple way the language of systems and networks. A primitive residentiary structure such as that of Melanesia may be thought of as a 'complex' or 'heap' of local, small-scale systems, each representing local groups within which production, social life and exchange are organized. They are interconnected by a web of links between kin and affines, exchange partners and friends, but there is an absence of higher-level integration. In a somewhat less primitive residentiary system, such as that of much of pre-modern Asia, the local complex is still present, but is subordinated to a higher level structure with more specialization of function, supported by long-distance trade, and structured politically into states and sometimes even loosely-knit empires. There is a centrally-organized pattern of space which is absent from the more primitive model, but the economy is still largely self-contained within each larger system.

Initially, these complexes have few dealings with one another, or with remote systems and complexes. The beginning of the colonial process can be likened to the sending out of tentacles from some remote system to contact peripheral elements of the residentiary complex. The very existence of these tentacles implies an organization capable of projecting its activities beyond the bounds of the origin system, and an expansionist will acting as driving force. Successful initial results lead to a strengthening of the tentacles, and to deeper penetration of the residentiary complex. The tentacles become in time the trunks of branching networks which extend deeper and deeper into the residentiary complex, creating a new pattern of nodes which become central points of a circulation system designed for trade and contact with the remote metropolitan system. The trunks become the long-haul routes, and the points at which these reach the edge of the residentiary complex and branch out into that complex are the ports of entry: they become centres for the exercise of colonial power over the residentiary complex, replacing existing centres in importance. Thus Rangoon replaced Mandalay, Lima replaced Cuzco, Calcutta, Madras and Bombay replaced the inland centres of power in India. More rarely, the invading force seizes the whole structure of a residentiary system by a *coup de main*, as in Cortes' conquest of Mexico, and adapts or modifies this structure for its own purposes.

An essential characteristic of colonialism is laid bare by this simplification. Colonialism is a multinational relationship linking metropolitan base with residentiary system. Commonly, more than one residentiary complex is linked with a single base, and sometimes there is overlap and interconnection within one residentiary complex between the invading systems of different metropolitan powers. Structures of this order demand large-scale organization, both in the absolute sense of size sufficient to sustain multinational linkages, and in the relative sense that these organizations must be large by comparison with organizations in the residentiary complex. This structural aspect of colonialism is fundamental. The largest structured corporations of early modern Europe were the big colonial companies such as the British East India Company. They were contrasted not only with the organizations of the residentiary complexes among which they operated, but also with the more diffuse structure of business in Europe at that period. They were eclipsed for a time with the rise of a great number of new capitalist organizations in the industrial revolution, but this form of essentially colonial organization has re-emerged in the multinational corporations of the present century.

Such multinational organization is not limited to the commercial field. Government itself has required to develop multinational dimensions, and to project the growing structure of metropolitan administration into the dependent territories. Missionary activity has not been unstructured. The Orders of the one great multinational Church provided an early means of organization, and other Churches have set up missionary organizations of their own. Similar structures have arisen in banking, in publishing, in the spread of education and university systems, in cultural diffusion, and in the whole range of agencies operating to transform the residentiary systems. Such multinational structures emerged ahead of political control; most have continued beyond political independence. They have operated in areas which have escaped the political phase of colonialism, and some of them operate more successfully today than at any time in the past, despite the widespread withdrawal of direct colonial rule.

This great simplification of the colonial process has its limitations. It does not describe the evolution of colonies of settlement, where the residentiary complex was either wholly or mainly swept aside to make way for settlers from the metropolitan regions and their servants. Nor does it cover the quite numerous instances in which new residentiary populations have been created, in subordinate relationship to the agencies of the colonial system proper, by the importation and settlement of great numbers of slaves or contract workers.

It may aid the conceptualization of the expansive forces, but has little to tell us about the residentiary reaction. This latter has varied enormously, from the speedy and total disappearance of the indigenous population from most of the Antilles to the completely successful resistance of the Japanese, who swiftly remodelled their own society so as not only to exclude the invading forces, but later to develop their own expanding networks. Between these two extremes lies an immense range of responses, and within this range falls the experience of Melanesia.

Melanesia is a remote region, which had little to attract the early agents of colonialism, and much to repel them. Its internal structure was quite inchoate, and its ability to mobilize resistance to the invading forces was minimal. Yet there has been a remarkable degree of survival of the old residentiary complex in greater or lesser transformation. This survival must be attributed to the rather light external impact. Even so there has been some settlement from metropolitan sources, and some creation of new residentiary populations, and as late as the 1920s many thought that the future of this region would lie with European settlers and entrepreneurs, together with their Asian servants. The inequality of both impact and response over the south Pacific region has created an unusually varied spatial pattern in modern times, and it is this variety that makes Melanesia particularly suitable as a laboratory for studying the processes of change.

SOCIETY AND ECONOMY UNDER COLONIALISM: 'PLURALISM' AND 'DUALISM'

This preliminary chapter is the place in which to explore concepts, and it will be helpful to go further in our generalization of colonialism. Society and economy under colonialism should differ from those in metropolitan countries as a result of the invasion: since any colonial society of the type we are discussing will contain both a residentiary complex and the agents of an exogenetic system, it follows that its population cannot be homogenous culturally, and that its economy must contain both locally and externally based organizations. Such conditions give rise to what Furnivall (1939, 1945, 1948) and Boeke (1953) termed respectively the 'plural society' and the 'dual economy'. Neither are conditions peculiar to colonial countries, but they were both first described in the southeast Asian colonial region, and tend to be more starkly exhibited in colonial lands than elsewhere: both are well developed in Melanesia.

A plural society exists when whole groups, differentiated by some attribute such as colour, language or national origin, possess value systems differing from one another, and combine only at the economic and political level to form a single national society. Group structure overrides the socially-differentiated stratification of the whole society, and primary loyalty is often to the group rather than to the nation. Often groups are characterized by their possession of different characteristic rôles in the whole society, frequently yielding unequal status, so that whole groups are ranked in a social hierarchy, irrespective of the relative standing of individuals within groups. The stereotyped behavioural patterns of pluralism may be remarkably persistent, and have an important effect on the nature and direction of action.

There is also the economic dimension, which is related to pluralism through the different rôle attribution of groups in the whole economy. The relation has rarely been explored, because it is customary to treat of dualism as though purely economic explanations can be invoked: an adequate interrelation of the economic theory of dualism with the social theory of pluralism has yet to be undertaken. Dualism means the presence within one integrated economic system, such as that of a state or territory, of sectors differing in scale, organization, efficiency and economic behaviour. As initially stated by Boeke (1953, 4) the contrast is sociological: 'Social dualism is the clashing of an imported social system with an indigenous social system of another style. Most frequently the imported social system is high capitalism.' The contrast is seen as that between East and West. Western enterprise is rational, profit-maximizing, capable of large-scale organization, able to use capital. Eastern enterprise, on the other hand, is lacking in organizing power and the profit motive; supply curves tend to slope backwards, so that a higher price may command less output than before; wants are limited, and society is moulded by 'fatalism and resignation'. Briefly, Westerners are optimizers while Easterners are satisficers, in a since-current terminology.

Boeke's thesis tended to be discredited in the one-world, one-mankind atmosphere of occidental liberalism after World War II, though there was little possibility of disputing his basic finding: 'dualism' is a hard fact of life in almost every underdeveloped country in the world. We may with reason argue that the sectoral division of the economy is in fact much more complex, and is plural rather than dual. Baldwin (1966) drew attention to important contrasts between plantations and mines in the 'external' sector, and many writers have observed that the enterprises of Asian migrants in foreign countries show behavioural patterns very different from those of indigenous enterprises, even though they may also be contrasted with European expatriate enterprises. But the fact that there are contrasts is self-evident, and Boeke's dichotomous approach may be accepted for its simplicity of analysis. Higgins (1959) provides a comprehensive review of Boeke's thesis, along with other theories of underdevelopment, and suggests that the contrast is explicable in economic and technological terms. He advanced what has been termed the 'factor-proportions' model of dualism, perhaps most simply set out in his Foreword to Geertz' *Agricultural Involution* (1963).

To Higgins, the 'industrial' (or highly-organized, capital-intensive) sector is characterized by relatively fixed proportions in which the factors of production may be combined, whereas in the 'rural' (small-scale, food- and handicrafts-producing) sector the proportions are variable: 'A wide range of techniques and of combinations of labor and capital will give the same output. Accordingly the proportions actually used will be adjusted to the factor endowment (and to the consequent relative prices of labor and capital)' (Higgins, 1959, 328). Thus so long as population increases faster than the rate of new capital injection, labour is unable to be absorbed into the industrial economy at the rate of its formation; it is thus forced into the more absorptive rural sector, where production becomes steadily more labour-intensive, leading to the condition of mutual shared poverty which Geertz (1963) elaborates. Fundamental to the model is a constant condition of labour surplus to both sectors.

The application of this model to Melanesia is a question of some interest. Resting on the substantive data presented here and there in later chapters, or in Brookfield with Hart (1971), it may be said now that Higgins' model is insufficient to explain the Melanesian case. He relies on population growth at a rate which exceeds that of capital formation or injection. Purely economic or technological forces are called upon, and this seems an unnecessary restriction in a colonial society. In Melanesia the required population explosion did not take place until a very late stage, after dualism had become firmly established. Labour did become scarce in both sectors, and there is limited evidence for the fixity of 'technological labour coefficients'. Indeed the proportion of labour to capital in the 'industrial sector' seems to have behaved rather as a dependent than as an independent variable: evidence suggests that it has been determined in large measure by the supply and cost of labour to the 'industrial' economy.

Attempts to refine Higgins' model have continued in the main to rely on economic forces, though Myint's (1964) cognitive description of dualism takes much more account of behavioural considerations and separates the discussion from that of population explosion. Other writers, such as Frank (1967), argue that dualism and the whole metropolitan-satellite structure which underlies it, together with the fact of underdevelopment, are direct derivates of the process of colonial capitalist exploitation. But this is also to oversimplify, persuasive though Frank's arguments are to an observer of the colonial scene. It is this writer's view that Boeke's original interpretation had some elements of truth which its over-sharp dichotomies tended to obscure, and indeed that he was merely over-stating observations first made many years earlier, as in Maine's classic contrast between 'status' and 'contractus', and Karl Marx' distinction between 'production for use' and 'production for gain'.

PRODUCTION FOR USE

It would be too much to say that Marx recognized the dual economy. He did not, even though he identified aspects of colonialism that were not made clear by the classical economists. But like all writers of his period and others as late as Schumpeter, he found it necessary to draw his empirical evidence on non-capitalist or 'non-modernized' societies from the ancient world: this is not surprising, since modern data on contemporary societies did not begin to emerge in usable form until around the time of World War I. Marx was therefore concerned not with a comparison of contemporary economies – although he does introduce some such comparisons as a secondary product of his analysis – but rather with the evolution of capitalism, and hence with pre-capitalist forms of organization. It needs only the so-called 'ergodic principle' – whereby differences through space or through time are treated as though they were differences through time or through space – to convert this into a primitive analysis of dualism. And as such it contains powerful insights.

Marx drew a valuable polar distinction between production which has the object of gaining wealth, which itself becomes the stimulus for further production, and production for purposes of consumption, which is a static (or satisficing) rather than an expanding (or maximizing) principle. Thus:

> the ancient conception, in which man always appears (in however narrowly national, religious or political a definition) as the aim of production, seems very much more exalted than the modern world, in which production is the aim of man and wealth the aim of production...Hence in one way the childlike world of the ancients appears to be superior; and this is so, in so far as we seek for closed shape, form and established limitation. The ancients provide a narrow satisfaction, whereas the modern world leaves us unsatisfied, or, where it appears to be satisfied with itself, is vulgar and mean (Marx/Hobsbawm, 1964, 84–5).

'Production for use', in the sense employed by Marx, includes the exchange within a community or even a city state. In such production the form of property that has principal value is land, and this is so whether land is individually held, communally held, or held in usufruct within a communally-protected territory. 'Property therefore means belonging to a tribe' (*ibid.*, 90). The use and development of capital demands the separation of labour from its own land, so that it can be hired or enslaved.

We do not need to follow Marx any further on this road. Many others have later developed the contrast between 'production for use' and 'production for gain'. Among these was Chayanov (1923/1966) who pointed out that under 'production for use' – again not excluding marketing if use is the ultimate intention of production – the inputs per operative vary directly with the number of dependants. Alternatively put, those who are least burdened by responsibilities put in the least effort. Recently, the anthropologist Sahlins (in press) has suggested that in any population, exceptions to this rule might be identified, and that these exceptions represent the ambitious, potentially innovative men in the society.

Sahlins has his finger on a question of major importance to this discussion. The modal 'producer-for-use' is narrowly a satisficer, in Marx' sense, but Sahlins' exceptions are not. If they are aiming at a satisfaction level, it is a variable one, capable of being influenced by new sources of information, and elastic in its response to opportunity. There is abundant empirical evidence that such individuals are to be found in a very wide range of societies. One encounters them among West Indian small farmers; they occur widely in Africa, in central America, and even Java, classic ground of dualism. Many are to be met with in Melanesia, and we shall encounter some in these pages. It would be too much to call them maximizers, or even rational economic men in the strict sense of the term, but they show much more acute awareness of benefit/cost considerations in planning their activities than does the modal peasant.

THE SUPPLY OF EFFORT AND RISK-TAKING IN PEASANT SOCIETIES

It is worthwhile to probe the question of motivation in peasant societies further, for it has great bearing on the problem of 'development', and on the understanding of reactions to colonialism. Contrary views are expressed. On the one hand we have the 'external' view that peasants are lacking in enterprise, and that the task of development is to force this enterprise along, cajoling, aiding and tempting the peasants into greater effort, and greater involvement with the cash economy. On the other hand we have the 'internal' view that peasant society is both adaptive and innovative, but is continually battering against barriers created by the external system, which engrosses a major share of the productive resources, natural and human, controls the linkages, and manipulates the system for its own benefit so assiduously that peasant enterprise is discouraged and even actively opposed. It will be useful to explore the question of peasant motivation more thoroughly before we turn to the nature of the external system, and its barrier effect.

An important part of the argument turns on the question of the backward slope of the supply curves of effort and risk-taking. The argument is that supply will increase only up to the point at which demand is satisfied, beyond which further rises in price or wage rates will only lead to reduction in peasant input, since demand can now be satisfied with less effort than before. This is the central prop of Boeke's argument. The supply curve turns back to parallel the demand curve, and does not intersect it and continue to rise with increased returns, as in the classical economic theory of supply and demand. Higgins (1959, 287) argues that such backward-sloping supply curves are by no means limited to peasant conditions. He notes their presence in the reaction of such groups as the Australian wharf-labourers to higher wages, and argues that they are common throughout the world in conditions where a satisfaction level has been reached: beyond this workers will prefer to optimize on leisure time, rather than seek higher and higher rewards by greater effort. He goes on to argue that such behaviour is a normal condition in static economies, and that in dynamic economies there is only an illusion of continuously-rising supply curves, due to progressive upward movement in the demand curves created by innovations, population growth, and the effect of informal or formal advertising. Since demand curves continually move to the right, the point of inflexion of backward-sloping supply curves will follow them, so that effort will continue to increase with rising rewards, all the time chasing rising demand, but never quite reaching satisfaction. This is as though to say that production is always for use rather than for gain, but that the level of utility is constantly rising, and never quite attained.

Fisk takes this argument a stage or two further in a clean and elegant model of development in a primitive society initially without any market production whatever (Fisk, 1962, 1964; Fisk and Shand, 1969). He unites demand and supply through the concept of utility of money to the population, which is at first minimal since there are few known wants that money can satisfy. The curve exhibiting the utility of money thus has the form of a backward-sloping supply curve, rising outward a small way from the point of origin, then curving backward toward zero utility as supply of money outruns limited known wants. The utility of money is increased through increased supply of goods available to the population, and a consequent widening of known wants. But the supply of goods will not be increased unless there is money available to buy them, so that the utility of money becomes, in effect, a function of the amount of money earned, and the process is inevitably halting. Only gradually does the tendency to backward slope diminish as wants increase and the utility of money rises: the demand barrier to progress is removed, in this model, when the possibility of earning more income itself becomes a sufficient incentive to greater input of effort and short-run demand is no longer readily satisfied.

Fisk goes on to emphasize other aspects of this process, which make any course of early development jumpy rather than smooth. Since demand is to some degree a function of the supply of available goods, and this supply is likely to be increased through the establishment of whole new trade stores rather than by simple increase in the scale of existing operations, it is subject to the 'lumpiness' of capital, and hence will increase by jumps. But the supply of money which creates the demand for available goods is also unlikely to increase smoothly. It depends on the level of returns to the peasant producer for his input, and initially these are likely to be very poor for want of adequate linkages to the market. Improvement in the linkages will again be jumpy: it depends on the construction of a new road or wharf, on the entry of a new buyer from the commercial system whose demand equals the supply of a fair number of peasant producers, on the addition of a new call to the itinerary of a ship, on the introduction of scale-economizing innovations such as a new processing plant. The combined effect of these irregularities will be to create a series of checks to the development process.

Fisk's theory recalls Schumpeter's old theory of 'unstable growth', except that he envisages a different, though related, process. Schumpeter relies on the irregular emergence of entrepreneurs in response to innovations, which tend to occur in clusters following periods of equilibrium. If for Schumpeter's entrepreneurs we read Sahlins' exceptions to the mass of satisficers who conform to Chayanov's rule, it is indeed likely that the thrust of such men might create new linkages so as to break through a stable equilibrium as conceived by Fisk. And equally, a loss of thrust for whatever reason might lead to a return to the stable equilibrium, and thus help explain the frequent disappointments that have occurred. But as we shall see in a later chapter, there are also other considerations that do not arise from this deductive search for explanation.

BEHAVIOUR IN THE INVADING SYSTEM

An important question now arises. Are behavioural conditions in fact totally different in the invading system, as Boeke suggests? Do we find the agents of the commercial invading system to be rational economic men? Does the theory of the firm hold good? Or does the real nature of the contrast between the two systems lie elsewhere?

It would be naive indeed to suppose that the entrepreneurial agents of the invading system were organized in a large number of competitive small firms whose numbers and activities were governed by the free operation of the market mechanism. This is true, or has been true, of only a limited sector of the invading population, principally the undercapitalized traders and planters who pioneered colonial enterprise and who have remained on the fringes of the system as a whole. The core of the system, as we saw above, became and has remained dominated by relatively large corporations, which had either to be multinational in origin, or else to develop multinational linkages in order to operate in their rôle of agency houses, growers, traders, shippers, manufacturers and *de facto* bankers. Vertical integration has been the key to their success, and at times and in places they have taken on a number of non-commercial rôles as well; the civil government and military control of colonies have sometimes been assigned to such corporations, and they have at all times exercised considerable political influence, if not power.

Since so large a part of colonial trade has been handled through these corporations, much of it has been effectively removed from the free play of market forces. This is true not only for the trade under direct corporation control, but also for business done with smaller entrepreneurs who have required credit, have fallen into debt to the corporations, and who buy from them and sell to them essentially against book entries. Latterly, bilateral trading agreements negotiated through governments have affected an increasing share of colonial trade, whether handed through the corporations or through marketing boards and other agencies; this too has often been separated by subsidies, special prices and other arrangements from the 'free' market. In one form or another, centralized control affects a very large part of the operations of a colonial system, and this has been a continuing feature, though it has grown in modern times.

Restriction of competition has been an essential corollary of this system, and would-be independent entrepreneurs have either had to accept this limitation, or else content themselves with less profitable, more risky or more arduous business opportunities. This is far less true of an expanding colonial economy, such as one being heavily primed with overseas loans and grants, metropolitan budgetary support, and new private investment. During such periods organizations multiply, and there is even opportunity for locally-based enterprises to ramify their interests and grow strong. But during phases of slow growth and stagnation the tendency seems always to reduce the number of small companies and entrepreneurs, and to concentrate the big corporation activities into fewer and simpler structures by mergers and takeovers. Especially during such periods the entrenched corporations have often become strongly conservative in policy toward production, trading and innovation. And they have at all times been a conservative force in employment and wage policy. It is possible for a multinational corporation to behave as a satisficer in some areas of its operation, while diverting resources for expansion and innovation elsewhere. Over long periods this has enabled such corporations to re-invest colonial profits in metropolitan countries, or to draw off profits from colonial areas where operations are closer to the economic margin to re-invest at more profitable centres.

It is frequently alleged that direct investment in colonial economies has led to net outflow of capital from these economies, and similar allegations have been made about the activities of commercial banks. Branches of metropolitan banks in colonial areas constitute a system of pipelines through which money can flow either in or out. In establishing branches, banks are often concerned more to tap sources of deposits than to act as lenders, though they sometimes also act as investors. It has been demonstrated that the ratio of loans to deposits in these banks is often very low, and that net outflow has taken place over long periods. This can occur even during periods of colonial prosperity. The centralized structure of the colonial commercial system and the dominant rôle of direct investment from overseas tend to restrict opportunity for profitable local investment by private individuals and locally-based organizations, such as marketing boards and cooperative societies. Such money can be more securely invested at deposit in the banks, which find their own more profitable and secure investments in the metropolitan countries. This is not always so; in Kenya for example a net outflow has been replaced by a net inflow in modern times. But Kenya has an unusually diversified economy, and especially in the smaller and less populous colonial countries the pattern is more disquieting. It sometimes seems as though a modern rôle of government has been to prime the pump by funding the colonial economy, only to have a substantial part of the inflow circulated back to the metropolis through the several other channels of the invading system.

Perhaps this is in the very nature of colonialism as a multinational process. The effect is precisely comparable with that of direct investment by American multinational industrial corporations in Canada, Australia or Europe. Substantial employment and taxation revenue are generated, and there is a valuable multiplier effect. But an important share of profits is repatriated, and it is a serious weakness that the primary loyalty of the executives is to the home-based shareholders, rather than to the host country. It is often against the interests of the parent corporation to allow the local branch-plants to become too innovative, to buy materials locally when they can be bought from organizations under corporation control, or to develop independent management. Corporation colonialism has the tendency to extend the economy and polity of the country of origin into another country. Under eighteenth-century mercantilism this was an overt policy, and it has never died because it is inherent in the system. The development of a colonial economy structured in this way thus implies an expansion of flows in both directions, in and out of the economy. This is among the reasons why the gross national product of a developing country is so unreliable an indicator of the true state of development; much of the expansion recorded may in fact flow only through the invading system, with limited benefit to the residentiary complex.

There is a wide range of views on this system. Its apologists point to the benefit obtained by the host countries in terms of revenue, employment, infrastructure and multiplier effects. They argue that the total sum of these provides much greater returns than could be obtained from locally-funded resource development. They point to the marketing and research organization created which has important spin-off effects to other parts of the economy. On the other hand we have Boeke's despair over the growing expatriate control over the economy of pre-1942 Indonesia, and the bitter views of many local economists in colonial and ex-colonial countries, such as the West Indies. To them, this 'plantation economy', as they describe the system, is a direct cause of underdevelopment in the residentiary complex. Such diverse interpretations demand that we make some attempt to examine and compare the two systems in combination.

STRUCTURE AND BEHAVIOUR IN A MIXED ECONOMY

There is a further set of differences that we have not yet taken into account. A widespread characteristic of peasant societies in the world is the prevalence of interpersonal reciprocal relationships having contractual force. This principle of organization, sometimes called the 'dyadic contract', is regarded by Polanyi (1957) and his associates as one of three forms in which economic relationships may be institutionalized. These three, market-exchange, redistribution and reciprocity, assume differential importance in different societies and at different historical periods. Market-exchange dominates in our own society, coupled with redistribution through a central authority via taxation and public spending. In peasant societies, and in what Marx termed 'archaic societies', the dominant form is reciprocity, meaning a face-to-face relationship in which every service to, or good provided to, another person creates a reciprocal obligation which may be returned in either goods or services at a later date. By giving, an individual assures his own future supply of gifts or services; by receiving, or seeking aid, he accepts an obligation to repay. The operation of this institution may be seen most clearly in major inter-group prestations, or in the formation of joint working parties on the land of one member of the party, but it runs through the whole fabric of peasant society and is, indeed, the very weft and warp of that society. It constitutes the system of social security; it is the web that links persons and groups; it provides the trading links through which goods are transferred across the complex; it provides a ready-made set of relationships into which market-exchange can also be fitted as a minor principle of transaction.

Reciprocity is a form of credit, and even the more formal granting of credit contains elements of reciprocity in peasant societies. Shopkeepers extend credit on a personal basis to their clients; the credit is never wholly repaid, and a continual relationship is maintained. Patron-client relationships operate between small landlords and their tenants. Small-scale redistribution itself is an extension of reciprocity, when a chief receives gifts and is expected to distribute them in a manner which will reduce inequalities. The loose systems of land tenure which operate in many peasant societies cannot be comprehended without understanding of reciprocity. Reciprocal relationships, widely enmeshed, serve both to reduce inequalities and also to create them, by facilitating temporary concentration of resources at points where they can be most opportunely used. Big men mobilize support for enterprises by calling in debts and seeking new support which in turn creates new obligations; if they acquire power they may be able to repay these debts in non-material ways, but otherwise a heavy burden is shouldered. A man who fails is likely to be forgiven his obligations, but is unlikely to be able to mobilize much credit in the future.

The contrasted structure of credit provision between peasant societies on the one hand, and more highly centralized and commercialized societies on the other, is of major importance. By its very nature, peasant credit is limited. Commercial credit, on the other hand, is backed up by a hierarchical system leading ultimately to the centres of financial power. In a colonial commercial system the ultimate control over commercial credit will rest in the hands of only a few men, who in turn are largely agents of ultimate overseas credit sources. The total volume of commercial credit may be less than the total volume of credit circulating in the residentiary complex, could this be adequately valued, but the latter is disorganized and its facility for concentration is very limited. The different forms of credit feed different forms of enterprise. Commercial credit feeds investment, though a substantial part of it is often in short-term bills to finance imports. But this is not the same as peasant credit for consumption, which is related to immediate needs. Peasant credit for investment creates major problems of repayment; commercial credit also depends on some personal knowledge of the applicant, however formally acquired, and on collateral, and it is not easy to extend such credit for investment into the diffuse peasant complex except through intermediaries, or by means of specially-created organizations.

This structural dualism perhaps goes further toward explanation of contrasts in the scale and behaviour of enterprises than any other explanation we have yet reviewed: in a sense it combines other explanations. But it does not follow that the problem is solely the extension of commercial credit into the peasant system. The mass of credit circulating within the peasant complex, including credit in labour and services, as well as in money and goods, is a source of great value. Efforts to mobilize it, either locally through Savings and Loan Societies, or on a much more ambitious scale, have enjoyed only limited success, but we should not assume that further efforts, and new approaches, will be similarly unrewarding. Imposition of external ideologies, whether capitalist or communist, encounters strong resistance from peasants unwilling to surrender the advantages of their own institutionalized economic system. But attempts are being made to evolve indigenous ideologies for the mobilization of resources, and these are worthy of close study. A closely meshed multi-tiered system of local organization might well provide acceptable redistributive channels which could build the public sector from below in a manner well suited to exploit the institutions of a residentiary complex.

A mixed economy, in which capitalist enterprise in the colonial commercial system is made socially accountable to the host country, and in which the resources of the peasant complex are more successfully mobilized so as to feed local capital-intensive enterprises, should not be an aim beyond reach. Unfortunately we lack prescriptions for the achievement of such an economy, which should be the logical and happy conclusion of the colonial process. Economists have been preoccupied in the main with models derived from a very different context; anthropologists have mainly been concerned to describe and analyse, rather than to model and prescribe. Attempts to model the historical emergence of dualism have been made, sometimes intuitively, sometimes with such abstraction and mathematical elegance as totally to lose sight of the real world. But all too little has been done to seek a way forward which will interrelate both invading system and residentiary complex so as optimally to use the resources of both. Nationalization by itself is a crude device, still without proven results. Socialism and capitalist economic man are both imported doctrines. The restrictions of the peasant way of life have declining appeal. But in this problem perhaps lies the ultimate challenge to the colonial process. It has wrought great transformations on the residentiary systems, and it has sometimes created new systems in new lands, in the image of the metropolitan systems. But where this has happened, most completely in North America and Australia, the remnants of the old residentiary complex are virtually rejects of society and economy. Nowhere in the world has any wholly satisfactory model of an integrated, mixed economy yet emerged from the colonial experience.

THE STAGES OF COLONIALISM

The argument of this chapter thus emerges in the following terms. The success or failure of the colonial process is to be measured not so much by its transformation or modernization of colonial economy and society in the metropolitan image, nor by the progress of the gross national product and other indices of wealth, nor by any conscious preservation of old cultural institutions. The colonial process is a revolutionary transformation of a society through invasion by agents of another society. If the invasion is to have been worthwhile it must have led to the creation of new indigenous institutions capable of taking over a part of its rôle in maintaining and developing the new external linkages. This does not mean the elimination of the invading system, but it does mean the 'taming' of that system so that it can operate as an equal member of the whole with locally-supported elements, all within the broad control of a post-colonial national administration. The measure of success or failure is thus the progress toward creation of a mixed economy which can retain and widen the external linkages created by colonialism but in a more equal partnership with the external world. This is a long process, and the ending of political colonialism is only one stage along it, albeit an essential one.

Intuitively, a number of stages can be recognized in the whole span of colonial experience; radically different conditions operate in each. The early colonial phase is the period of penetration of the residentiary complex and establishment of the basic structures of the invading system. External political control is usually achieved within this period, but not necessarily at an early stage. The succeeding period of high colonialism witnesses major transformation of the residentiary complex under dominance by the external agencies. Dualism emerges strongly, and empire is seen as a semi-permanent condition. But the stability is illusory, for forces are evolving both within the residentiary complex and in the metropolitan countries which will lead to new striving on the one hand, and weakening expansionist will on the other. The succeeding late colonial phase is characterized especially by growth of the public sector, the resultant of both sets of forces. Political independence comes at some stage in this period, but a true post-colonial phase can hardly yet be recognized, except in former colonies of settlement which have become new societies in the metropolitan image.

This is not seen as in any way a determined sequence. Reversal is possible, and indeed has occurred in some measure through the new mercantilism of multinational corporations since World War II. This may even be the initial phase of a new colonialism, but if so it is likely to encounter a very different residentiary reaction from the first, and to experience a different sort of historical process. Interpretation and explanation such as is essayed here has to be primarily retrospective, and in regard to the future the most we can do is to project alternative possible courses from present trends.

In so far as it can be described as such, this is the model of the colonial sequence which is adopted as framework for the descriptive account which follows. We shall examine the experience of Melanesia within it, paying attention both to the invading systems and the residentiary complex, and to the relationship between them. Because the invading system enters from a wider world, and latterly the residentiary population is also becoming more fully cognizant of trends in that integument, we cannot discuss the Melanesian experience without reference to its context. But the discussion is not comparative: the focus of interest is a group of islands in the south Pacific and their people. We shall, I believe, find them to provide a microcosm of events played out on a much wider scene.

REFERENCES AND SOURCES

The literature on economic development theory is barely sampled in this chapter, but comprehensive reviews are given in Higgins (1959, 2nd ed. 1968). The approach taken here is a development of views previously expressed in more diffuse form (Brookfield with Hart, 1971), and derives a comforting measure of support from the writings of students of colonialism and underdevelopment in the Americas such as Furtado (1964), Best (1968), Levitt and Best (1969) and Levitt (1970). In a wider sense there is also present the understanding provided by Myrdal (1957) and Myint (1964).

In terms of antecedents to my approach among geographers, I would call first on Robequain (1954) who succeeded – as I have not – in uniting in one book of deep insight an understanding of the spatial, ecological and temporal processes of colonialism.

CHAPTER 2

COLONIAL BEGINNINGS

The colonial experience of Melanesia did not begin until the nineteenth century. There is a prehistory of discovery by Europeans beginning in the sixteenth century, and even one early attempt at colonization by Mendaña's second expedition to the Solomon Islands. Before this, western New Guinea was visited for slaves and a little trade by seamen from eastern Indonesia, and the Indonesian settlement at Fakfak at the western end of that island perhaps dates from the fourteenth century. There seems to have been a major period of voyaging by the ancestors of the present Melanesian population in the first millennium A.D., but the earlier prehistory, involving the anciently settled Papuan people, the Melanesians and some Polynesian groups is shrouded in mist. Man has probably been in New Guinea at least 20,000 years, but in the eastern islands for only a much shorter period. Crop and livestock complexes, and agricultural methods, seem to have entered the Melanesian region successively from the west over a long period of time; some crops were indigenously domesticated, and some techniques may have been locally invented. The Spanish entry into the Philippines in the sixteenth century was followed by the introduction of new crops, which found their way to Melanesia along established trading routes; sweet potatoes seem to have entered New Guinea and became the dominant crop in the central highlands only after this event. Occasional exploratory vessels sailed through the islands during the seventeenth and eighteenth centuries, but few made landings, and in 1800 Melanesia remained about the least known maritime area on earth.

The turning point in the whole history of the south Pacific islands is the British establishment of a penal colony at Sydney, New South Wales, in 1788. Here was a *point d'appui* which, however unsuitable it may have been as a base from which to penetrate the Australian continent, was from the first an excellent base for operation in the Pacific islands. The very poverty of the colony in agricultural resources encouraged a scouring of the islands as far away as Tahiti in search of food. In short succession, the provision traders were followed by American whalers, *bêche de mer* and shellfish traders, then, after 1804, by sandalwood traders who set up the first shore-based establishments in the islands. Sandalwood, of high value for incense-burning in China and hence a means of trade for the purchase of Chinese tea, was discovered at Bua bay on the island of Vanua Levu, Fiji, and later in other islands, including Hawaii, the Marquesas, the New Hebrides and New Caledonia. This exploitative business led to sharp conflicts with the indigenes, and to early experiences of forced labour and forced supply. It also created, as Shineberg (1966, 1968) has shown, the beginnings of indigenous demand for such goods as tobacco, cloth, iron goods and muskets, which were traded for the sandalwood. In one area after another, this business and the associated trade in reef products continued as the main *raison d'être* of contact until after the middle of the century.

These scattered contacts led to wider European knowledge of the islands, and introduced the islanders not only to a rather biased sample of the agents of expansion, but also to the wares of a trading and industrial society, and to a more comprehensive range of hitherto unknown diseases. There was also created a scattered population of beachcombers, castaways and escaped convicts, some of whom played an important rôle in local events, though others lived a precarious and often rather brief existence. But among these men were to be found the earliest agents of a rather more durable colonial penetration.

THE INVADING SYSTEM AND THE RESIDENTIARY COMPLEX AT CONTACT

The remoteness of Melanesia protected the region from the earlier phases of European colonial expansion between the fifteenth and eighteenth centuries, during which time activity was concentrated upon a few areas of known or early-developed value. The navigational risks of the reef-strewn seas of Melanesia added further protection even after the eastern Pacific islands were already penetrated, and the hostility and perceived savagery of the population also discouraged contact until greater force became available, or until the islanders learned of the power that lay behind the individual vessels arriving from an unknown outer world. The northwest European metropolitan countries were already well into the industrial revolution in the early nineteenth century, completely confident in the superiority of their own society and polity, religion and ethos, over all others. Their mood was one of expansionism based more and more on the doctrines of free trade, to permit full scope for individual enterprise. Trade would bring peace and enlargement of life to all peoples, and the mercantilist doctrines of the previous centuries were increasingly seen as restrictive practices fit only for discard. The anti-slavery movement was rapidly gaining in influence, and its successive victories from 1807 onward inspired a sense of lofty purpose, especially among the British, who became the policemen of anti-slavery throughout the world. This compared badly with the harsh treatment administered to convicts in New South Wales, but even in this remote colony the supporters of free enterprise gradually gained sway against the authoritarian rule of government. It was a ruthless age that rewarded success handsomely, but offered little or nothing to the failures. Cross-cutting this harshness, however, was a growing sense of humanitarianism, inherited in part from thinkers of the previous century. Thus while Melanesia was subjected to some unusually rapacious self-interest among its earlier exploiters, it was also protected from their excesses before these could become utterly destructive.

But perhaps as significant as the ethos of the invading agents was their comparative weakness. Individuals and small parties had to survive as much by their wits as by force, and it was not until mid-century that the organized power of naval vessels began to become onerous, and able to enforce the peace for the benefit of entrepreneurs and missionaries. Inland in the larger islands there was only the most limited penetration until much later. The hill tribes of Viti Levu, Fiji, were not subdued until the 1870s, and in New Guinea there was minimal inland penetration until the present century. The parties which explored central New Guinea in the 1930s relied on their wits almost as much as the seaborne pioneers in eastern Melanesia a century earlier. And in 1959 it was still possible for local big men in the hills around the Baliem valley, in West New Guinea, to send messages to the Dutch Controleur inviting a visit, as they wished to eat his liver.

Some of the characteristics of the residentiary complex have already been briefly outlined. Except only in eastern Fiji, where there was limited centralization, local organization in Melanesia was atomized to an extraordinary degree. Here and there loose federations, alliances, or groups recognizing common origin as a basis for cooperation might number a few thousand people, but even within these, smaller and more local groups had considerable autonomy. In most parts of Melanesia the effective maximal group numbered only a few hundred persons and was often fewer than one hundred in population. There was a complex cross-cutting system of local groups, based on common residence in a village or locality, and descent-based groups which showed only partial accordance with the local group pattern. Leadership was generally achieved by vigorous men within each generation, and even in Fiji, where there was a strongly-developed ranking system, hereditary right did not ensure achievement of power. Most people lived in villages of from twenty to several hundred people, though patterns of scattered hamlets and dispersed houses prevailed in some areas. Except for a coastal and swampland population that lived by fish and the extraction of sago, Melanesians were dominantly agriculturalists, practising root-crop cultivation by methods that varied in intensity from the simplest forms of shifting cultivation to highly elaborate and intensive technologies, including swamp reclamation and terrace irrigation. But the incidence of the latter technologies did not correlate with any more complex organization of society.

Specialization of labour was minimal. There were some communities and individuals who lived mainly by trade or manufacture and leadership was to some degree a specialized occupation. Other than this there was well-developed division of labour between the sexes, often accompanied by residential separation. Young unmarried men formed a separate class who participated little in production and reciprocal exchange, but constituted the core-group of the armed force on which each community relied for its protection and, if necessary, aggrandisement. But though land was sometimes taken in warfare, and women were seized or sometimes 'given' as wives in a peace settlement, men were never taken prisoner or enslaved. There were land-poor men in many societies, but only very rarely did economic disadvantage of individuals extend to limiting their access to necessary subsistence. There was no wage employment, and though land-borrowing was widespread, there were no landlords. Patron-client relationships occurred widely, but they were not rigid or necessarily continuing; indeed the social institutions of many societies had the effect of ensuring that such relationships need not persist from generation to generation. Life was certainly precarious, but it was not mean. Even in Fiji the class structure did not develop the rigidity and exercise of privilege which it acquired in some of the Polynesian kingdoms.

Most of these features are discussed in much greater detail in Brookfield with Hart (1971), and in the voluminous literature on particular societies and small areas. Any brief statement that goes beyond the most sweeping of generalities must contain such a list of exceptions as to be quite unhelpful. My purpose here is simply to outline the sort of residentiary complex that awaited the invasion; more detail on particular aspects will emerge from time to time in what follows.

FATAL IMPACT?

It is a common view that destruction was the dominant characteristic of early colonialism in the Pacific. Alan Moorehead (1966) entitled his readable gloss on the discovery and early settlement of the region 'The fatal impact'. It is argued that rapaciousness, disease and general disruption overwhelmed the fabric of indigenous society and led to widespread depopulation. This certainly happened in large parts of Australia and in Hawaii and some other Polynesian areas, and within Melanesia there was quite severe population decline in the eastern islands, though nothing to compare with the annihilation that took place in the Antilles after Spanish colonization in the fifteenth century. But by the second half of the nineteenth century it was apparent that the population of all contacted areas of Melanesia was in decline, and by the end of the century there were many who felt that the only remaining duty of the European colonialists was to smooth the pillow of the dying islanders. In New Caledonia a first census showed a Melanesian population of 42,000 in 1887 after some years of decline; a low point of 27,000 was reached in 1918. In Fiji a series of epidemics brought population down to about 140,500 by the first reliable estimate in 1874. A measles epidemic in 1875 wrought further damage, and the first census in 1879 showed a Melanesian-Fijian population of between 110,000 and 112,000. The lowest recorded total was only 84,475 in 1921, after the 1918 influenza epidemic.

Further west the response was varied. Some coastal and island areas of New Guinea gained population between 1906 and 1940. Others remained static, while still others lost population right through the period. A series of epidemics virtually extinguished the population of some small islands. The classic ground for this discussion is the New Hebrides where literal decimation has been postulated, but on rather flimsy evidence. Recent detailed study of the documentary evidence for certain islands in this group (McArthur and Yaxley, 1968) has suggested that the argument was based on overestimation of pre-contact populations coupled with under-estimation of modern populations, so that the decline has been enormously exaggerated. But there has been decline: there is field evidence of former intensive cultivation in depopulated areas, and there are eye-witness acounts such as the following:

Of all the diseases introduced the one that ranks first as a depopulator is dysentery... I personally know of whole populous villages of over 100 that were swept away by this disease... When I arrived at Port Stanley, Malekula, there was a population well over 500...made up of three fairly large villages. In 1904 there was a severe epidemic of dysentery and the people died at such a rate that they could not be buried. By 1910 there were not 150 people left and now there are not 50...

In 1905 during a Naval punitive expedition, at one village, Nevaar, Malekula, we rounded up 140 adult men and many got away. That village is now extinct and the survivors formed a small village not far away – there are 12 of them left (Corlette, n.d. [*c.* 1942]).

It has been argued, very reasonably, that some of the 'decline' is to be explained by the movement of people from inland to coastal villages following colonization. It is also suggested that decline has simply been assumed in line with expectation based on evidence elsewhere. But a widespread reduction is evident in all coastal areas: the only major exception seems to be inland New Guinea, where no sustained decline is reported following contact and pacification in the present century.

The loss of residentiary population led to much speculation and inquiry. Disease was generally recognized as the main cause, including epidemics of dysentery, measles, smallpox and influenza, and also the chronic effects on fertility of gonorrhoea. Many writers felt that there were also psychological factors, a death-wish arising from a sense of complete hopelessness in face of the invasion. Though discredited, this view is still sometimes given credence, as by Doumenge (1966, 157, translated):

> The collapse of [indigenous] beliefs, evangelization that was sometimes too rapid and too rigorous, and arbitrary administrative policy that moved people off their land: these were often followed by a rapid decline in population. Life ceased to be worth living [*dégout de vivre*], and people lost the desire to reproduce their kind [*se perpétuer*]. Some tribes in New Caledonia almost organized their own disappearance.

We shall see below how the disappearance of some tribes in New Caledonia was, in fact, 'organized', but it must be noted that these interpretations have had an important effect on action. It was reasonable to assume that development through the residentiary population was not worth the effort, that 'vacant' land could be taken without doing harm, that since the causes were psychological, no major health programme would have any effect. When, a little later on, colonial administrations felt it to be their duty to discourage any tendencies to 'organize disappearance', this too had effects. Absence of large numbers of male migrant workers, either overseas or on local plantations, has certainly been a supplementary cause of birth-rate reduction, by lengthening birth intervals in societies where marriage is a relatively stable institution. When population counts have shown a tendency to decline (from whatever cause), it became the practice to 'close' areas to labour recruitment (not distinguishing married from single men) until such time as absentees returned home, and stayed home long enough to do that which was expected of them;* recruiting could then safely be resumed.

Concern over the decline of population went on for two decades after Melanesian numbers had begun the upturn which led into the rapid upsurge of the present day: speculation on causes of decline gave way, almost without intermediate stage, to speculation on the dangers of overpopulation. That this occurred is itself a commentary on the poverty of the data base, and the heavy reliance on guesswork. But it should be added that there were always those who did not fear disappearance of the residentiary population over any large area, whether or not their thinking was any the more constructive in consequence of their insight.

* 'To repair their houses, plant their gardens, and leave their wives pregnant', according to one officer in the Australian administration.

THE ENTRY OF THE INVADING COLONIAL SYSTEM

By about 1840 both traders and missionaries were established in the eastern islands of Melanesia, and throughout Polynesia to the east. The missionaries, lacking in adequate financial support, were often the first to introduce trade in coconuts and coconut oil; sandalwood and reef-products were handled mainly by private entrepreneurs. The timing of the invasion had much to do with the early and sustained interest in coconut products. The early-nineteenth-century discoveries of Chevreul on the constitution of fats, and of Leblanc on the extraction of alkali from common salt, had begun to be applied to the manufacture of soap and candles. Use of vegetable oils began to supplant use of animal tallow, and by 1840 West African palm oil, American cottonseed oil, and widely-gathered coconut oil were all being imported into Europe. Coconut oil made by Pacific islanders was discoloured and often rancid, but it was transportable in barrels and, until the development of suitable machinery for the large-scale extraction of oil from copra in the 1850s, it was the preferred form. The business was initially quite disorganized, but in the 1850s Goddefroy und Sohn of Hamburg began to operate as buyers and agents at Apia in Samoa, and demand spread rapidly, ahead of the agents of the system. When in 1853 the Tongans conquered the east-Fijian island of Moala they collected tax in coconut oil (Sahlins, 1962).

The product improvement that followed processing of coconut oil from copra in the importing countries both increased total demand and changed the nature of the supply side of the industry. Dried portions of coconut meat – copra – were now sought, and though the technology of copra making is extremely simple and diffused quickly, profits could be obtained by the trader who bought whole nuts and made copra using his own supervised labour. Some also planted coconuts themselves on land obtained from islanders. But the growth of coconut planting was slow, in part because of the long gap between planting and maturation of the palms; the plantation industry began with shorter-term crops including coffee, tobacco, maize, sugar cane and cotton.

Land alienation began seriously in New Caledonia and Fiji in the 1850s, often by direct seizure in the former territory, by negotiation and pressure in the latter, where rudimentary kingdoms had emerged in the eastern part of the country. An American demand for a large indemnity, against damage sustained by one of their citizens, was intermittently pressed and led to a large – fortunately never wholly-implemented – grant to an Australian company which offered to meet the debt. There were expectations of British annexation in the late 1850s, and a consul was appointed. The 30 to 40 Europeans resident in Fiji in 1858 were augmented swiftly in the 1860s as the price of cotton soared following outbreak of the American Civil War. Land sales increased, and though most plantations remained very small over 30 gins were in operation by 1867. Fijians failed to offer themselves as workers in sufficient numbers, and by 1870 over 1,200 workers had been imported from surrounding island groups. Cotton plantations were also established in New Caledonia and in the central New Hebrides. When the market for cotton collapsed in the 1870s, planters shifted to maize sold for livestock feed in eastern Australia, but also began more seriously to turn to the planting of coconuts.

By 1870 there were already strong colonial establishments in New Caledonia and Fiji, including a European penal colony in the former territory, still the only one under effective political control. There was a much smaller establishment on Efaté in the central New Hebrides, but the Solomon Islands and the whole of New Guinea were still without any shore-based colonial activity whatsoever. Further east in the Pacific there were major colonial establishments in Samoa and Tahiti, while in Hawaii American commercial dominance was already leading to demands for annexation. The Spanish empire still slumbered from the Philippines across Micronesia, and to the north in Japan the Meiji restoration was just two years old.

THE MINERS

There was one group of invaders who ranged more widely even than the planters, missionaries and traders. A roving population of men, working in many trades, but experienced in prospecting for gold, was loose in the Pacific in the years after the Californian gold rush of 1849. Such men found gold in Australia and New Zealand, and their numbers were further augmented. Mainly European, they included also some Chinese, whose presence in Australia led to grave fears. When sub-humid New Caledonia was annexed by France in 1853 the sandalwood trade there was already approaching its end, and entrepreneurs brought in cattle to graze the western grasslands. As this business expanded, especially after 1860, it attracted many Australians with experience as stockmen; some of these had worked in the goldfields, and by 1863 small finds were already being made. Nickel was first identified in 1867, and in 1870 there was a major gold strike at Fern Hill, in the north of the island. A mine was developed, and this led in turn to the mining of copper, discovered in the same region shortly afterwards. Development remained ephemeral until the full value of the nickel deposits was realized in 1875 and quickly developed by the Anglo-Irish entrepreneur Higginson, who had earlier organized the gold and copper exploitation. Concentrated veins of six to twelve per cent nickel were mined, and a first fusion works was set up at Nouméa in 1887. Cobalt was discovered in 1875, and exploited by small miners at several points on the west coast, and there was also early development of iron ore, antimony and manganese. Chrome was discovered in 1875, but not developed until 1895. For a short period in the last years of the nineteenth century, New Caledonia was the world's leading producer of three alloy minerals – nickel, cobalt and chrome. Though quantities produced were small, their export from New Caledonia stimulated metallurgical developments which in turn stimulated discovery and exploitation elsewhere. There was a remarkably early geological survey and a tolerably complete geological map was completed in the 1890s. This development was almost in opposition to the plans of government for New Caledonia, but it laid the foundation for the ultimate form of the territorial economy, and foreshadowed transformations elsewhere in Melanesia that are only now coming to fruition.

Elsewhere there was early interest only in gold. Early indications in eastern New Guinea were not followed up, but there was a minor rush to Port Moresby in 1877, and a larger movement into the islands off the east end of Papua in 1888. Prospectors moved onto the mainland in the 1890s, advancing steadily westward and inland, reaching valleys north of the central range before 1914. Here, in the valley system inland of Lae, came the major strikes of 1922 and 1926, leading to the firm establishment of a mining industry in the Bulolo valley in the 1930s. Prospectors fanned out from this area. Some penetrated the long-hidden valleys of the populous central highlands in 1930, and had scoured this whole region by 1936. Others found and worked small deposits in Bougainville and in the Solomon Islands, leading to the first indication of much greater mineral discoveries. Some moved into Fiji, where a major strike was not made until the 1930s. Often, and most outstandingly in the discovery of the populous highland valleys of central New Guinea, the miners moved well ahead of all other forms of colonial penetration. Though the individual prospector has now given way to the multinational mining corporation, the pioneer rôle of the mining industry continues. As we shall see, the contribution of mining has never been unimportant in this region, and is burgeoning to major importance in the 1970s.

REFERENCES AND SOURCES

There are few general sources on the early colonial history of the western Pacific, perhaps the most complete accounts being in Naval Intelligence Division (1943–5), written mainly by J. W. Davidson, and in J. M. Ward (1948). There is also much material, with emphasis mainly on the French Pacific, in Doumenge (1966). Most of the research is presented in specialized articles, especially in the *Journal of the Polynesian Society* (Wellington, N.Z.) and since 1966 in the *Journal of Pacific History* (Canberra, Australia). There are also valuable collections in Maude (1968) and in the collection of papers in Waigani Seminars (1969). Shineberg (1968) deals with an important aspect of the early contact period in her review of the sandalwood trade.

There is much more on particular territories. Still the most compendious source on Fiji before cession is Derrick (1946), while France (1969) deals exhaustively and elegantly with the story of land in this group. Among a massive literature on New Guinea particular mention might be made of Klein (1953–4), Souter (1964) and the historical material in Rowley (1965).

The argument over population 'decline' also has a very large literature. Two major early sources, both convinced of rapid decline, are Rivers (1922) and Roberts (1927); Baker (1928) analyses the New Hebrides material in detail. The modern counter-view is forcibly expressed by McArthur (1967) and with reference to the New Hebrides by McArthur and Yaxley (1968).

Modern sources on the history of mining in Melanesia are few: Healy (1967) provides the most detailed single account of gold mining in New Guinea, and there is also much material in Doumenge (1966). There is a very large early literature on New Caledonia, which has been utilized here, and a selection of more accessible titles would include Garnier (1867, 1876), Le Chartier (1885), Cordeil (1885), Bridon (1890), Benoit (1892), Pelatan (1892) and Bernard (1894) - the last named being a published doctoral thesis of great value.

CHAPTER 3

DIFFUSION AND ESTABLISHMENT

Melanesia is an archipelago, and only navigational constraints stood in the way of giving any coastal place an equal chance of selection by the invaders. This being so, it is perhaps surprising that the nineteenth-century colonialists did not behave as did the Spaniards in the Antilles around 1500; these latter by-passed the outer screen of small islands, and made their bases on the large islands that lay beyond. Yet even though the western tip of New Guinea lies close to the earliest centres of colonial activity in the Moluccas, and nearest to the old-established Dutch base in Java, the effective penetration of this region began in the southeast and rolled across the archipelago to enter the westernmost territory last of all. Approach using the southeasterly variables, or Trades, may have influenced this pattern, and the presence of malaria in almost all parts of the region but Fiji and New Caledonia may have operated as an additional constraint, but the more fundamental consideration perhaps arises from the nature of Pacific colonialism. Only in New Caledonia was it at first a national enterprise with military force. Elsewhere the early invaders were in small groups on individual vessels; they had to move cautiously, establish themselves generally on small islands and peninsulas and retain contact with early centres of establishment in the Polynesian islands made known and enticing by tales of the eighteenth-century navigators.

By about 1870 there was a fairly clear distinction between a partly-colonized Melanesia in the three southeastern groups, a fringe still undergoing initial penetration in the Solomon Islands and the coastlands of eastern New Guinea, and the virtually uncontacted mass of central and western New Guinea. The next two decades saw the establishment of a new major centre of diffusion in the Bismarck Archipelago north of New Guinea, and of scattered bases around the eastern New Guinea coast and in the Solomon Islands. During these same two decades the formation of a colonial economy underwent rapid strides in the southeastern groups, where this was the period of establishment. Establishment came in the period 1890–1910 further to the northwest, and in much of inland eastern New Guinea it was delayed until after 1950 by a succession of events which slowed the rate of advance.

Generally speaking, the first major call of the colonial economy on a newly penetrated region has been on its resources in labour. Demand for land has followed and has been succeeded by investment. Some areas have never experienced the second and third stages, and have moved directly from the first to a fourth: development within the residentiary complex itself under the initiative of government.

THE LABOUR TRADE

Even in its beginnings, the Pacific labour trade confronted Victorian colonialism with a dilemma. While convinced of the virtues of permitting private enterprise to operate free of 'miserable legislation', Victorian Europeans were at the same time almost habituated in the ethical doctrines of a once-fiery anti-slavery movement. The British especially were convinced of the folly of extending rule where this cost was not counterbalanced by gains in trade, and on such grounds resisted the acquisition of empire in the Pacific islands for more than fifty years. Yet the ethical motive drew them steadily deeper into the region, and if rivalry with France and Germany precipitated the final scramble, it was concern over protection and evangelization of the 'savages' which brought Britain to the position of emerging dominant from that scramble.

The Pacific labour trade began in the 1850s, when a few islanders were taken to Australia and later to Fiji. In 1862 came the forced recruitment of Polynesians for the mines and plantations in Peru, followed by swift protest and control. The next year saw the beginning of serious recruitment for New Caledonia, Fiji and also Queensland, while smaller numbers were also taken to Samoa, Tahiti and Hawaii. The New Hebrides were the first major source area, and recruiting there continued until the end of the century. Recruiting schooners soon moved on to the Solomon Islands, and later to eastern Papua, but the mainland of New Guinea was hardly touched until plantations were established in the Bismarck Archipelago.

There was never slavery, but terms of contract were at best vague, and methods of recruitment often questionable. Many reported abuses are reviewed by writers such as J. M. Ward (1948), Parnaby (1964) and Scarr (1967a). Wawn, a recruiter who was himself ultimately suspended for such abuses, describes the more honest aspects of the business in some detail:

> A knife and a tomohawk, a handful of beads, half-a-pound of tobacco, a few pipes and a fathom of calico were considered sufficient payment for a man or woman ...But the demand for firearms was rapidly increasing and two years after this I had to give a musket as well as tobacco and pipes before a man was allowed to leave the shore (Wawn, 1893, 8–9).

There were many incidents, and some vessels were overwhelmed by revengeful islanders, yet individuals were often very willing to go. Giles, a passenger on a recruiting schooner in the 1870s, recounts how youngsters in Santo, New Hebrides, leapt into the ship's boat and remained deaf to the entreaties of their womenfolk to return (Giles, 1968). Recruits preferred to go to Australia, rather than to Fiji where they felt out of touch with civilization.

Queensland absorbed the bulk of Melanesian labour, and from the late 1860s until 1901 a running battle continued between white labour interests and the sugar plantation and other companies over the question of the 'Kanakas'. The first controlling Act was in 1868. In 1880 the right to employ islanders was restricted to persons engaged in tropical agriculture, and in 1884 this was further narrowed to the sugar industry. Recruitment was halted in 1890, when there were about 10,000 islanders in the colony, mostly on three-year contracts and paid 50p a month, and keep. Twenty-two per cent of the population of North Queensland was then non-European. Recruiting recommenced in 1892, but the first Italian workers arrived in 1891, and from then on white labour became increasingly available. The cost of island labour also increased sharply. In 1901 it was said that the recruitment of each worker cost £25.00, and that with wages then up to 50p a week and keep, the total cost of a Kanaka was between 12p and 15p a day (Mackey, ms. marginal note in: Mitchell Library [Sydney], Cuttings on Coloured Labour, 8/6/1901). Numbers remained between 7,000 and 10,000, but a final decision to repatriate was taken in 1901, and in 1906 some 4,500 labourers were returned to the islands. The trade in island labour to Fiji continued a few years more, but the last Solomon Islanders recruited for Fiji were returned home in 1912.

ISLANDERS, CONVICTS AND ASIANS IN NEW CALEDONIA

France annexed New Caledonia in 1853 as a naval station, but early efforts were made to establish agricultural and pastoral settlement. Labourers were recruited from the nearby Loyalty Islands and after 1860 from the New Hebrides. When nickel mining began in 1875 the skilled workers came mainly from Australia, the black labourers from the New Hebrides and only in small numbers from the local population: in 1874 some 2,500 New Hebrideans were at work in New Caledonia. In 1884, when only 800 remained, they were employed at about 6p per week plus keep at about 2p a day (Lemire, 1884, 53).

The colonists wished to expand use of island labour, but New Caledonia became a penal colony in 1863, and transportation continued in various forms until 1897. Most of the convicts were criminal transportees, their number reaching 10,500 by 1887. The law required that each transportee sentenced for a period of seven years or less should remain in the colony after sentence for a period equal to the term, as a *libéré*, free, but still subject to control. Those sentenced for eight years or longer remained for life. The convict population was overwhelmingly male, and few *libérés* succeeded as farmers; as their number grew the problem of finding employment became severe.

The 'simple transportees' were augmented after 1871 by 3,900 of the Paris Communards who, together with political prisoners from Algeria after 1874, were employed mainly in direct labour at a settlement on the Ile des Pins. Few remained after an amnesty in 1880. The colony got little from them, nor from habitual criminals who were transported for life after 1885 over fierce protests among the free settlers.

To ease the problem of finding private employment for a convict and *libéré* workforce which exceeded 10,000, the government arbitrarily halted immigration of island workers in 1882, and again in 1885 after a short resumption. Recruitment recommenced in 1889, but though there were 3,000 New Hebrideans in the colony in 1893 labour shortage persisted and threatened to become acute as transportation came to an end, since the residentiary population seemed to be vanishing. A few Chinese were imported in 1883, and in 1893 the nickel company imported the first 600 Japanese; numbers grew to reach 2,500 by 1900. Some Vietnamese political prisoners were sent to New Caledonia in 1891 and other Vietnamese were recruited by private employers. The first Javanese workers arrived in 1901, and by 1921 there were almost 4,000 Asian workers in the colony. Their number was further augmented after World War I, as we shall see below.

New Caledonia offers a microcosmic, but interesting, opportunity to compare the rôle of four distinct sources of labour: the residentiary Melanesians, imported islanders, European convicts and tied settlers, and Asians. Residentiary Melanesians were never employed in large numbers, though 300 were at work in Nouméa at the time of the 1878 rebellion. They could slip away too easily, and even when deprived of their own land they were able to acquire land elsewhere through kin and affines, and were unwilling to work for the low wages offered. Immigrant islanders from the Loyalties and New Hebrides were far more readily controlled, and the cost could thus be more accurately budgeted. For a long time they were seen as the main hope of private enterprise, and some important political action was initiated on the basis of this assessment. Convicts were cheap, but very unwilling, workers. They were paid at 48p a month, fed and lodged by the employer except in Nouméa and were thus more costly than islanders. *Libérés* cost far more, at an average of £3.00 a month plus food and lodging (Lemire, 1884; 55, 251–2). It was remarked of them that they were:

unsuitable for agriculture...possible only as workers for the state and industry ...Even if they were good workers...they would still be unsuitable for most rural employers; they cost too much. Is one going to pay 25p or 30p a day for picking coffee or making copra? This work needs to be done by cheap labour. We find these workers among the natives (Cordeil, 1885, 111, translated).

Convicts were thus engaged mainly in public works, and did much to give Nouméa its present air of established permanence. *Libérés* were often settled on the land in agricultural concessions, but being entirely without capital were unable to specialize in cash crops, and often eked out a miserable existence aided by administration support. Only 1,200 were on the land in 1893, against a planned total of 13,000. Demoralized, penniless *libérés*, dispossessed of their concessions as failures, made poor workers. Asians were cheap, cheaper than islanders. They could be disciplined more readily, often organized their own work gangs, and gave better value to their employers. They showed their resentments less than did the islanders, but – especially among the Vietnamese – there was a harvest of hatred against the French that was reaped in time.

THE WEST INDIAN MODEL IN FIJI

Planters in Fiji encountered the same problem of labour shortage as their counterparts in New Caledonia, notwithstanding the much larger residentiary population. Fijians could not be persuaded to work regularly or consistently, and efforts to recruit islanders encountered competition from Queensland and New Caledonia. Just before cession in 1874, a settler-dominated 'independent' government introduced a poll tax designed to force Fijians to work in order to raise the necessary money, but it was quickly abolished by the new colonial administration and the whole system of regulation in Fiji, and in the island labour trade, was tightened up by the Islanders' Protection Act of 1875.

Islander labour continued to be a main source until 1890, and was employed especially in the coconut industry, and in efforts to plant other long-term crops. However, the new governor proposed that Indians be imported on the pattern of Mauritius, Natal, Trinidad and British Guiana. Arrangements were made in 1878 and the first five-year contract labourers arrived in 1879. It was argued that such introduction would protect the Fijians from exploitation and guard their 'way of life', much the arguments that de las Casas used in advocating Negro slaves for the Antilles in the sixteenth century. There were no opposing interests protecting white labourers, or the employment of convicts, and the prospect of an assured supply of Asian labour had important consequences.

The growing sugar industry of northern Queensland faced an uncertain future in 1880 in view of mounting white labour agitation. The successful Colonial Sugar Refining Company of Sydney decided to hedge its bets by extending activities to the more tolerant environment of Fiji and sustained this policy through the next twenty-five years of growing doubts over its prospects in Australia (Colonial Sugar Refining Company, Reports, 1890, 1891). Other companies followed, and a strong sugar plantation industry developed throughout the dry zone of the two main islands, and in parts of the wet zone of Viti Levu. The development might have been even greater but for a long period of depressed prices, and CSR, as the most powerful company, was consistently the main importer of labour. After 1882, Government came to the aid of private planters who might otherwise have been eliminated, but it was not until economic conditions improved after 1900 that small planters became significant employers of Indians.

The sugar plantations replicated the characteristic Caribbean model of a 'total institution', the company being employer, provider and immediate authority, with minimum Government control. Wages, at 5p a day for men, 4p a day for women, were not increased from beginning to end of the system, though there were some late improvements in working conditions. But Government regulation of the rules of importation did have an important effect. It was required that 40 per cent of the immigrants be women, and that workers have the option of remaining in Fiji on expiry of contract. More than half remained, renting land from the company and freeholders, or leasing it from Fijians on terms that were only very gradually regulated. They continued to grow sugar, but now under contract to the company which provided planting material and advice. A small stream of free immigrants, mainly Punjabi and Gujerati, began to follow the contract workers after 1903, and initiated a movement into Suva and other nascent towns. By 1908 some 18,600 ha of land were held on some form of tenure by Indians, against one ha in 1888, and the firm establishment of an Indo-Fijian population was assured.

For the planters, static wages meant declining real costs, and with an improvement in returns the demand for Indian labour grew steadily; immigration exceeded 3,000 per annum in several years after 1900 and reached a peak in 1911. As the supply of island labour finally dried up, Indians were also employed in other plantation industries, and by 1916 only two-thirds of Indians under contract were in the sugar industry (Gillion, 1962, 95–102). The Indian immigration was of immense economic benefit to the Fijian national economy, and the colony built up a commanding position in the islands. But the social and political cost was enormous, to Fijians and Indians alike, and the whole sum of the bill has by no means yet been presented.

LAND AT A SHILLING AN ACRE

Labour, not land, was the scarce resource for the colonial system in this establishment period, and in a great degree it was the supply of labour that guided and regulated the flow of capital. Land was almost incredibly easy to acquire, and resistance, where it was encountered, was usually swept aside at small cost. We shall examine the reasons in a later chapter, but the effect was that title was acquired to huge areas, far beyond any possibility of development with the labour and capital available.

Small offshore islands were often the first choice, because they presented no delimitation problems and offered more security. On the larger islands the method was often as follows. Having, for a consideration, obtained the right to land, the would-be alienator would walk around it blazing trees – tiring work – and over-estimate its area. The estimated acreage would then appear on a document to which the indigenous 'owners' would put their marks. Survey pegs might be placed, but they would soon vanish, and perhaps be replaced further out. Thus initial 'grants' of 100 ha would become holdings of 500. The cost was so small that it is meaningless to relate it to potential production. A few axes, tobacco and trade goods sufficed for many years. In 1873, the would-be settler in the New Hebrides with 'pluck and some capital' was advised to:

> arrive in time to commence cotton planting. The first thing you have to do on landing is to buy your land – an easy matter generally, unless you take a fancy to some of the natives' reserves [cultivated areas]. A shilling per acre will generally procure you as much as you want, and leave the natives none the worse (Campbell, 1873, 186).

As late as 1893, in the same group, buying land was still easy, for '£50.00 in cash or judiciously selected trade ought to purchase from two to five hundred acres' (Lindt, 1893, 33). By contrast, the labour recruiters were then asking £10.00 for delivery of each new worker.

This situation led to overlapping claims, and to the almost complete alienation of wide tracts of land. As in the labour trade, control of excesses in land alienation was an early objective of belatedly-established administrations. A land commission set up in Fiji confirmed less than half the claims presented to it, and comparable, if smaller, reductions were made elsewhere. Once Government was established, it became possible for speculators to realize higher returns on land they had acquired earlier, and there was some improvement in the prices paid to indigenous holders. On Guadalcanal, Solomon Islands, 8,000 ha were bought for £60 in trade goods in 1886, were transferred for £200 in 1905, and for £40,000 in 1907 after partial development. Nine hundred and ninety ha were bought in 1902 for 3,000 porpoise teeth, five cases of trade tobacco, and some calico, pipes and matches valued at £5.00. In 1903 the land was resold for £400 (Lasaqa, 1972). Government itself cashed in on the market by employing 'waste lands' legislation, under which all allegedly unused land fell to the Crown, and could then be leased to occupiers at a rising rental.

In some areas the methods employed were very rough indeed. We have seen that initial occupation of western New Caledonia was pastoral, and hence required large areas of land for unfenced range. This had serious consequences for an indigenous agriculture based in part on complex irrigation systems, without fencing. Legislation to create 'reserves' was promulgated as early as 1868, and was applied vigorously. Opposition, or the slaughtering of errant cattle, was punished by sequestration of land, and most of the immediate hinterland of Nouméa was cleared in this way by the mid-1860s. A rebellion in the north in 1862 was followed by clearing of a large area. A reporter in 1878 contrasted the behaviour of two lessees who found villages on their new concessions. One allowed the villagers to harvest their standing crops before he evicted them; the other threw them off at once, burned the village, and sold the dispossessed Melanesians the yams and taro they had planted (*Sydney Morning Herald*, 12 October 1878). The end result of all this, and later events in New Caledonia, is that the Melanesian reserves now occupy only 8.5 per cent of the area of the main island.

More varied methods were used in New Guinea. The German chartered company in the northeast received the exclusive right to occupy or dispose of 'vacant' land, and to conclude deals for purchase of occupied land. In the central areas of closer occupation the Imperial Government which took over in 1899 made serious attempts to learn the indigenous land tenure system, and operate in relation to it. But pressures from settlers were strong. In 1900 a certain Wolff became interested in an area near Mt Varzin on the Gazelle Peninsula of New Britain. He bought 320 ha for a quantity of trade goods, and began his plantation. The residentiary matrilineage disagreed over boundaries, and over the authority of the elder who had made the sale. In 1902 the plantation was attacked, and Wolff's wife and son were killed. An acting governor decided this was a signal for a general uprising and took punitive action, killing many people and sequestering a large parcel of their land, some of which was later added to Wolff's plantation (Leyser, 1965). In more outlying areas it was sometimes found convenient to offer licence to an entrepreneur to 'pacify' an area, and claim such land as he wanted as his reward.

Matters were under tighter control in the British-administered area of Papua, where an early governor legislated the sole right of alienation to Government – a practice which has since become general throughout the region. Land became available to settlers only on leasehold, with the condition that one-fifth of the lease was to be planted by the end of the fifth year, on pain of forfeiture. This condition was applied, so that leasehold land fell from a peak of almost 150,000 ha in 1911 to only 81,000 ha in 1915.

But land never became scarce. The situation as described by the Governor of German New Guinea in 1913 would stand for almost the whole of Melanesia:

> The principles of land concession have become familiar and appear to meet the requirements of the particular kind of cultivation in the colony. The great impetus to European plantation economies was largely the result of the accessibility to the natives arising through their pacification and to the conditions of land concession. One may affirm that today European economic enterprise (up to the present numerically predominantly German) is only limited by its dependence on the possibility of obtaining labour. Capital was available in an increasing degree, in fact more rapidly than was compatible with the opening up [for recruitment of labour] of the districts not yet pacified (German New Guinea Reports [in translation], 1912–13, 170).

THE RÔLE OF CAPITAL IN THE ESTABLISHMENT PERIOD

Capital was needed from an early stage to develop the land, but more especially to provide the infrastructure and organization needed to establish trade. The first company to operate in the region was Godeffroy's firm of copra and coconut oil buyers. By offering credit, this company like all its successors soon acquired control over private traders and small planters, and became a planter in its own right. Godeffroy's company failed, but its successor, the Deutsche Handels- und Plantagen-Gesellschaft der Sudsee Inseln zu Hamburg, spread its tentacles over a very large part of the Pacific, trading, planting, and buying land both from speculators and directly from indigenes. It was the model of the vertically integrated, multinationally operating corporation that has since been widely replicated. By the 1870s three or four trading and planting companies were already operating out of Australia, and these gradually fell into the hands of two main corporations in a manner we shall describe below. The Colonial Sugar Refining Company brought another and more specialized type of operation from Australia to Fiji, while in New Caledonia Higginson's first Société le Nickel was formed in 1875, mainly by local interests, but it fell increasingly under the sway of the Banque Rothschild in Paris, which became the main controlling interest in 1896.

A number of trading and planting companies were formed in the islands, the better to mobilize capital. A number survive, especially in New Caledonia and to a lesser degree in Australian New Guinea, but others have fallen under the sway of the larger corporations. Though small by world standards, the companies operating in the south Pacific achieved considerable influence by the late nineteenth century, and some of them had an important political rôle.

German enterprise was strongest in this area. The chartered Neu-Guinea Compagnie was formed in 1883 to annex land in New Guinea, and to administer and develop it on behalf of the Imperial Government. Their charter was abrogated in 1899, but the Compagnie continued as the largest land development company in German New Guinea until 1919. The Jaluit Gesellschaft had a similar commercial-administrative rôle in the Marshall Islands until it too was absorbed into the imperial system based on German New Guinea in the first decade of this century.

Though there was a British attempt in the Solomon Islands, the chartered company system was not adopted elsewhere. But the political rôle of the private company was strong in several territories, especially in the New Hebrides, where New Caledonian interests made a serious attempt to force the hand of their metropolitan government in the 1880s. The basic issue was labour. The 2,500 free settlers in New Caledonia were fearful of being swamped by the *libérés*, and increasingly concerned at the growing dominance of the penal administration in government and land holding. When in 1882 the right to import New Hebridean labour was suddenly abrogated there was a sharp reaction. Under the leadership of Higginson and other miners, a Compagnie Calédonienne des Nouvelles-Hébrides was formed in Nouméa, and its capital fully subscribed. In effect a partly-owned subsidiary of Higginson's Société le Nickel, the Compagnie Calédonienne sought to buy out all Anglo-Australian landholders in the New Hebrides, acquire additional land from the indigenes, and establish a French settlement so as to oblige the French Government to tear up their non-intervention agreement of 1878 with Britain, and annex the group: the labour of the New Hebrides would thus become freely and exclusively available to New Caledonia (Lemire, 1884; Cordeil, 1885).

By October 1882 the Compagnie was already at work, and within two years had acquired most of the Anglo-Australian holdings from owners very ready to sell at the prices offered. Several anglophone planters who remained were working for the Compagnie. Other land was acquired from New Hebrideans by methods which marked perhaps the lowest ebb in ethical standards: 'local tradition has it that [one company agent, Bartelémy Gaspard] had enticed the bushmen aboard, made them drunk, then got them to name the hills and other physical features ashore; these were then entered upon a "deed of sale", to which their marks were obtained' (Scarr, 1967a,

199). Plantations of coffee and coconuts were established, and though many of them failed a firm colony was established on Efaté and in southeast Santo. By 1908 it was not unfairly stated that while the 'British' were drifters, the French were: 'a fixed element, in close relation with the soil; they hold almost all the agricultural land, on which for the most part they live with their families...for them, to hold the land is to conquer' (Brunet, 1908, 104, translated).

But there was opposition, mainly from the one organized body on the anglophone side. The Australian Presbyterian Mission sometimes forestalled the Compagnie in buying land, and sought support in Australia. They obtained it from a Presbyterian entrepreneur then just beginning to extend his Queensland business into the islands, James Burns, who supported the foundation of an Australasian New Hebrides Company with the avowed object of 'securing of these islands for the British and the expulsion of the French' (Scarr, 1967a, 203; O'Reilly, 1957, 29–30). They gained a subsidy from the New South Wales Government to operate a shipping service, and set up planters.

Both companies operated continually at a loss, and neither survived the depression of the 1890s. The Australian company required more and more support from Burns, and was taken over by his company, Burns Philp, in 1896. The Compagnie Calédonienne was involved in Higginson's bankruptcy in 1894, but the French Government supported a new Société Française des Nouvelles-Hébrides to take over its interests. This was reconstituted in 1904 with the solid and lasting support of the Saigon-based Banque de l'Indo-Chine. The deadlock between British-Australian and French-New Caledonian interests became insoluble, and led to the political compromise of 1906.

Corporation influence in public affairs is also evident in the Solomon Islands. Until a British Protectorate was finally established in 1894 there was minimum control over either recruiting or land alienation, and in the 1880s considerable tracts were 'acquired' by private entrepreneurs, by the Compagnie Calédonienne and by the Deutsche Handels- und Plantagen-Gesellschaft: so little was done with this land that sometimes it was only in seeking to register later alienations that the earlier title was discovered. In 1898 an ambitious Pacific Islands Company was formed in London and Sydney, incorporating interests over a wide area of the Pacific. The company sought a ninety-nine-year occupation licence over large parts of the Solomon Islands, offered to assume burdens of administration, and bought out some existing holders, including the French and German holdings. However, they preferred a 'waste land' rule applied in their favour, so that government would declare unused land to be 'waste', claim it and then lease it to private companies. Problems over definition of such 'waste land' led to prolonged delays.

The Pacific Islands Company had land, and support in high places, but lacked capital. In 1900 they had a windfall in the discovery of high-grade rock phosphate on Ocean Island and Nauru, the latter unfortunately under the control of the German Jaluit Gesellschaft. Capital and swift action were both needed, when in 1901 one of the company's directors found himself on board ship from Sydney to Vancouver in company with the British soap manufacturer, Lever. Lever's 'Sunlight Soap' business had been built up on the use of palm oil and coconut oil, and became an early multinational corporation with interests in many countries. It was to inspect factories in Australia and Canada that Lever made his world tour. The time was opportune, since he was contemplating further vertical integration by acquiring direct control of copra production in the Pacific. Lever was thus persuaded to invest handsomely in a phosphate-mining subsidiary to be formed by the Pacific Islands Company, in return for a large share of the company's scattered and little-developed holdings. A subsidiary, Lever's Pacific Plantations, was formed in Sydney to develop this land. It was at first a bad bargain, though the influx of funds enabled the phosphate company to treat successfully with the Jaluit Gesellschaft before the German Government had time to realize what was happening. Lever's Pacific Plantations decided to concentrate only in the Solomons, disposing of the other holdings mainly to Burns Philp – a transaction which led to a long-lived working arrangement for shipping services. In 1905 and 1906 Lever took over all the Pacific Islands Company's land in the Solomons, including the occupation licence to 'waste land', which was somehow extended from 99 to 999 years in the process! (Wilson, 1954, 159–63; Lasaqa, 1972; Scarr, 1967a). Development was rapid, and over 2,000 ha were planted to coconuts in the three years 1907–9 alone (LPPL Report, 1927). The company had acquired over 120,000 ha of land by 1913, when more rigid controls over alienation were at last applied by Government.

Land was thus available in abundance, and no contemporary Pacific enterprise had such a backing in capital, but the problem was labour. In 1911 it was estimated that the local supply in the Solomon Islands was only about 5,000 at any one time, so that 'foreign labour of some sort will before long be required to supplement local supply' (BSIP Handbook, 1911, 47). This statement was part of a campaign to obtain Indian labour. The Colonial Office was sympathetic, but there was opposition in Australia, which at that time was expected to take over administration of the Solomon Islands. An alternative proposal to introduce 'free' Indian immigrants was then advanced, but now rejected by the Government of India. Lever therefore shifted capital input to more kindly fields of enterprise in Africa, and growth in the Solomons was slowed. Most of the land acquired remained undeveloped, including huge tracts on Kolombangara Island, once described by Lever as 'an ideal spot for Indians [whence] they would spread all over the Solomon Islands' (Wilson, 1954, 164).

THE BURDEN OF WHITE MAN'S GOVERNMENT

With the exception only of the French in New Caledonia, and of the Australian colonies in Papua, governments were very reluctant to assume the costs of administration in these remote and seemingly-worthless lands. Since trade was supposed to develop best in the absence of government interference, and civilization should follow trade, the arguments for establishing colonial rule were based either on the need to protect some established interest from foreign interference, or on the need to regulate unbridled excesses of private colonialists. The Netherland Government laid claim to western New Guinea in 1828 simply to forestall a dimly feared British move that might place foreign entrepreneurs close to the Moluccas: they did almost nothing with their acquisition until the end of the century, and then only in response to British and German activity in the east of the big island, which might threaten their right to retain an unoccupied territorial claim. France acquired New Caledonia in 1853 with more positive intent, under the imperialist government of Louis Napoléon. There was desire to obtain some territorial stake, however small, in a southwest Pacific where French explorers had once been as active as the British, but more than this was the navy's need for a way station between Tahiti and the main field of French Asian enterprise in Indo-China. New Caledonia was administered by naval officers for many years. But even France was reluctant to go further. The Loyalty Islands were definitively annexed only in 1864, for fear of the political influence of British missionaries established there, and the filibuster of the Compagnie Calédonienne in the New Hebrides was not supported until it was too late to obtain an exclusively French solution.

Britain was drawn into Fiji by local entrepreneurs of British extraction. A seeming American threat in the 1850s was countered by the appointment of a British consul and an 'offer' of cession, which was refused. In the 1870s the settlers – planters and traders – supported the proclamation of the ruler of the Bau federation, Cakobau, as 'King' of Fiji; however, the King's Government ruled not from Bau, but from the settlers' base at Levuka on Ovalau Island to the north. The Government failed to control a deteriorating situation, and in 1873 a new offer of cession was made, this time to be accepted.

The establishment of British rule in Fiji in 1874 transformed the situation in the whole region. A Western Pacific High Commission based on Fiji was formed to regulate the labour trade in 1877, and to control and protect British subjects in a wide area including Tonga, the Line Islands, the Gilberts, Marshalls and Carolines, New Guinea, the Solomon Islands, and all other areas not under a regular government. The navy was the only means of implementation, and as relations with the navy were not made clear, the system of gunboat government from the high seas did not work well. But the statement of British paramountcy stimulated other metropolitan powers to reconsider their own intentions, and there was a rapid sequence of events.

German trading vessels from Apia had operated as far afield as the Caroline Islands and the Bismarck Archipelago since 1870, and shore stations were set up in the New Britain area in the mid-seventies. The pace accelerated after 1877, and the Queensland Government put increasing pressure on its metropole to annex New Guinea. In 1883 the Resident Magistrate from Thursday Island raised the British flag at Port Moresby. The action was repudiated, but was followed immediately by the annexations of the Neu-Guinea Compagnie, which in turn led to a hasty turnabout of British policy, and annexation of the southeastern part of the island. The Spaniards successfully challenged German penetration in the Carolines two years later, but in the resulting arbitration the Marshall Islands fell into the German sphere. In 1886 the tropical western Pacific was, by agreement, divided into British and German 'spheres of influence', but with a declaration of reciprocal freedom of trade. In 1899, at the time of the Spanish-American war, the German Imperial Government moved swiftly to acquire the Carolines and Marianas, and at the same time, or soon thereafter, took over direct administration of northeastern New Guinea and the Marshall Islands from the chartered companies. An organized west Pacific empire was designed, with successive improvement in communications, until by 1910 the Imperial Government was ready to proceed to administrative integration, based on the new capital at Rabaul in New Britain.

British moves were less purposeful, but in 1893 the Western Pacific High Commission was reconstituted to empower the setting up of land-based governments in areas where British subjects had established residence. 'Protectorates' were established under this system in the Solomon Islands and in the Gilbert and Ellice Islands. The Santa Cruz group north of the New Hebrides was attached to the Solomon Islands Protectorate without much objection from France, and a new division of the Pacific between Britain and Germany in 1899 gave all the Solomons group but Bougainville to Britain. There remained the New Hebrides, where a policy of 'joint minimum intervention' by Britain and France proved increasingly ineffective as their citizens fought a commercial war on the land. After discussions delayed only by the intransigence of Australia, the 'temporary' solution of the

Anglo-French Condominium was decreed in 1906, and a government set up under its provisions in 1907. The treaty, which flowed out of the new spirit of *entente cordiale*, was a compromise throughout: agreement was truly arrived at on only one fundamental point – that the arrangement was transitory, and that the other party must ultimately go. This was the great age of jingoism, when it could be written by a New Hebridean colonist of British origin that: 'The British empire is in its infancy, and is yearly gathering strength. The trivial interests of an unexpanding power like France must give way before its path' (Jacomb, 1914, 203).

ON BEING COLONIZED

Little has survived in the written record of the residentiary reaction to all this, but its nature can be pieced together readily enough from the evidence. In the early phases the reaction was far from passive, except in response to the disastrous epidemics. Melanesians, like Polynesians, saw in the early visitors an opportunity to acquire goods, new forms of organization, new access to power over their enemies. The success of Kamehameha I in conquering almost all of Hawaii early in the nineteenth century was paralleled by the reunification of Tonga and the extension of a Tongan empire into eastern Fiji by mid-century, and by the wars between the east-Fiji federations which ended in the narrow victory of Bau in 1854. The delicate balance between Bau and the Tongans which ensued for the next twenty years was never satisfactorily resolved, and provided opportunities for the small European colony to establish its hegemony. Deeper within Melanesia the wars were in smaller compass, but they had devastating local effect.

There was everywhere the same active interest in manipulating contact and trade to advantage, in using the opportunities of labour recruitment to learn about a wider world, and in exploiting every perceived opportunity to gain access to the wealth of the outsiders and its secrets. Shineberg (1968, 215–16) has cogently argued of the early sandalwood traders that:

> Their importance to the Pacific islanders was that they gave them access to the only aspect of western civilization in which they showed an immediate and sustained interest – namely, to the European material culture in general and to the use of iron in particular...the islanders played a very lively part in their relations with the Europeans and...endeavoured to turn the coming of the white men to their best possible advantage.

There were many consequences of this behavioural response. In order to obtain closer contact with the sources of goods and information many villages were relocated on the seaboard, where they were accessible to traders and missionaries. Land was given up, without understanding in many cases that the transfer was to be permanent, in exchange rather for contact with the invading system than for the trinkets and consumables actually received. It was felt, as it still was in the 1950s and early 1960s in central New Guinea, that to have a resident white trader or planter was an advantage, giving new opportunities not only to acquire goods, but also to study the newcomers at close quarters and learn the secrets of their success. It was hoped to manipulate the newcomers to advantage, and only when it became evident that a disastrous mistake had been made did the reaction harden. We examine this problem more closely in Chapter 13. Sometimes there were sharper reactions, unpredictable and seemingly unjustifiable attacks and murders, perhaps of men whose aims were the least exploitative, such as missionaries. Desire for goods was often the major motive, as in more friendly reactions, but there may also have been suspicions of sorcery (a common cause of intra-Melanesian murder), simple bravado, fear, or a will to right some wrong, or some insult. The severity of the punitive action that followed such incidents in the later period may have quieted the immediate reactions, but also led to a withdrawal of cooperation that was sometimes very persistent indeed.

Where the impact became heavy, there was often a reaction of hopelessness verging on desperation. True colonial wars in the African pattern are absent from the history of Melanesia, but there was a fairly stiff campaign to subdue the recalcitrant hill tribes of Viti Levu in the later 1870s, and in New Caledonia there was a series of rebellions, none of which can have had any real hope of achieving success. The biggest of these was in 1878–9, in which almost 300 Europeans and a much greater number of Melanesians lost their lives. A naval officer who took part in the campaign is fairly clear on the basic causes:

> Perhaps there were a few isolated arbitary acts, or some bad treatment, but these were not sufficient to cause a revolt. A more serious burden was seizure of native lands, more or less justified, and the irruption of cattle onto the lands left to the natives...But the main cause of the rising, one might even say the sole cause, was the antagonism that one always finds between a conquered people and the conquerors. The conquered must either be absorbed, or disappear (Rivière, 1881, 281, translated).

New Caledonia, alone of the Melanesian islands, was made into a colony of settlement, much on the Australian model. Niceties of land alienation were little observed, and as we have seen, treatment was often savage. In the heavily penetrated west coast region, residentiary reaction was desperate. A minor incident led to arrest of some chiefs. The next night the post at Boulouparis was attacked and over 80 were killed. Panic followed, and in Nouméa many colonists fled on to ships in the harbour. A military force seeking to repair the cut telegraph line was ambushed, and its commander killed.

A policy of severe repression was put into effect, but nervousness and folly led to a spread of the rebellion. East coast tribes remained 'loyal', and were persuaded to aid in the suppression of traditional enemies. By October, after four months of punitive action:

Col. Wendling considers the revolt stamped out at Bouloupari. All the villages, to the number of nearly fifty, the plantations, coconuts, bananas, taro, sugarcane, every ordinary means of subsistence, are utterly demolished... The soldiers have had no feather-bed of it – every second day marching over fearful mountains, accompanied by a hard-working band of friendly natives whose abilities for destruction are described by the Colonel as something remarkable. The few remaining natives of the Bouloupari tribes are reported to have fled toward Bourail to join the new insurgents there (*Sydney Morning Herald*, 5 October 1878).

In November, however, the rebels were still troublesome at Bouloupari, and it was months before the revolt was finally quelled. A correspondent, who unlike the special correspondent quoted above, had no sympathy with the rebels, expressed his astonishment in these terms:

When it is taken into consideration that these men fighting to the very death... (have been)... as a rule well and kindly treated whenever they visited the colonists in all parts of the island, regarded in the same manner as are the aborigines by the Australian squatter upon stations occupied thirty or forty years, their present action against the colonists is inexplicable (*Sydney Morning Herald*, 15 November 1878).

Perhaps he showed perspicacity in his Australian comparisons. The whole western region where the rebellion was centred is today alienated land, almost bare of Melanesian villages and cultivation. But in 1880 a new law required colonists to fence in their cattle: the rebellion achieved that much.

But even in New Caledonia the conquered did not disappear. Widely ranging kin and affinal ties were availed by refugees to regroup in the limited areas remaining to the Melanesians, and as everywhere in the region individuals, if not society as a whole, found niches in the new system. It was out of this more adaptive and resilient approach to the invasion that, ultimately, the new Melanesia has been forged.

REFERENCES AND SOURCES

Many of the sources noted for Chapter 2 are also applicable here. J. M. Ward (1948) and the papers in Waigani Seminars (1969) are especially significant.

On the labour trade a rapidly growing literature is supplementing the early accounts of J. M. Ward and by Parnaby (1956, 1964), and the writings of contemporary participants such as Wawn (1893); a number of other contemporary accounts is now being republished. Scarr (1967a, 1967b, Introduction to Giles, 1968) has made a major contribution to new understanding, and further progress has been achieved by Corris (1968, 1970). Numerous data are given in the contemporary New Caledonian sources, and in a series of Parliamentary Papers and contemporary tracts and surveys surrounding the long controversy over Pacific Island labour in Queensland. Convict labour in New Caledonia is discussed in the sources cited for Chapter 2, while Maisonneuve (1872) provides some additional detail on convict settlements. On Asian labour at this period only Biskup (1970) has yet treated the subject significantly outside Fiji, but there is an excellent literature on Indian migration to and settlement in Fiji, especially Gillion (1962), and Mayer (1961, 1963). Much ancillary information is also provided by Lowndes (1956) and R. G. Ward (1965, 1969). Among contemporary accounts the most significant is that of Burton (1910).

Land alienation is touched on in a very large number of sources, and important detail is provided by Doumenge (1966), Scarr (1967a), R. G. Ward (1969), France (1969) and Lasaqa (1972), to mention only a few. Sack (1969, 1971) reviews German land policy with new eyes. There is an immense body of data in the records of the Fiji Land Claims Commission, the Lands Department of the New Hebrides Joint Court and other sources, and in view of the rising political significance of this topic fuller use of these data is to be expected.

The history of the companies is not so well documented, perhaps the only comprehensive accounts being in Couper (1967) and Brookfield with Hart (1971). The early history of Burns Philp is traced by Bolton (1967), and there is much incidental material in the 'bio-bibliographic' surveys of colonists in New Caledonia and the New Hebrides by O'Reilly (1953, 1957). The companies themselves provide brief histories in their advertising statements in *Pacific Islands Yearbook*. Wilson's (1954) history of the Unilever corporation has a useful review of the company's Pacific activities.

The establishment of government, on the other hand, is exhaustively treated. A selection of principal sources is represented by Derrick (1946), J. M. Ward (1948), Grattan (1963), Van der Veur (1966), Scarr (1967a) and Waigani Seminars (1969). There is also a large periodical literature.

There is still no fully adequate history of the New Caledonian rebellions, and many contemporary accounts are surprisingly silent on the subject. Rivière (1881) offers one of the fullest eye-witness accounts, and there is also valuable reportage in the *Sydney Morning Herald* for 1878–9 from two correspondents of very different views. Guiart (1968) analyses the effect of the war on the tribes most closely involved. Elsewhere in Melanesia there is an account of the 1873 rising of the Viti Levu hill peoples in Derrick (1946), and on risings around Madang in New Guinea in Lawrence (1961). References to many minor skirmishes are scattered through the literature.

CHAPTER 4

HIGH NOON: MELANESIA IN A WHITE MAN'S WORLD

Melanesia was awakened late on the morning of colonialism, and high noon came swiftly. The political territorial pattern took final shape only between 1899 and 1906, but the white man's burden was now everywhere shouldered, and his task was to plan progress in an orderly manner. In the years between 1910 and 1914 each administration was congratulating itself on its successes to date, and looking forward to a bountiful future. The depression of the 1890s was over, raw material prices had improved consistently over several years, and there was an unprecedented flow of capital investment, in Melanesia as in almost all the developing world. European emigration to the Americas and Australia peaked during these years; so did Indian emigration to Fiji. In this last and greatest era of *laissez-faire*, Melanesia had become part of one economic world, and shared its boom with that larger world. But those who really shared in the benefits were the agents of the colonial system: the others got a cut of the cake only in so far as they were useful.

FIRM ESTABLISHMENT OF EXPORT STAPLES IN FIJI AND NEW CALEDONIA

The two southeastern territories had each established access to sufficient labour from Asian sources by 1900, and entrepreneurs could proceed with a controllable development in which inputs of land, labour and capital might be adjusted in accordance with decision, without uncertainty arising from dealings with the residentiary complex. In Fiji the sugar industry grew steadily, mainly on a plantation basis. The dominant CSR company proceeded to rationalize both transport and milling: the last large mill was built at Lautoka in 1903, and further extensions of the cane area were linked to the existing mills by rail, rather than being provided with new mills. The area of land leased to Indians and small European planters grew; some Indian cane farmers even employed contract workers themselves. The copra industry also flourished, and there was a significant development of banana plantations. The growing free Indian population provided an increasingly important source of small entrepreneurs, while the Fijian population – still much the most numerous element – concerned itself with adaptation to the complex official systems for regulation of its land tenure, social life and economy, evolved out of an interpretation of traditional practice by a paternalistic administration. With Asian workers so readily and cheaply available, employers showed growing reluctance to employ Fijians at all.

In New Caledonia troubles with the indigenous population still smouldered, erupting in a last rising as late as 1917. The indigenes had been effectively removed from the colonial economy – though by means somewhat different from those adopted in Fiji. Governor Feillet, who had brought transportation of convicts to an end in the 1890s, made a major effort to attract free colonists to a series of agricultural settlements: over 500 families were established on the land, and much firmer foundations were laid for a small-plantation system of coffee growing. Entry of the disease *Hemileia vastatrix* threatened to destroy the coffee groves in 1910–11, but prompt planting with new strains, coupled with the dry climate of western New Caledonia, saved this industry which had become the base of the European agricultural economy. The cattle industry still dominated most of the land, and more and more of the properties fell into the hands of a few large companies.

Far more critical for the future of New Caledonia was the fate of the mining industries. When Société le Nickel began operations in 1875 the main end use of nickel was in coinage, and demand was very limited. The supply from New Caledonia brought down the market price from over $US 8/kg to around $US 1.30/kg by 1885. Development of the sulphide ores at Sudbury, Ontario, brought additional supplies on to the market in 1888, but in the next year a technical breakthrough in Britain created a major new use for nickel, alloyed with steel to make armour plate. Despite massive expansion of Canadian production, it was not until 1896 that supply was sufficient to compete with SLN in the European market. When it did, however, New Caledonia almost went out of the mining business. Growth of the armaments industry after 1900 saved the situation, and under conditions of rising demand the technical problems involved in using the low-grade laterite ores were solved. In 1909 the trading company already dominant in New Caledonia, Maison Ballande of Bordeaux, set up the first of a series of fusion works just north of Nouméa, and they were followed by SLN in 1912. With adequate supplies of labour from the Tonkin delta region of northern Indo-China, the industry entered a new period of expansion.

Cobalt mining, always an activity of individual miners, did not recover from the fall in price that followed development of larger reserves elsewhere in the world. But chrome mining, also stimulated by metallurgical developments around the turn of the century, only began in 1908, and continued for many years. The firm mining orientation of the New Caledonian economy was now definitively established, and plans to develop closer agricultural settlement faded away.

THE RELUCTANT HEGEMONY OF COPRA

Elsewhere in Melanesia, except in Papua where gold production continued to be the main revenue-earner until after 1910, the pattern of development shifted more and more firmly to reliance on tree-crop plantations, and especially on the coconut. Among a complex of reasons, some concerned with the excessive price fluctuations which affected field crops such as cotton and maize, or tobacco, the one consistent causal factor is the persistent shortage of labour, in relation to the scale and speed of the development effort. As the last German report on New Guinea put it:

> The labour question today takes precedence in importance and incisive effect over all other problems, both economic and cultural. If the planting obligations of the country already taken up are to be discharged, the numbers of recruits will have to be almost doubled. The opening up of the island spheres [the Marianas, Carolines and Marshalls] of Kaiser-Wilhelmsland [the New Guinea mainland] and New Pomerania [New Britain outside the Gazelle Peninsula] may bring relief for the next few years (German New Guinea Reports [in translation], 1912–13, 596).

What was happening was a major attempt to utilize the available capital by developing as much as possible of the huge areas alienated in the previous decades, and still being alienated. There was a process of spread which fed on itself. With a residentiary complex in which human needs were tolerably well satisfied – sometimes called a condition of 'primitive affluence', perhaps rather inappropriately – it was hard to secure a stable labour force unless the recruits could be removed from their home areas. The reluctance of residentiary populations to work for wages except for short periods was augmented by another consideration: planters depended on the local populations for supply, as well as for labour. During the establishment period of plantations most planters made an income mainly by trading in indigenous copra, or by buying whole nuts and making copra from them. Most copra exported from both parts of New Guinea was produced from indigenous palms until 1910, and some 'chiefs' were said to receive as much as £15 a month from the business. In 1911 the German administration claimed to have instigated the planting of over 32,000 Melanesian-owned palms.

This was a situation in which planters might have been expected to raise wages in order to secure local labour. But a cheaper alternative was available. Away from the plantation areas the indigenous population had no local source of cash income with which to obtain the desired material goods. They were therefore willing to be recruited as long-term contract workers, and such recruits provided the planters with the stable work force that they required. In regions of small islands, where most of the people were within easy reach of the sea, recruiting could be done from vessels, often operated by the planters themselves. The same vessels carried outward cargoes of trade goods for sale, thus creating the demand for money that yielded the inward cargoes of labour. But in the larger land masses this method was less rewarding; universally prevalent local warfare not only made the areas dangerous for visitors, but also greatly limited the mobility of potential recruits toward the recruiter.

Hence it was necessary to pacify areas, develop a basic infrastructure, and create the conditions leading toward a demand for money, before a sufficient supply of labour could be tapped. Government activity in this area was constrained by a minimal administrative staff and budget, hence pacification could only be achieved by establishing private agents of the colonial system, as missionaries, traders or planters. So the economy continued to spread, and by spreading aggravated its problems of transport, and denied itself the economies of concentration. Foci of plantation activity did develop, but they were fed with labour from an enormous area. Thus of 9,268 new workers recruited in the whole German colony in 1912, 67 per cent came from islands in the Bismarcks, the Admiralties and Bougainville, 22 per cent from the New Guinea mainland, and 11 per cent from the Micronesian islands to the north. At this time 76 per cent of the planted area was in northern New Britain, New Ireland and on the north coast of Bougainville. Under the boom conditions of 1910–14 the spread of land alienation continued apace, but labour became more and more a critical constraint to development.

It was the same in other territories. Lt Governor Murray of Papua drew up a 'plan' for development of the colony in 1911, estimating labour requirements, and proposing a planned and balanced growth around three plantation crops: coconuts, rubber and sugar cane. He preferred that plantation development should remain concentrated in only two or three areas, but this happened only in the case of rubber; the coconut industry became widely dispersed. There was spread also in the Solomon Islands, even within the Lever organization, where undue dispersal of plantations had to be rationalized by a later and more cost-conscious generation of management. And in the New Hebrides and northern Fiji the same pattern was evolved. The consequence was the uneconomically wide spread of the coconut plantation industry which, coupled with the very small size of many plantations, created a legacy of inefficient operation that has held back progress in the industry as a whole. High fixed costs, due to remote location and small size, have reinforced pressures to hold down wages, and hence to continue use of unskilled migrant labour recruited from an ever-more-distant labour frontier. The principal benefit has been the provision of infrastructure to the same wide labour field; in time, this has become useful in local development.

Persistent labour shortage also explains the choice of crop. With capital investment in plantation development continually pressing beyond the limits of labour availability, there was constant economic pressure to economize on the use of labour. But capital-intensive methods of tropical crop production were then unknown, and are still wanting in many crops; the only available strategy was to concentrate on those crops having the least required density of labour. The field crops were thus excluded, except as catch crops grown during the maturation period when labour was not required for harvesting. More than this, it became increasingly difficult to cultivate labour-intensive crops such as coffee and cocoa, even though these had given excellent results and offered much higher income per ha. Coffee was developed in New Caledonia ultimately with Javanese labour. In the New Hebrides a population long accustomed to work for wages, and cut off from former outlets in Australia, facilitated the active planting of such crops after 1900. Even so, coconuts became increasingly the base crop of the economy.

This occurred in spite of strong efforts to diversify the plantation economies. In the German territory, an unsuccessful effort was made in the 1890s to grow tobacco near Madang, using Chinese labour. Failure seems to have been brought about by uneconomical loss of workers through mortality, but tobacco does well in this same area today. The Neu-Guinea Compagnie, and still more the Imperial Government after 1899, systematically sought to introduce a range of crops, and their botanical collections have formed the basis of the major centre for tropical crop research in Melanesia in modern times. Particularly great efforts were made to develop a rubber industry, based on *Ficus* for want of *Hevea* planting material, and collecting expeditions for *Ficus* and gutta-percha ranged far and wide between 1900 and 1910. *Ficus* was a failure, but on the southern side of the island the new Australian administration imported rubber seedlings on a large scale from Singapore in 1906, and established the basis of a continuing industry. Yet the proportion of the planted area under coconuts rose steadily in Papua, as elsewhere. From 67 per cent in 1910, it rose to 70 per cent in 1913 and reached 74 per cent in 1920. In German New Guinea, 84 per cent of the planted area was under coconuts in 1905, and the proportion exceeded 90 per cent by 1920. In the Solomon Islands the proportion of the total developed plantation area under coconuts never fell below 95 per cent, and stood at 99 per cent in 1946.

The peculiar flexibility of operation available to coconut planters has been discussed at length in an earlier book (Brookfield with Hart, 1971). It was possible to combine coconuts with other crops, to reduce labour requirements on maintenance of the plantation floor, either by neglect, or by using cattle rather than labour. These advantages were appreciated early, and they were combined with the further advantage that coconuts were a relatively 'safe' crop, proving less liable to strong cyclic price fluctuations than the more intensively-grown, high return crops. And notwithstanding the general boom, there were such cyclic price fluctuations during the period between 1900 and 1914. All these conditions led inexorably to the hegemony of copra, plans and policies notwithstanding. And they led also to the diffusion of coconut growing from plantation to peasant, for the same advantages of flexibility made the crop admirably suited to the irregular work input characteristic of Melanesian societies. This in turn provided continuing support for the plantations, which could thus gain valuable supplementary income by trade in Melanesian nuts or copra. The low level of skills needed was acquired quickly and widely, and economy of specialization compensated to some degree for lack of economies of concentration.

GOVERNMENT, INFRASTRUCTURE AND THE GROWTH OF TOWNS

The rôle of Government in all this was regulative more than it was creative, even though there were some notable initiatives, and though the publications of governments become in this period the best data source on economic affairs – most of this discussion is based on them. A fundamental division separates those governments which facilitated Asian immigration from those which did not. Australia's white labour policies negated action in this matter not only in Papua, which became an Australian territory, but also in the Solomon Islands which remained British. The Germans had no such inhibitions, and the Neu-Guinea Compagnie brought in small numbers of both Chinese and Japanese in various capacities, but Germany lacked an Asian empire and the Imperial Government preferred to rely on local resources despite periodic appeals from planters. Had Germany been more successful in its late bid for a territorial stake in China, the story might well have been different.

The regulatory activities of the governments extended quite widely during this period. Free land alienation came to an end, and there was growing insistence not only on investigation before registration, but on the principle that the State should intervene as intermediary in land transactions between the residentiary populations and private operators in the commercial system. Though policy vacillated, even in Fiji, all of Melanesia had by 1914 moved close to a system under which only the State could buy land from residentiary owners, or lay claim to 'waste land'; private occupiers then had to treat with the State, which made land available more and more on lease rather than in fee simple. Regulation of the labour trade virtually halted interterritorial recruiting, and controlled the conditions under which labour might be recruited internally. Contract terms were more rigidly defined, and there were the beginnings of control over wage levels, ration scales and the housing and clothing of workers. Private employers still had very free disciplinary powers in some territories – though far too much has been made of the German employers' right to flog labour; practice differed only in small degree from that followed elsewhere. However, labour contracts became legally enforceable, and desertion was made a criminal offence in most territories.

Systems of local government were set up among the indigenous population. A strong start was made in Fiji, where the Fijian regulations created what was virtually a state within a state, segmented downward from a central department advised by the Council of Chiefs, through intermediate levels to village officials and recognized chiefs. German efforts to comprehend the land tenure and organization of the Tolai people in northern New Britain led to the creation of a system which ultimately became standard over a large part of New Guinea. *Luluais*, from the Tolai *lulalua* or big man, were appointed over each group, aided by a *tultul* or messenger. These men were responsible to Government, as intermediaries in a system of direct rule. In Papua a village constable carried out the same functions, and village headmen were recognized in the New Hebrides. Here the 1906 Convention was modified by a new Protocol in 1914; one major change was to introduce a system of District administration, with French and British Agents to each District. A district subdivision of administration was also introduced in the other territories during these years, the only exception being New Caledonia. Here the whole island was divided into communes on the model of French local government. The indigenes were excluded from this system. *Grands-chefs* and *chefs-de-tribu* were appointed in each Reserve, and the whole Régime de l'indigénat was under the direct control of the Gendarmerie Nationale. It is noteworthy that both Fiji and New Caledonia adopted separate systems of administrations for the Melanesian population: in the other territories this system meshed more directly into the district and national government.

Governments had an important effect on the location of economic activity by their restriction of foreign trade to a few ports of entry, chief among which was always the colonial capital itself. Though overseas vessels continued to follow multiple-port itineraries inherited from an earlier period, and made necessary by the dispersal of the plantation industry, there was growing concentration of trade, resulting in the emergence of local shipping services based on each main port. Suva and Levuka in Fiji, Nouméa in New Caledonia, Port Moresby and Samarai in Papua, Vila in the New Hebrides, Herbertshöhe (Kokopo), Madang and after 1910 Rabaul in German New Guinea –

these few ports commanded the bulk of the trade by the early years of the twentieth century. Suva developed an entrepôt function based on its political rôle as capital of the Western Pacific High Commission, and from 1910 Rabaul developed more and more as focal point for the whole of northern New Guinea and Micronesia. The statistical appendix (Table 1) shows how the northern New Britain region had become much the most economically significant and most agriculturally diversified part of the German empire. It was also the centre of the first strong Government-sponsored effort in education of Melanesian boys: a German-language senior school was established, and it was planned to develop others. However, this effort was nipped in the bud in 1914, when this 'centre of German indoctrination' was closed by the Australians. No replacement was provided for more than a generation.

The institutions of government provided the first stable urban hierarchy and the first stable network of communications. Before annexation, aggregations of traders sometimes formed embryonic towns, but it was the firm entry of government that gave structure to the urban system. The housing, roads, wharves and health facilities which governments had to create for their own use were also used by private members of the colonial system. Only the larger corporations could afford to duplicate this infrastructure on sites of their own choosing. In this way, the mere fact of government had a major rôle in forming the colonial space economy. More direct official participation in designing the space economy was limited, by both constraints on finance and conception of the rôle of government, but even the little that was done was of major importance.

To comprehend the government rôle, we must again separate the few large corporations, such as CSR, Lever's and the SLN, from the mass of smaller entrepreneurs. The former could create their own company towns and systems of transport, but the latter were spatially disorganized, relying on the trading companies and government for their linkages with the world economy. As in most colonial territories, the rôle of government was of great importance, most especially in the creation of the earliest road systems. The penal administration in New Caledonia provided a crude network of roads in the southwestern part of the island, and the Fijian Government established the basis of a network radiating from Suva – much less dense, however, than the rail and road system created by CSR in the sugar districts. Little was done in Papua, the New Hebrides and the Solomon Islands, but in German New Guinea the creation of a basic road network was prosecuted with energy in northern New Britain, New Ireland, and on Bougainville. The work was done at very low cost with what is best described as 'persuaded labour' – neither wholly voluntary nor wholly compulsory – but it absorbed an important share of government revenues from land sales, taxation, and the £45,000 subsidy received from Berlin. Roads were initially only walking tracks, but after 1910 certain of them were improved to take motor vehicles. Governments also subsidized shipping services, and made special arrangements with long-haul carriers; the German administration did this with Norddeutscher Lloyd and the Australians with Burns Philp. Thus governments relied heavily on cooperation with the companies, and in so doing they contributed to the growing power of these companies in the whole economy.

In all this, it is the work of the German administration that emerges most impressively at this period. Though there was also considerable progress in Fiji and New Caledonia, both these territories enjoyed far more powerful commercial support. The German administration not only facilitated the expansion of a strong plantation industry, but also assisted the diffusion of development among the Melanesian population with particular vigour. Trade more than doubled between 1910 and 1913 alone, and in the last year over 17,000 Melanesians were in employment. Nearly 19,000 pupils were in school in New Guinea, and the foundations of a German-language education system had been laid. Exploration of the interior had been actively pursued, and a significant body of serious scientific work was undertaken. But perhaps the greatest achievement was the administrative, and increasingly the commercial, integration of a widely scattered empire covering an area as large as Europe. Fifteen government stations, all but two established after 1900, were coordinated through the new capital at Rabaul. Only the large populations of the central highlands of New Guinea remained to be discovered, and explorations in 1914 yielded clues that would certainly have been followed up in 1915 and 1916: discovery of this large population would have resolved the labour difficulties of the colony and might have facilitated the rapid evolution of a colonial state with a strongly based and centralized economy, with significant consequences for the subsequent history of the region. But faraway events determined that a different course was to be followed.

REFERENCES AND SOURCES

From this chapter forward the official reports and other publications of colonial governments become a major source of data: from early in the century there is good annual reportage for Fiji, German New Guinea and Papua. Material from German sources on New Guinea forms the basis of accounts of the pre-1914 period in Mackenzie (1927) and Rowley (1958), and has been subjected to modern analysis by Biskup, Moses and Sack in Waigani Seminars (1969), and elsewhere by Biskup (1970), T. Scarlett Epstein (1968), A. L. Epstein (1969), Lawrence (1964), Sack (1971) and Salisbury (1970). A more sketchy account of German New Guinea is given by Lyng (1919), and a useful source for the investigator with limited German is a selected translation of official reports by H. A. Thomson, a typescript of which is held in the Commonwealth National Library, Canberra: this latter is the source of the quotations given in this book.

On the region as a whole the main non-government sources are those already cited, including Klein (1953–4), Lowndes (1956), Gillion (1962), R. G. Ward (1965), Scarr (1967a) and Waigani Seminars (1969). On more specific aspects, Couper (1967) and Lasaqa (1972) are particularly useful. Unfortunately, however, this halcyon period of colonialism in the Pacific tends to suffer in coverage from a tendency among historians to be more interested in the genesis and establishment of the system than in its apogee.

CHAPTER 5

TREMORS FROM FARAWAY CONVULSIONS – 1905-1920

A colonial system is interdependent with a wider world, and though colonial events may change the course of metropolitan history – as events in the Americas did for Europe in the eighteenth century – the pattern has more commonly been that colonies are the almost passive recipients of changes emanating from abroad. In the period which we have just reviewed there were important long-term changes in metropolitan policy, the effect of which came to Melanesia as accidents from without, and others of which no initial ripple was even felt in these remote islands, but which were ultimately to transform the conditions of life.

The rôle of faraway convulsions was important even in the nineteenth century. The American civil war initiated the first plantation boom. The Franco-German war of 1870 set off a chain of events that brought Germany into the Pacific as an imperial nation, and which engendered in the French a proud anger toward all foreigners that had its consequences for the New Hebrides. But by the end of the nineteenth century powerful shocks were being generated closer to Melanesia. The final jockeying for territory in the Pacific islands was not only an echo of the contemporary 'scramble for Africa'; it was also related to a potentially much greater 'scramble' that was brewing after 1880 in China, where the powers were jostling on the starting line of what seemed an imminent race to gobble up the remains of the Manchu empire, and open all of China to capitalist enterprise. In writing his geography of Britain early in the new century, Mackinder (1907, 342–51) considered that tendencies for the British empire to dissolve into a loose federation would be checked by naval competition from other powers, and he singled out competition in the China seas for special mention.

The powers were deadlocked in China, against one another rather than the Chinese, and they remained deadlocked until the moment of opportunity had passed away. Japan entered the tangle in 1895, then in 1905 startled the world by decisively defeating the Russians both on land and sea at Mukden and Tsushima. To the Japanese this victory was part of their imperialist expansion, but in tropical Asia the success was viewed very differently. That

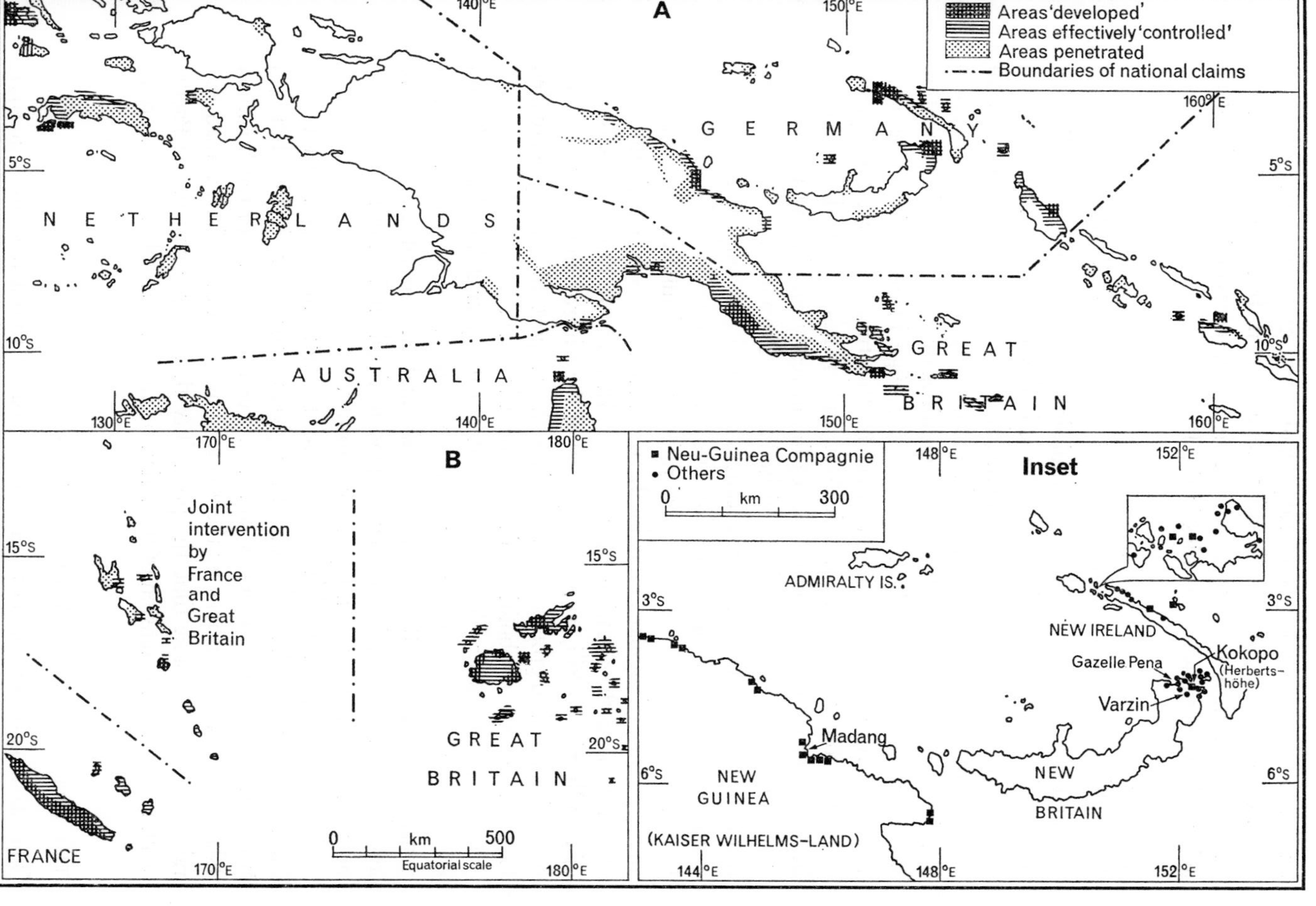

Figure 2. A and B: the region about 1905, showing areas of effective operation of the colonial economic system. Inset: part of German New Guinea, indicating plantations

an Asian country could successfully challenge a great Western power did much to encourage infant nationalist movements in India, Indo-China and Indonesia. In the following years the newly arisen forces of Asian nationalism achieved two significant victories in the Pacific.

TERMINATION OF THE FIJI CONTRACT LABOUR SUPPLY

The first successes were achieved by India in Fiji. The growing centralization of administration in India facilitated the activities of both the Indian National Congress and the newer Muslim League, and they gained greater power with a reform of the Legislative Council in 1909. A focus of discontent was provided by the disabilities of Indian communities overseas, to which attention was being called by Gandhi's vigorous campaign in South Africa between 1891 and 1914. Fiji and Guyana were by this time the largest recipients of Indian contract workers outside Asia, and criticism of conditions in Fiji by a missionary writer (Burton, 1910) found ready ears in India. Gokhale, leader of the Congress moderates, visited South Africa in 1912; on his return from meetings with Natal Indian leaders he called for complete abolition of contract recruitment, and for freedom and equality of status for the established Indian communities overseas. Some reforms in Fiji followed the agitation, and there was triangular discussion between London, New Delhi and Suva, but all the time the agitation grew stronger. In 1915 two European associates of Gandhi visited Fiji, with the approval of the Viceroy and funds provided by Indian political groups. On the basis of their report the Viceroy persuaded London to agree to abolition of recruitment in 1916.

Colonial interests rallied, and negotiated a five-year delay. The agitation then became a mass movement in India, and gained support in labour-conscious Australia. Recruitment ceased, and in Fiji all contracts were abrogated on the first day of 1920. Thenceforth all Indians in Fiji were free men, though scarcely with equal opportunity.

But for the rise of Indian nationalism, it is not only certain that Indian immigration would have continued for several more years in Fiji, but also probable that Indian labour would have been introduced to the Solomon Islands and New Hebrides by the 1920s. The status of Indians abroad was raised, but at the same time the possibility that a large part of the Pacific would become an extension of the Asian oecumene was definitively averted.

THE ENTRY OF AUSTRALIA AND JAPAN

The six Australian colonies were finally coaxed into a federation in 1901, and in 1906 the British Government transferred its New Guinea territory to

Australian administration. The British were in these years interested in the devolution of imperial responsibility among the new 'dominions'. Policy in southern Africa had as its ultimate aim the creation of a federated state from the Cape to Lake Malawi; encouragement was given to suggestions that Canada might assume responsibility for at least some of the West Indies. It had been seriously proposed earlier that New Zealand should federate with Fiji, and Papua had in fact been administered mainly by Australians for several years before the transfer. When war broke out in 1914, the Imperial Government's requests to New Zealand to occupy Samoa, and to Australia to occupy the German West Pacific colony, were a logical consequence of this policy.

An Australian task force was quickly organized, and reached New Britain early in September. After a few brief skirmishes the Australian commander received the surrender of all German forces in the colony on 17 September and, as he thought, also the surrender of the whole colony. However, strong German naval forces were still at large in the Pacific, and despite prodding from London the Australians did not feel strong enough to sail into the regions north of New Guinea until November. But Japan entered the war in mid-September in order to seize the German holdings in China, which they did with British help in three months. In mid-October Japanese naval units, less timorous or better informed than the Australians, moved into the undefended Micronesian islands, and in November the Japanese decided to stay. They exerted pressure through London to halt the Australian expedition belatedly mounted to 'relieve' them, and on 3 December the equator was agreed on as a boundary between occupation zones. Toward the end of the war, following an agreement with Britain, the Japanese set up civil administration in the islands north of the equator.

The course of Australian military administration in German New Guinea has been described in considerable detail by Mackenzie (1927) and Rowley (1958). Takeover was slow, and it was mid-1915 before all German posts were occupied. German planters, confident of victory in Europe, continued to develop their plantations, and between 1914 and 1919 the planted area increased from 34,000 ha to 54,000 ha. The indigenous labour force rose from 17,000 to 30,000 and copra production from 14,000 to 30,000 tons per annum. Very little but copra was produced, but the new areas planted were sufficient to double production again by the time all had reached maturity, about 1927. The economy was set firmly on its feet, but the planters reckoned without the mood of the victorious allies in 1919. Almost all non-mission property was expropriated, and resold by the Australian authorities for their own benefit. The proceeds thus compensated Australia for the 'harm' done to her by Germany during the war. The dispossessed planters were to be compensated by the German Government, but many were overtaken by the collapse of the mark in 1923, and got nothing at all. Apart from the mission estates, almost all that survived of the extensive German properties in the New Guinea region were some small holdings in the neutral Dutch territory of West New Guinea, the largest of which was later sold to a Japanese group.

The rupture between the New Guinea and Micronesian portions of the German empire was complete – so complete that even in 1972 there is still no direct air service or two-way shipping service between the two regions. Their evolution was henceforth totally separate, and the Micronesian region underwent violent reversals in its orientation – first toward Japan, and now toward Honolulu and the mainland USA. The few Japanese who had resided in German New Guinea were eased out by means never made wholly clear. But though the empires of two west-Pacific nations now faced each other across the equator, they were not acquired in the fee-simple title of former times. Some important changes had taken place in the conditions of colonialism since 1914.

LENIN, WILSON AND ANTI-COLONIALISM

Colonial expansionism had become the universal and unashamed philosophy of all the major powers in the last years of the nineteenth century, when something approaching Schumpeter's popular imperialism gripped the powers for a brief space. Only Britain pursued its supremely confident path of devolution of authority to new nations created, or forced, into its own image. In the 1890s the streams of 'manifest destiny' and economic expansionism finally came together in the United States, and led in a short space to the annexations of Puerto Rico, Guam, Samoa, the Philippines and Hawaii. This was not accomplished without serious opposition within the United States, as the suppression of the Afrikaner Republics was not achieved without opposition in Britain. The Philippine insurrection, the prolonged Afrikaner resistance, and the defeat of Russia in 1905 not only dented confidence, but gave strength to anti-imperialist disquiet among people of many political persuasions. Wilson's Government proclaimed a policy of ultimate American withdrawal from the Philippines in 1916, and though this remained no more than a policy until the Tydings-Duffy legislation of 1934, it marked a definite stage in the American retreat from territorial expansionism. Major events followed swiftly.

On 8 November 1917, Lenin called for peace without annexations or indemnities, and for the surrender of pre-war conquests and colonies by all powers. Treating colonialism as a last stage in capitalism, he linked colonial revolution with proletarian revolution in the metropoles. There was little practical effect even on Russian policy, but the ideological identification of anti-colonialism with Bolshevism influenced the alignment of nationalist movements in several Asian countries. Between 1920 and 1923, communist parties came into existence in every major south and east Asian country except Japan. In Indonesia, communist activity precipitated a wave of strikes and local revolts in 1926 and 1927, and while these were defeated there were two consequences of some significance for Melanesia. A concentration camp for political prisoners was formed at Tanahmerah, deep in the forests of the upper Digul system in West New Guinea, and many of the post-1945 leaders of Indonesia spent time there. In Java, a new nationalist party was formed on a wide base, under the leadership of a young man named Sukarno.

Two months after Lenin's address President Wilson put forward his Fourteen Points as a programme of peace. Included among them were calls for fair settlement of colonial issues, autonomy for small nationalities, and a general association of nations. Modern anti-colonialism now achieved force in world affairs, strongly at variance with the aspirations of the west-European powers, and also of Japan and Australia.

The Wilsonian world view came into sharp conflict with national colonialism at the Versailles peace negotations in 1919. The conference readily agreed to form a League of Nations, and rather less readily to the proposal that the middle-eastern territories of the former Turkish empire be allocated as 'mandates' under its aegis, rather than being simply redistributed as colonies. It was only on Wilson's insistence, however, that the German African and Pacific colonies were also brought into this system. As reported by Isaiah Bowman (in Miller, 1928; 1, 43), Wilson held that: 'the German colonies should be declared the common property of the League of Nations and administered by small countries. The resources of each colony should be available to all members of the League' [italics omitted]. Here was the old 'open door' policy, in head-on collision with national economic and political interests. A compromise was reached, under which full national rights would be given, with only an obligation to secure equal commercial opportunities for other members of the League. The obligation could be largely disregarded, but outright annexation was thus disallowed.

Neither Australia nor Japan were very pleased with this outcome. Both went to the conference determined to hold what they had, and keen to gain at least commercial access to the other part of the former German colony. Hughes of Australia was especially vehement, hopeful even of gaining German Micronesia, and determined to avoid any provision that might oblige him to admit Japanese migrants south of the equator. Miller (1928; 1, 114) suggests that Wilson's opposition to Pacific annexations was motivated in part by concern at the Japanese position across the sea lane between Hawaii and the Philippines, but whether this is so or not it was because of Wilson that the Australians got so much less than they had sought.

THE BEGINNINGS OF ECONOMIC DISASTER

Only slightly disturbed by the uncomfortable proximity of the Japanese, the victorious colonial powers of the south Pacific now settled down to take up the peaceful development of their properties. The climate was changed by the emergence of Australia as the dominant colonial power in the region, and by the imminent closure of access to Asian labour for all but the French. The prospects, however, were excellent. There was a boom of unprecedented dimensions in world trade due to a universal desire to replenish stocks, and supported by a continuation of wartime deficit budgeting. But the boom was short lived. Prices began to fall sharply in March 1920, and by the second half of the year the received prices of the Melanesian primary products had fallen to levels below those ruling in the 1910–13 period. For Melanesia this was the beginning of a bad period that lasted so long as to come to seem like normality. The improvement of the late 1920s was by no means so pronounced as it was in the advanced countries, and the subsequent depression was worse. High noon had been brief, and it was followed by a prolonged grey period that was to leave a deep mark on the whole region.

REFERENCES AND SOURCES

Sources for this chapter are inevitably widespread: for the general history of Melanesia in this period Grattan (1963) is perhaps the major source. Gillion (1962) reviews the events in Fiji, while writings by participants in the affair include Burton (1910) and Andrews (1937). On the events of World War I in the Pacific the most important participant source is Mackenzie (1927). Miller (1928) provides considerable detail on the mandates discussion at Versailles, and some useful background material is given in the first volume of Hancock's (1962) biography of Smuts.

CHAPTER 6

THE ILLS OF MERCANTILISM

President Wilson's hope that the resources of the ex-German colonies would be freely open to all, which we noted in the last chapter, was already an anachronism in 1919. The old British view that trade should flow freely across political boundaries, and its corollary that political colonialism was inimical to economic integration, had been espoused by policy makers in several countries in its time. It influenced the prolonged reluctance to claim new territory in the Pacific, as in Africa (Robinson, Gallagher and Denny, 1961), and it may perhaps be argued that it collapsed for the same basic reasons as in Africa: beyond a certain point trade could not advance without empire, and once competing national economic interests began to perceive this truth the establishment of empire came quickly. Germany on its own behalf, Britain mainly and often reluctantly on behalf of Australia, France egged on by its tiny but vociferous band of colonists in New Caledonia, were thus urged into competitive annexations, and the jockeying for strategic position in the looming conflict for China completed the bill of sufficient causes.

Even so, a considerable measure of free access survived until 1914. German traders were strongly represented in Fiji and Tonga, even though the Germans complained of discrimination against their nationals in Fiji. Australian traders, planters and especially missionaries were active in German New Guinea and in New Caledonia. Rationalization of the invading systems on national lines was progressive, and it was encouraged by governments, but rarely forced. All this was changed in 1919. Australia moved swiftly to remove the German system root and branch from New Guinea, and balked only at the missions. More than this, the Government of Australia applied mercantilist legislation designed to restrict participation in the development of eastern New Guinea to British nationals, and in great measure only to Australians. France supported national enterprise in New Caledonia and the New Hebrides by both direct and indirect means, with considerable vigour, and took strong steps to oppose or discourage foreign enterprise. Britain applied a more open policy, but one which benefited Australian corporations. The rôle of such organizations now becomes critical: they were the agents of a new mercantilism.

THE ASCENDANCY OF SYDNEY

Sydney, New South Wales, has a fine harbour incredibly made beautiful by the growth of a city around it. From the harbour ferries, the clustered towers of the city centre rising above the green Domain and the Opera House, and framed to the right by the great but unlovely bridge, present a panorama worthy of Canaletto. Here, among the soaring modern towers and old brown sandstone of central Sydney, has lain for most of a century the real focus of the tropical southwest Pacific, thus integrated in a manner not fully paralleled in any other colonial region. The earliest traders for pork and sandalwood operated out of Sydney, and by the 1870s there was a whole range of small Sydney trading companies at work, many of them with shore establishments in the territories already colonized. Then in the 1880s came greater centralization as CSR extended its operations to Fiji, and the Queensland firm of Burns Philp first moved its base to Sydney, then projected its activities into the islands. By the early years of the twentieth century, Burns Philp was operating shipping and agency business, and was directly involved in land dealings and plantation development from Singapore to Samoa, in the territories of the Netherlands, Germany, Britain, France and the United States. The Solomon Islands were being developed from Sydney by Lever, Burns Philp and smaller companies; British enterprise in the New Hebrides depended heavily on Sydney capital; the main shipping services to the German colony were still provided from Sydney, though this branch of the network was about to be displaced by the competition of Norddeutscher Lloyd.

More substantial opposition was encountered in the French territories, where few Australian companies found direct investment feasible. French trading companies, either of metropolitan origin or with local backing, controlled most of the activity, and they were increasingly supported by the Saigon-based Banque de l'Indo-Chine, which became more and more deeply involved in the affairs of New Caledonia and the New Hebrides. Yet even these territories imported increasingly from Australia, and the Nouméa companies either maintained their own Sydney offices, or dealt with Sydney agencies. Sydney was the main entrepôt for the island trade inward and outward until after 1909, though a growing share of business thereafter passed through Singapore via Norddeutscher Lloyd. Thanks mainly to the growing strength of the Australian labour movement, Sydney became a more and more expensive port and its trans-shipment business declined rapidly. There thus developed a directional imbalance in the islands trading networks; still importing consumption goods mainly from Australia, they sought export outlets to Europe and North America either by Singapore or by direct charters. The opening of the Panama Canal in 1914 created new opportunities here, and the first regular service to exploit them was operated by the French company, Messageries Maritimes, which opened a trans-Pacific route in 1923. Burns Philp, meanwhile, sought cheaper outlets by chartering California-Alaska schooners during the winter season to carry copra directly to North American ports.

It was at this point that the elimination of Germany had its most immediate effect. In the mandated territory, the Expropriation Board took over not only plantations, but also the total assets of the German companies, and disposed of these readily to Australian houses. Burns Philp were quickly on the scene, and a new Sydney company formed by W. R. Carpenter, a former employee of Burns Philp, was able to acquire the assets of the Neu-Guinea Compagnie. Burns Philp provided the main shipping service with a subsidy and a guarantee of trade.

This became highly important, for the Australian Government now extended its Navigation Act to both New Guinea territories. This Act required that all coastal cargo in Australian waters be carried in Australian vessels, except by special licence that was not readily given. Except, therefore, where there was sufficient cargo to fill a whole overseas vessel, all exports had to be shipped through Sydney. The Expropriation Board in the mandated territory was able to charter overseas vessels by operating until 1925 as a central marketing agency for plantations still held by the Board. When the plantations began to be sold in 1925 it was noted that:

> The change will be attended by new difficulties, as the new owners will not have the advantage of a central selling agency for their produce such as the Rabaul office of the Expropriation Board furnished for the plantations under their charge. Dealing with large quantities of copra the Expropriation Board selling agency was enabled to charter steamers and could thus obtain cheap freight rates direct to European markets (Annual Report on the Administration of the Trust Territory of New Guinea (TNGR), 1925–6, 14).

The effect on Papua was more serious, for production was far smaller and insufficient to attract shipping, Papuan copra production peaked at a mere 12,000 tons in 1928, against 75,000 tons from the mandated territory in the same year, and soon after the War the Lt. Governor reported bitterly that:

> Agricultural development has, temporarily at least, come to an end. The low price of rubber and copra is responsible for this: but even should prices rise again it is improbable that there will be any further development so long as the law confines our trade relations with Australia (Territory of Papua Reports (TPR), 1920–1, 7).

The effect of Australian mercantilism was felt through the whole western Pacific. By their expansion not only in New Guinea, but also in Fiji and

Samoa, the Australian-based companies tied the consumer goods trade of the whole region to Australian and New Zealand sources. At the same time the competing German shipping service was removed, and with the export trade of the largest producing area funnelled through Australia at high cost, the remainder of the region was too lean in cargoes to attract more than occasional Norwegian and Japanese tramp vessels. CSR had its separate arrangements, and New Caledonia and the New Hebrides had service to France, but the general trade was very poorly served indeed. In 1925 protests in Papua and the mandated territory led to withdrawal of the Navigation Act from both these territories: it was finally realized that mercantilism was of little service without some efforts to develop a better metropolitan market for produce. Freight rates certainly fell: the Papuan Government plantation at Kemp Welch reported that it cost £19.00/ton to freight rubber to London via Sydney in 1924 (TPR, 1923–4, 51), but only £8.82½/ton by direct service in 1928 (*ibid.*, 1927–8, 43). But the damage was done. It was still hard to get shipping, and appeals for a new service to Singapore fell on deaf ears. The situation did not really change until 1932 when the British Bank Line, a subsidiary of Unilever, began to operate regular traders through the islands by the Panama route, and was soon picking up most of the copra and other agricultural exports.

Australian mercantilism most certainly did not end in 1925. The Sydney companies continued to expand their activities, absorbing several of their competitors during the depression years, and further extending control over indebted planters and small traders. After World War II there was some withdrawal, when the companies refused to return to the Solomon Islands because the British refused war-damage compensation, did not return to West New Guinea, and sold remaining interests in the French territories. But all but one of the significant locally-based companies in Australian New Guinea were absorbed by the Big Two, and in Fiji Carpenters gained control of a large local company with extensive multiterritorial interests in 1956. Australian banks have also increased their activity, and other Australian-based companies have entered the region. Most regional air transport is operated either directly by Australian airlines, or by companies in which Australian capital represents a significant share of ownership. Australian shipping serving New Guinea still carries Australian crews at trade union insistence. We shall see the effect of all this below, but must presently conclude that – except that Collins Street, Melbourne, has also acquired an important share – the dominance of central Sydney in the commerce of these islands is as pervasive as ever in 1972.

A FRENCH NATIONAL ECONOMY IN THE NEW HEBRIDES

Just after World War I, there was a brief possibility that Australian interests might overturn the dominant French position in the New Hebrides by a *coup de main.* In 1921 there were 677 French to only 226 British subjects in the group – the Melanesians being without citizenship. The Condominium Joint Court had still not started its work of hearing and registering claims to land, and French interests claimed 52 per cent of the estimated occupiable and arable area of the whole group; British interests claimed 11 per cent, leaving only 37 per cent in undisputed possession of the New Hebrideans. Cultivated land in 1914 covered just over 14,500 ha, of which 75 per cent was owned by French subjects. French companies handled almost three-quarters of the trade, against only one half in 1906. Then in 1921 the impecunious Higginson estate offered its 8,000 profitless but controlling shares in the Société Française des Nouvelles-Hébrides (SFNH) to the Australian Government, which was ready to buy. The French Government denied permission, and was forced hastily to support purchase of the shares by the Banque de l'Indo-Chine.

The French now determined on a major effort to oust the Anglo-Australians by economic means: 'C'est une lutte incessante qui s'y livre. Deux actions rivales y sont perpetuellement en présence, qui cherchent mutuellement à s'annihiler et à s'exclure' (There is an unceasing struggle. The two rival parties are at all times opposed, each seeking to annihilate and exclude the other) (Pelleray, 1922, 67). The basic problem was, as everywhere, that of labour. Copra, cocoa and coffee grew well, but covered insufficient area. New Hebrideans were becoming less and less willing to engage on contract, more and more demanding in terms of wages. The French blamed this on 'laziness', on the 'bad habits' of private copra buyers who gave as good a price to indigenous growers as to European planters, but above all on their arch-enemy, the Australian Presbyterian Mission, which was supposed to be discouraging New Hebrideans from working for the French by any and every means at its disposal. Each recruiting voyage cost more and yielded less, and labour was growing desperately short. Only 3,150 New Hebrideans were employed in 1922, fewer than before 1914.

French planters enviously watched the successful efforts of their compatriots in New Caledonia to re-open the pre-war labour traffic from Java and Tonkin. Out of 1,000 Tonkinese recruited for the south Pacific in 1920, 124 came to the New Hebrides and a private planter obtained more by a personal visit to Hanoi in 1923. Late in 1923 agreement was reached on regular recruitment, but with the firm proviso that these labourers from French Asia should be available only to French nationals: indeed the British administration for several years refused their own nationals permission to employ Tonkinese.

Land was abundant, and labour was now available to the French, though in competition with New Caledonian employers: efforts to tap also the Javanese supply to New Caledonia proved unsuccessful. Capital, however, was not available as freely as before 1914, and the State had to intervene, partly through the Société Française des Nouvelles-Hébrides, partly through the Banque de l'Indo-Chine. It was decided, very unwisely in view of the still-tight labour situation, to make a new attempt to grow cotton, a crop which – unlike coconuts, cocoa and coffee – would show immediate results. Only a short-stapled, rather coarse variety could be grown, and pests and diseases which appeared after 1926 checked production. But investment continued, and grew heavier in the more favourable economic climate of the late 1920s.

Capital was initially obtained from the sale of SFNH land to New Caledonian investors. A Compagnie Cotonnière des Nouvelles-Hébrides was formed, and created a large plantation on Malekula, against some Melanesian opposition. Private planters more prudently grew cotton mainly as a catch crop under new coconuts. A series of further development companies was formed, and three ginning works were ultimately set up with a combined capacity of 5,000 tons per annum. There was much trading in unimproved land, and it is estimated that some 500 million francs were invested, at least on paper, up to 1929. Credit was extraordinarily free, and Government itself offered credit to development companies against unimproved and untried land, much of it not even confirmed in title. The Banque de l'Indo-Chine and the trading companies permitted growing overdrafts and mounting credit accounts, and the companies also undertook direct investment. All the elements of a 'South-sea Bubble' were present, and actual achievement lagged far behind expectations.

There was continued difficulty over labour. Like the British before them, the French had to pay regard to agitation over the conditions of contract labour in Indo-China; recruiting was briefly halted in 1926 for this reason. Due to high recruitment costs, requiring planters to go into debt, numbers of Tonkinese grew rather slowly to reach only 2,500 in 1925, 5,000 in 1929. Cotton production never surpassed 1,000 tons per annum, and actually declined a little after 1926. Copra, cocoa and coffee production however improved, though a growing share, especially of copra, was produced by New Hebrideans; these latter virtually ceased to engage as labour by 1928. There was thus the characteristic separation of the residentiary population from the supposed growth-sectors of the economy, similar to that which had followed the use of alien labour in New Caledonia and Fiji at earlier dates. But in the

New Hebrides there was a large planting of coconuts by the New Hebrideans, and this later made possible substantial increases in copra production, well above the 12,000-ton level attained in the 1920s, during and after World War II.

When prices began a catastrophic decline in 1929 there was at first no diminution in the flow of credit, or even in the increase of quite useless cotton-ginning capacity. By 1930, however, the situation became more serious, and the Banque de l'Indo-Chine allowed one of the three French trading companies to fail. A second, which had seen the danger soonest, was less deeply involved, but the dominant Maison Ballande was allowed to build up overdrafts. The plight of the colonists was desperate. Many could not pay their labour, and the workers were returned to Tonkin at Government expense: their number in the New Hebrides fell to 600 by 1935. All work ceased on many plantations. In 1931, Government intervened by means of the Crédit National: 5 million francs were advanced for relief of French planters. The loans made in the boom were mostly never repaid, and it was estimated that 50 million francs were still outstanding in 1934. In that year, the French Government took over large areas of land from SFNH in return for payments through the Banque de l'Indo-Chine to the principal creditors. In the end, some 80 per cent of the debts were written off, and with them the last great attempt to establish national colonialism through European rural enterprise in the islands.

There were some lasting consequences. Effective control of SFNH now passed to the State, in fact to the Government of Indo-China. The development companies were reorganized into one group, Plantations Réunies des Nouvelles-Hébrides, whose main tangible asset was the former Compagnie Cotonnière plantation on Malekula, now under young coconuts. Again virtual control was in the hands of the Banque de l'Indo-Chine, which was closely linked to the State. New Hebrideans again entered employment after 1930, when they could no longer sell copra remuneratively. By 1935, 1,500 were employed, but at wages as low as $1 to $3 per month, against $2 to $5 in 1931. Casual labour in the capital received 70 cents a day in the 1920s, but only 10 to 20 cents in the mid-1930s. Finally, in 1935, the condition of the economy began to recover. Tonkinese recruitment was resumed, now for both British and French planters, and cocoa and coffee cultivation again expanded. But there was no return to cotton, and the net balance of the economy as between British and French was not changed substantially from its 1921 condition. The main change was that a more important rôle was now open to the New Hebrideans.

BACKWASH OF MERCANTILISM: THE SOLOMON ISLANDS AND WEST NEW GUINEA

Mercantilism as a development strategy requires emphasis on the links with the metropole, and on maximization of potential returns to the metropole. While judgement may be faulty, the basic strategy is implicit in the philosophy of the whole policy system, and its locational emphasis is thus far more likely to be toward the cores, or to rich new resources perceived as exploitable, than toward the periphery of either territory or economy. Social considerations may not be lost from sight, but they are secondary. The colony must pay for itself, as soon as possible if not at once, and if it is more profitable in the short term to import labour as well as capital, and to isolate the residentiary population from the growing points of the economy, this is done. The first responsibility is to the backers, be these the metropolitan taxpayers or the shareholders of a multinational corporation, or bank.

Such was the basis of policy in the interwar period in both the colonies discussed above. When Australia took over German New Guinea, her Government did not continue the pre-war subsidy, and it was the evident failure of the Navigation Act to permit the colony any profitable operation that brought about the withdrawal of the Act. A small subsidy was paid for 'native purposes' after the mid-twenties, but it remained minimal. In the New Hebrides the object of the French activity was the rapid development of a prosperous colony which could repay the loans and bring profit to the backers. The excessive granting of credit was motivated by a desire for speed, coupled with anxiety to outplay the Australian interests. In fact there was some spread effect of this investment and easy money supply which benefited the Australian sector of the economy, notwithstanding French policy to the contrary.

In Fiji mercantilism took an unusual form. An Australian-based multinational corporation created a whole economy in the sugar districts, importing both labour and capital. Government, meanwhile, concerned itself little with the sugar economy, and instead devoted its attention to the Fijian population, seeking to 'protect' it from harmful influences, but also involving Fijians in the business of Government. The police and the military forces were thus recruited largely from the Fijians; the Fijian chiefly class received education and limited responsibility; the Indians were isolated to a great degree from the political processes of the colony. In developing education and defence, Government persisted with an older New Zealand connexion, while the sugar economy and the trading companies were linked with Australia. Even within the southwest Pacific area there was thus a dualism of outlook, which limited the spread effects of social and economic development alike.

Two Melanesian territories lay outside the scope of any development thrust, whether Government or private, during almost all the interwar period. They were starved of capital and skilled manpower, and while no labour was drawn from them, the absence of inputs led to stagnation. There was no carryover from any strong earlier impetus to help them through a period of slack investment, as there was in Fiji and the mandated Territory of New Guinea in the 1920s. There were no major gold discoveries to provide limited new impetus, as in the same two territories in the 1930s. Together to some degree with Papua, these territories – the Solomon Islands and West New Guinea – slumbered in the backwash of mercantilist development.

In the Solomon Islands coconut planting came to a virtual end in 1920, and there was the minimum of further investment in the plantation industry until the 1950s. As trees matured, production climbed from 5,400 tons in 1914 to 12,000 tons in 1921 and 22,000 tons in 1926–7. Thereafter production fluctuated between a maximum of 25,000 tons and a minimum of 18,000 tons. About 30 per cent consistently came from Lever's plantations; there was a small but slowly growing proportion from Melanesian groves, and this supply tended to be more elastic in response to price variations than supply from the plantations.

With the blithe insouciance toward indigenous production that characterized the time, it was observed in 1927 that 'with the exception of the copra industry there is no agriculture in the Solomon Islands' (Annual Report, British Solomon Islands Protectorate (BSIPR), 1927, 5). A few attempts to experiment with other crops were undertaken about 1929, but they were not sustained. Denied the right to employ Asian workers, planters contented themselves with what they had, and indeed raised wages quite distinctly above New Guinea levels. In the 1920s labourers in the mandated territory got 25p a month, and those in Papua 50p a month. The 6,000 Solomon Islanders at work received £1.00 a month, and employers were consequently rather more economical in the use of labour: like New Hebridean planters they made much more use of cattle in keeping plantations clean than was normal in New Guinea. Numbers of workers were reduced after 1927, and fell to only 3,000 in 1935, when many planters ceased all maintenance work on their plantations. Wages were halved in 1934, and were not again increased before 1942.

The Solomons were very much on the frontier in those days. Tulagi, the capital and only town, occupied four small islands in a bay on the south coast of Nggela. By no means the whole Protectorate was pacified, and Government – with a total budget less than that of the Local Government Councils in 1960 – lacked the means to do more. In 1931 two officers were murdered in the Malaita bush while trying to collect taxes. Europeans rallied, and a motley 'army' of planters and traders, transported to Malaita on an Australian warship opportunely available, made a fatal 'example' of some thirty men, women and children before the original murderers were arrested. Such was Government at the end of the line in the stagnant years.

West New Guinea had lain at the end of the line for a century. The first missionaries were established in 1855, but Government set up no permanent posts until 1898, fourteen years after the establishment of colonial rule in the east. Up to that time New Guinea was merely a buffer zone beyond the limits of Dutch oecumene in the Moluccas and Halmahera: it now became a frontier. In 1902 the area was divided into three subdistricts (*Afdelingen*) of the Residency of Ternate. There followed a period of active scientific exploration by military parties, paralleling the German expeditions of the same period, and both Government and the missions expanded their activities. Commerce followed. Trading companies from Ternate and Amboina (Ambon) set up depots where they bought copal, crocodile skins and the plumes of the bird of paradise: Malay traders penetrated deep inland in search of these plumes, some crossing into the eastern territories. Burns Philp set up a store in the south, and there was some land alienation on the north coast, mainly to German companies and individuals. Some Japanese also arrived as traders. It was the old penetration phase of colonialism replicated, but during the years of high noon for the established colonial enterprises elsewhere in Melanesia.

For a brief space from 1920 to 1923 West New Guinea achieved the dignity of a separate Residency, based at Fakfak in the far west, but budgetary retrenchment brought about re-attachment to Amboina and Ternate. Control over the coastal region continued to extend until 1930, when some five-sixths of the coast were under administration, but there were substantial withdrawals in the 1930s, so that a few areas controlled in the 1920s were not again under administration until the 1960s.

Economic development was minimal until the end of the 1930s. Dutch nationals had a few small coconut, coffee and kapok plantations scattered along the northern coast and islands, and one German plantation survived. A large German holding on Geelvink Bay (Teluk Tjenderawasih) was sold to a Japanese group which tried to grow cotton, and collected copal over a wide area. There was one American plantation on an outlying northern island – a remnant of late nineteenth-century interest in the Marianas, isolated in Dutch territory by a boundary delimitation. Each plantation recruited its own labour, and most also traded in copal, skins and plumes.

Assignment to New Guinea in the Dutch service was most often a punishment, though there were a few volunteers who included some remarkable men. The Dutch had plans for the territory. Some Javanese prisoners were settled near Merauke on the south coast in 1906, and they were later joined by Timorese, Butanese, Tanimbarese and Kaiese, and by 50 internees allowed to leave the prison camp at Tanamherah, deep inland. There were proposals to settle more Javanese in this area, but they were not put into operation. On the other hand, plans to settle Eurasians from Java were implemented by two private organizations. Poorer Eurasians found life increasingly difficult in Java, and after the troubles of 1926 the Vereniging Kolonisatie Nieuw-Guinea was formed, followed by a competing organization, supported by the Koninklijk Pakkevart Maatschappij (the shipping company) in 1929. In 1930 the second organization established settlers at Manokwari, while the VKN established 'villages' inland of Hollandia. The settlers received a diminutive stipend during the initial period, but had no capital or equipment other than hand tools, and cleared the land either themselves or with local labour. Most turned to shifting cultivation for their own subsistence; few grew the cash crops hoped for by the promoters and still fewer succeeded. A 1937 Government inquiry – the first official interest in the schemes – revealed 225 persons cultivating only 219 ha at Manokwari, and 12 families cultivating only 82 ha near Hollandia. The Hollandia colony was abandoned between 1937 and 1941.

Commercial interest appeared at last in 1930, when a consortium of Shell Petroleum and two American companies began to investigate oil seepages in the western Vogelkop peninsula. Oil was struck in 1935 at shallow depth, and 16 wells were prepared, at Sorong and on MacCleur Gulf, by 1941. Pipelines and storage facilities were almost complete by the end of that year when the Japanese attacked. The oil business was managed entirely from without, using labour from central and eastern Indonesia. Even as ultimately developed in 1948, it was another instance of an economy developed with outside capital and labour, virtually excluding the residentiary population from participation. Nothing else in western New Guinea attracted capital in those years, for the Dutch had more worthwhile things to occupy them, and they discouraged outsiders even from mineral search. But major discoveries of new concentrations of people in the central highlands at least made news, as they did in the same period in Australian New Guinea. This new colonial frontier was, however, to be penetrated and developed very much more tardily than its counterpart in the east.

REFERENCES AND SOURCES

Government reports, by now regular and either annual or biennial for most territories, provide the major source for this chapter and the next, supplemented by a number of official papers on specific aspects. Useful material on Australian neomercantilism in New Guinea is provided in a series of papers brought together by Eggleston (1928), and from 1930 onward the expatriate colonial community found a voice with the foundation by R. W. Robson of *Pacific Islands Monthly*, which becomes an invaluable source on opinion and a rather less reliable source on facts from this date forward.

The discussion of the boom and its collapse in the New Hebrides also relies largely on periodical literature, mainly in a series of articles in the monthly *Revue du Pacifique* from 1922 to 1936. I am indebted to Mrs M. Dunn for an analysis of this material which she carried out as research assistant in 1965. There are also rather better informed articles in *L'Océanie Française*, especially by Caillard (1924), Barateau (1931) and Théry (1931). Geslin (1948) and Leaney and Lea (1967) additionally provide some valuable summary material, and there is useful incidental data in O'Reilly (1957), and in sundry minor sources.

Material on the Solomon Islands and West New Guinea is strikingly lean, but an invaluable summary of what little is available on the latter is provided by Groenewegen and Van de Kaa (1964). The Eurasian settlements, and the story of oil exploration are discussed in papers in Klein (1953–4).

Also invaluable throughout are Grattan (1963) and Couper (1967).

CHAPTER 7

HARD TIMES AND NEW BEGINNINGS

The average price of copra at New Guinea main ports reached a peak of £32 per ton in 1919. By 1922 it had fallen to only £18 per ton. A gradual recovery followed to a new low peak of £22 per ton in 1925–6, but after this there began a slide which took it to only £3.64 ($9.10) in 1933–4. Though there was a new recovery to £12.90 ($32.23) in 1936–7, a further rapid fall brought the average price back to only £6.80 ($17.00) a ton in 1939–40.* It was the same in all territories, and the consequence was a gradual withering of early post-war optimism, so that after all pre-1920 plantings had come into bearing, leading to a peak of production in the late 1920s, the output of copra thereafter varied directly with the price, bottoming between 1933 and 1935, then recovering only gradually in the last years before World War II. Indigenous production was more elastic than that of the planters, who had no alternative but to produce or to cease operation. The planters pared down costs of production in every way possible, reducing work on maintenance, cutting and making copra less frequently, going more and more deeply into debt. An unknown number fell under the direct management of their creditors, the trading companies. For many it was impossible to operate at a profit for a period of years, and after 1931 quite a number gave up and abandoned their holdings. Growers of rubber, cocoa and coffee experienced rather more volatile prices, but though there were periods of optimism there was little expansion. Only late in the period, in the middle 1930s, did the shaken-down plantation industry begin a new period of rather low-level investment, and this was abruptly halted on the outbreak of the new war. Shipping difficulties created a new slump in this remote region, and in 1941 it was reported in Papua that 'most planters have paid off their labourers and ceased production owing to the collapse of the market' (TPR 1940–1, 6).

READJUSTMENT IN THE COLONIAL COMMERCIAL SYSTEM

Though the 1920s were a hard period, the first thought was of only a temporary setback. New companies were formed on private initiative, and the initial trend was toward multiplication of elements, rather than centralization,

* See Note on Conventions on p. xv: £ are pounds sterling; $ are Australian dollars.

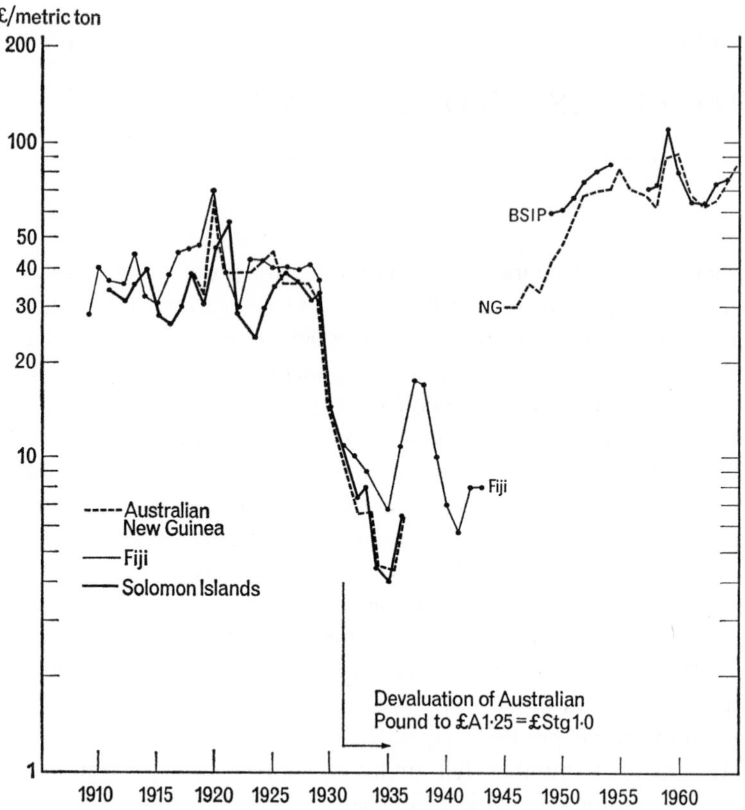

Figure 3. Variation of average price of smoke-dried copra at main ports in three Melanesian territories, 1909–65 (in pounds sterling to 1931, then Australian): from official sources

in the commercial network. In the 1930s this enthusiasm gave way to concentration of control into fewer hands, and this applied not only within the islands, but also in the international system to which island business was linked: the copra business in particular became heavily dependent on the policy of the single Unilever organization, which employed technical advances in the substitution of different types of oils and fats to switch buying emphasis toward the more weakly priced products in the interests of reducing its own costs.

Taken as a whole, the commercial system displayed very great flexibility during these years, so that the strongest firms continued to show profits and pay dividends, and were able to invest in promising new lines of activity both in the islands and the metropoles. By extension of credit, or by providing management services, the companies were able to keep the greater part of the scattered plantation and trading business intact – which may not have been a wholly wise strategy – and there was thus comparatively little permanent abandonment of plantations. To keep control of a greater share of a diminished total business, they discouraged the buying of indigenous copra and other crops which had been an important activity during earlier expanding phases. On the other hand there was one instance in which the plantation collapsed as a viable institution, and here the strategy was a sharp switch to encouragement of peasant production, to keep the whole industry and its well-capitalized facilities in being.

This instance was the complete changeover of the Fiji sugar industry from a plantation to a peasant-producer basis, so complete that the plantation has become less important in the total production pattern in Fiji than in any other major sugar-exporting region. When labour contracts for all Indians were cancelled on 1 January 1920, Colonial Sugar and the lesser companies at first experimented with a variety of devices, including new attempts to attract Fijian labour, conversion of plantations into something very like feudal estates, and a shift of wage arrangements from a time basis to task-rates and piece-rates. Before long, however, they settled for the widespread adoption of practices that had already been pioneered during the preceding thirty years. Indians and second-generation Indo-Fijians who obtained land on lease or tenancy-at-will from Fijian land holders were offered contracts for purchase of their cane, while the plantations were divided up into tenant farms under tight company control, but with a guaranteed market. The old plantation areas became cane districts and sectors, each under a field supervisor. The company provided the plant-cane and fertilizer, and loans as necessary, and the tenants delivered cut cane on a determined time-table that gave each grower an opportunity to cut some cane at the peak of its sucrose content, while cutting other cane early and late in the season. Transportation continued to be provided by the CSR rail system, with a uniform price at each siding so that the company equalized the cost of long-haul transport to the mills. Growers were then paid a price based on the average return for the whole industry, less the costs incurred by the company on their behalf, and some other profits that were not distributed. The result was hardly freedom, but it rescued the industry: five-year moving means show that the decline in sugar production which began early in World War I was arrested by the mid-twenties and replaced by a slow but continued growth. The cane area increased slowly year by year almost right through the period.

The reasons why this system was successful, while alternatives failed, lie in the demographic and land tenure conditions of the colony, coupled with the monopoly control of milling and marketing which CSR held from 1920 onward, as other companies either withdrew or entered into contracts with CSR. The population of Fiji in 1921 was a little below 160,000, among whom only 38 per cent were Indian. The Indian and Indo-Fijian population was deprived of significant new recruitment, but it did not diminish; rather it continued to increase, as did also the Fijian population from this census date onward. There was thus continued slow growth in the potential work force, but this work force was not sufficient in numbers to provide a large excess willing to continue unpopular work on the plantations. The Indians held very little land in freehold, but they were able to obtain land fairly readily from the Fijians at this stage, while other land became available for rental and lease as private European planters ceased production, but retained their land. Thus while there was insufficient landless Indian labour to keep the plantation system going, and very few Fijians lacked land at this stage, there was abundant scope to use willing labour on its own land. Once the costs of conversion were met, the continued operation of the industry was in fact more assured than it had been before the change.

There were further advantages. The experience with sugar was not wasted, and the Indo-Fijian tenants and contractors found themselves with little alternative means of gaining cash. Though received prices fell fairly steeply during this period and into the thirties, supply of cane proved to be rather inelastic from a population of growers to whom money income was an essential, not merely a desideratum. The rapid growth in Indo-Fijian population, on small land holdings, ensured continuance of this condition. It was, however, only very slowly that any considerable number of Fijians could be persuaded to enter the system.

The main transformation was complete by 1928, but some plantations continued to operate until World War II: most of these were smaller European-owned plantations under contract to CSR. At the beginning of the 1930s some 3,000 workers were still permanently employed on plantations, with an additional 1,000 during the crush season. Among the tenants and contractors a system of cane-cutting gangs was evolved for greater efficiency. Contracts and agreements required that each grower should join such a gang, under a *sirdar*, and that the gang should cut the cane through its whole area. The result was thus a modified system, neither wholly divorced from the plantation base, nor wholly a peasant system. So successful did it prove, however, that it has continued right down into the 1970s with few significant modifications except in areas of new cane extension since 1950, where the gang system and the controlled delivery with its equalized transport costs have not been put into operation.

THE GROWTH OF GOVERNMENT INTERVENTION IN THE ECONOMY

There is almost no stage from 1860 on during which we can say that Government had no rôle in the economy anywhere in Melanesia. Its rôle was of major importance in New Caledonia during the convict period, and we have seen above the disastrous intervention of nationalistically-inspired Government policy in the New Hebrides after 1920. In German New Guinea the Neu-Guinea Compagnie was both commerce and Government before 1899, and in Papua Government set up and directly operated a small number of plantations with the object of leading the way for private investors. The Expropriation Board in the mandated New Guinea territory operated as producer, landlord and agent from 1919 until the late 1920s, though it would have been wound up far more swiftly under a kindlier economic climate. In general, however, the aim of Government in all territories until the 1930s was to withdraw ultimately from the economic field. This has continued to be the long-term aim in later government enterprises, but it has grown more and more difficult to achieve, and meanwhile several forms of direct intervention have become firmly established.

During the worst of the depression in the early 1930s the governments of several territories in the Pacific had to provide aid to the planters, either directly or indirectly, in order to keep them in business. This aid was accompanied by strong deflationary measures, applied especially on the wages of indigenous workers where cuts of an order quite inconceivable in metropolitan countries were imposed. This was not only facilitated by legislation, but governments as leading employers themselves took a part in reducing wage levels. Then governments began also to intervene in marketing, and establish marketing boards, though progress in this direction was still very limited in 1942. Most significant of all were the extensions of tariff protection to the colonial producers that gained ground rapidly after 1929. Fiji benefited enormously from the institution of Imperial Preference in its sugar exports after 1931: the price decline was cushioned and the depression was by no means as severe as for the copra industry.

Substantial direct spending by governments in public works was confined virtually to Fiji and New Caledonia, where large-scale road construction programmes were undertaken. The hand of Government was, however, much more deeply involved than elsewhere in New Caledonia, though this was very largely through the Banque de l'Indo-Chine which continued to hold a monopoly of finance in the colony to all concerns but the Société le Nickel, in which 51 per cent of the shares were held by the Banque Rothschild of Paris. Thus in 1934 the pastoral industry was rescued from disaster by a Government contract to provide tinned meat for the army, coupled with loans from the Banque de l'Indo-Chine. The successive reorganizations of the nickel industry were also negotiated with Government aid. When electro-metallurgy was first undertaken by SLN in the 1920s, provision of the necessary hydro-electric system was aided by Government. Bounties on colonial produce, subsidies and preferential tariff arrangements were widely employed over the whole range of New Caledonian production and commerce. The ultimate reorganization of the nickel industry into a reconstituted SLN in 1937, coming at a time of heavy demand for nickel for armaments, was certainly carried out with the active interest of Government, though they were not participants.

At the very end of the inter-war period a new principle began to emerge in colonial affairs. A number of loans and outright grants were made to colonial administrations during the 1930s, and budget subsidies were again increased toward the end of the period – though still measured only in thousands of pounds or dollars. This was not universal: though the subsidy to Papua was increased to £36,000 ($90,000) at the end of the 1930s, the Solomon Islands budget for 1938–9 included only a loan of £3.20 ($8.00) for some unspecified purpose, in a total estimate of £49,800 ($132,000). But much more substantial loans were made to Fiji and to some of the British African colonies. In 1940 the British parliament formalized this new policy with the passing of the Colonial Development and Welfare Act, authorizing expenditure of £5,000,000 ($12,500,000) annually on welfare and on comprehensive plans for development. Commenting on this small beginning of the ultimately massive CD&W programme, Lord Hailey noted that it was significant:

> that the terms in which the Act was put forward to Parliament marked a definite acceptance by the Government of its responsibility for improving the standards of life in the dependencies, and that it secured a wide approval from the public and the press...[the public] is now able to view the problems presented as being in line with those of the 'depressed' areas in Great Britain itself, the treatment of which had become a matter of engrossing concern in domestic policies (Hailey, 1943, 16).

The flowering of this new metropolitan approach to colonialism was delayed until after World War II, but already by the end of the 1930s it represented the effect of growing metropolitan opposition to exploitative colonialism first clearly expressed in 1917, and reinforced through Imperial Preference and similar devices during the inter-war period. Observations of the serious consequences of the Great Depression for the primary-producing colonies provided a further nudge toward the adoption of 'New Deal' philosophies in the colonies. Above all, however, the basic change was that these philosophies now began to embrace development of colonies through and for the residentiary populations.

SOME CONSEQUENCES OF THE COLLAPSE OF CURRENCIES

For all its immediate hardship and dislocation, there are several senses in which the period 1929–31 marks the beginning of modern trends in the history of Melanesia. In 1929 the police and almost the whole indigenous work force in Rabaul, capital of the mandated territory of New Guinea, went on strike for higher wages. The strike, which took Government and employers completely by surprise, was quickly ended and the leaders were rather savagely treated, but the event was the first true Melanesian urban-based protest, and it is likely to gain historical stature with time. Also in 1929 Australia, and with it the two east New Guinea territories, abandoned convertibility with sterling; in January 1931 the Australian currency was devalued, and after a short floating period was pegged at the rate of £A1.00 = £0.80 ($2.50 = £1.00) which endured from December 1931 to November 1967.* Up to this time Australian currency had for some years been rather seriously overvalued, and the change eased both Australia's and New Guinea's export position. Then in September 1932 Britain abandoned the gold standard, and a favourable balance of trade emerged for Australia. France held on much longer, and did not finally depreciate its currency in terms of gold until 1936.

The result of all this was twofold. In the first place Melanesia gained its first improvement in terms of trade since 1919, easing the budgetary positions of its governments. But even more significant was the improvement in the price of gold, occurring at a time of falling labour costs, and reduced prices for imported machinery. The mandated territory of New Guinea was the first to benefit, for the major gold strike at Edie Creek in 1926 had been followed by discovery of the large alluvial deposits in the Bulolo valley. Exploration and initial development of the dredging areas was completed by 1932, and production soared. Government took a 5 per cent royalty on the value of gold mined in the territory, and by the end of the 1930s this royalty exceeded £80,000 ($200,000) a year, about a quarter of the territorial revenue. Hence came the enthusiasm with which governments all over Melanesia except in Dutch New Guinea encouraged miners to penetrate new areas with their pans, shovels and experienced eyes.

Exploration for gold became very extensive. Some old mining areas in Papua were re-opened, and prospectors ranged throughout the Bismarcks, Solomon Islands and Fiji. There was a major strike in Viti Levu in 1932, and a large deposit in metasediments was developed by means of three mines opened in 1934–6, operated by an Australian company and worked with Fijian and Rotuman labour, deliberately making minimal use of Indo-Fijians. For a short period at about the beginning of World War II, gold became the

* See Note on Conventions on p. xvi.

principal export of the colony. There were no similar strikes elsewhere, though a small deposit was located on Guadalcanal in the Solomon Islands in 1937. But this discovery, like some others, had consequences. In Guadalcanal, and Bougainville, gold was found in association with large bodies of low-grade copper ore, the quality of which was then too low to offer any prospect of development. In West New Guinea, too, a Government-sponsored expedition failed to find gold, but a geologist attached to an expedition which climbed the summits of the Carstensz Toppen (Djajatop) in 1936 found a massive body of gold-bearing copper ore just above the tree line. The samples brought back were unfortunately deeply weathered, and the brief interest flickered away. However, all these discoveries remained in the records, and became the basis for major developments thirty years later.

DISCOVERY AND PENETRATION OF A NEW COLONIAL FRONTIER

By far the most immediately dramatic, and ultimately far-reaching, of the consequences of gold exploration was, however, the discovery of a million people, about a quarter of the total Melanesian population, in the valleys of the central New Guinea highlands. The first party to penetrate these valleys and report its findings was a small group of miners in 1930: seeking the source of gold traces in the gravels of the Ramu river, they ascended the low ranges in this area and found large populations in the grassland plateaux and valleys beyond. Later exploration was similarly conducted by prospectors, though supported by Government, and not until after 1935 did Government take over the whole task of exploration; by this time initial hopes of gold had proved to be unrewarding.

It is remarkable that this discovery did not take place sooner. Both the German and Australian administrations explored in the foothills of the central ranges during the decade 1900–10, and an outlying valley of the highland cultural area was in fact penetrated from the Papuan side in 1910. Some outlying groups in West New Guinea were contacted about the same time by expeditions to the 'snow mountains'. Detzner, a German boundary surveyor who spent the 1914–18 period in hiding in the New Guinea interior, wrote a report of large populations in the central mountains in 1921, but his account is garbled and partly fictional. Also it was published in German. In 1921–2 a Dutch expedition passed right across the West New Guinea highlands at a sparsely populated point, finding nothing almost by random chance. But evidence was accumulating, and it is strange that the discoveries of 1930 should have come as a total surprise.

The major discoveries followed in 1932–3, when a better-financed party revealed the existence of almost 350,000 people in the Chimbu-Wahgi area.

Between 1933 and 1939 almost all remaining groups in the Australian colonies were located, partly by prospectors and Government officers from the north, partly by the most hazardous of all expeditions from the south. This party travelled right across an intensely difficult belt of limestone country, and passed through the whole width of the Tari and Mendi valleys under constant attack, ravaged by sickness and hunger. Spurning the indignity of seeking aid in their extremity, by crossing the border to an already-established mandated territory mission a few days' easy walk north of where they stood, they turned back across the limestone into Papua.

Comparable discoveries were also made in West New Guinea, especially in 1936 and 1938, when the two major population concentrations were both sighted initially from the air, then penetrated on the ground by expeditions backed by strong Government forces. But this early effort was not followed up: though the Wissel Lakes area received a Government post in 1938 and was occupied by the Japanese in 1943, the great Baliem valley was only briefly revisited until 1957, when a permanent post was finally set up. Some valleys close to the border were not explored until 1959–60.

Nothing is more revealing of the cultural gap between the colonizers and the residentiary populations than this history of late and almost random discovery. The highland population concentrations were physically separate from the lowlanders, and culturally distinct in a number of ways, but they were from the most ancient times in trading and social contact with fringe and lowland people by multiple routes. Hughes has shown how European penetration of the Chimbu-Wahgi region was preceded almost thirty years before by an innovation wave of accelerated trade coming up these multiple routes, introducing new goods which included a few European tools. Contact with fringe groups of highlanders was made as early as 1905, yet no information passed or was credited. The highlanders in their turn perhaps heard rumours of new men, but these were without any comprehensible reference, and the exploring parties were generally greeted with astonishment. The first reaction varied greatly: sometimes fearful, sometimes friendly in the hope of gain, sometimes overwhelmed by an apparent return of ancestral spirits. Rarely was the reaction immediately hostile, but hostility usually followed, and there were both extensive thieving and some mass attacks. There were also murders of isolated individuals, mostly prospectors and missionaries, and even though other individuals had been able to roam in safety over great distances, the Australian administration in 1934 determined to close the new frontier to random penetration. This wide extension of the 'uncontrolled areas regulations', first implemented to limit Government responsibility for wandering gold prospectors in 1926, represented a new departure in Melanesian colonial policy. It had important consequences.

Late discovery protected the highlanders from many of the effects of colonial penetration as experienced by others. Especially once it was established that their homeland was without valuable minerals, the colonial commercial system could not make direct use of any of its resources but labour. Linkage was initially, and for many years, almost wholly by air, and while the methods of 'air-lift' had been pioneered for the whole world in New Guinea, in the Morobe goldfields, the longer haul and greater flying hazards of the central highlands made this still an impracticable method of mass carriage for either goods or persons. Further, discovery of the large labour pool came at a time when labour demand was at a low ebb because of the general depression. Hence there was little opposition to the humanitarian urgings of some early officers and private individuals, who argued that these populations were largely non-immune to malaria, and hence would suffer heavy mortality if recruited for the coast. Such motives were to prove of small effect in a period of rising labour demand after 1946, but they had the effect of softening the initial penetration period in a manner experienced by no other Melanesian area. The 'uncontrolled areas regulations' further meant that Government must establish control of a sort before either missionaries or private entrepreneurs could enter and begin work. Despite the killing sometimes involved, the establishment of control was widely welcomed, by bringing a new security into life hitherto lived in a climate of constant feuding, skirmish, ambush and warfare. There was little disastrous introduction of disease, even though some Europeans and many police were active among the highland women. Hence there was also no widespread reservoir of hostility built up in this initial period except toward some of the lowland indigenous servants of the Government. These exceptional initial conditions have had important continuing consequences.

The significance of this protection received by the highlanders can be more readily appreciated by contrasting the experience and reaction of some other populations first penetrated during the same period. The inland areas of the Sepik District, around Maprik, were lightly explored in German times, but the first substantial ingression was by gold prospectors and miners who entered in fair numbers during the 1930s. In this more accessible region, open to approach by the Sepik River, they were accompanied also by professional labour recruiters who began a drain of men away to the plantations in the Bismarck archipelago. The miners were a rough group, and many nasty incidents occurred before Government established its control in 1936–9. Missionaries also entered freely, and there was often bitter competition for converts. The period of initial penetration is remembered as a very bad time in this area, and when the Japanese replaced the Australians here in 1942 they were warmly welcomed: indeed in this one area, the Japanese were able to recruit a force of local auxiliaries to resist the return of the Australians in 1944–5, and resentment has continued to this day.

Except in West New Guinea, where initial penetration was widely delayed until the 1950s and 1960s – even the 1970s in some areas – the 1930s saw the substantial completion of colonial penetration in Melanesia. At the beginning of the decade fully a quarter of the total regional population was still without knowledge of the existence of the new outside forces and their agents; by its end only a residuum remained in total ignorance. But the new penetration was only locally in the unpoliced hands of private venturers; for most of the newly colonized people it was an experience very different from that felt by earlier generations in the coastal New Guinea areas and especially the eastern islands. This great extension of colonial penetration took place at a time of stagnation – even retrogression – in most of the older-colonized parts of the region. Commercial drive was very limited, and even missionary drive was constrained for lack of support. Government was rarely far behind the advance, and usually in the van. The rôle of government itself was thus transformed, with feedback running all the way to metropolitan attitudes in Australia and the Netherlands. This was indeed an almost unique event in colonial history, but it was one which meshed readily with new trends arising in response to widespread forces in the colonial and metropolitan worlds. Before these trends could become clear, however, a new cataclysm swept the world, this time with a major storm centre in the Melanesian islands themselves.

REFERENCES AND SOURCES

Basic sources for this chapter are much the same as for Chapter 6: there is useful material on the interwar period in Naval Intelligence Division (1943–5) and also in Doumenge (1966). Stanner (1953), and other writing of observers who knew Melanesia in these years, is also of great value.

The sugar industry of Fiji in this period is surveyed in Lowndes (1956) and R. G. Ward (1965): there is also valuable material in Robertson (1931), Shephard (1945) and Watters (1963). On New Caledonia, Faivre, Poirier and Routhier (1955) and Le Borgne (1964) have much useful data on the interwar period, and there is a valuable review of events in the north of the island in Rocheteau (1966).

There is an extensive literature on the discovery and penetration of central New Guinea, summarized in part in Brookfield (1961a). Among contemporary sources by participants and observers, the following are some of the most important, and interesting: Chinnery (1934), Hides (1936), Leahy and Crain (1937), Colijn (1937), Redaktie TKNAG (1940), Archbold, Rand and Brass (1942) and Le Roux (1948–50).

The most thorough survey of gold mining in this period is Healy's (1967) history of the Bulolo field, but there is a great deal of information in more recent geological reports, especially those dealing with the Solomon Islands. A summary of the history of mineral development is given in Brookfield with Hart (1971).

CHAPTER 8

TRAUMA – 1940-1946

The initial effect of the outbreak of war in 1939 was merely to halt the gradual recovery from the worst of the Great Depression. Though prices improved, most especially for nickel in New Caledonia, shipping difficulties quickly became acute, and withdrawal of personnel for the armed forces led to a cessation of the expansion of Government activity. There were some political consequences of the fall of France in 1940, but not until 1941 did the growing threat of a Pacific war begin to influence activity. The Japanese irruption in 1942 was swift, disastrous for the Europeans, but not at all damaging in a physical sense. But the reconquest from 1942 to 1945 had a major and lasting effect on the whole region: in a real sense it is the major event of modern Melanesian history.

DETACHMENT FROM THE METROPOLES: 1940–1942

In May and June 1940 both the Netherlands and France were overrun by the German armies. The Netherlands Indies as a whole became a virtually self-governing colony, still run as before, selling to and importing from new trading partners, but in no great distress. For West New Guinea the effect was minimal to nil. The fall of France had more serious local consequences, leading quickly to the first active emergence of latent separatist forces among the small European colony in New Caledonia. On 20 June 1940, General de Gaulle issued his call to the French nation from London, and the first territory to respond was the French administration in the New Hebrides which declared for 'Free France' with only a few dissenting voices among local planters. In New Caledonia the locally-elected Conseil Général voted on 26 June to continue the war, but the governor was promptly deposed by the Vichyist military commander who remained in touch with his superiors in Saigon.

Long-established forces now guided the course of events. Descendants of both free colonists and convicts inherited a tradition of opposition to metropolitan rule, and the oligopoly exercised by the SLN, the Banque de l'Indo-Chine, and the Maison Ballande pressed hard on them at all times, but most especially during the depression years. Small businessmen, sub-contract miners, farmers and pastoralists had a common focus of resentment which they shared to some degree even with the Melanesians. Resentment focused as much on Saigon, immediate source of financial control, as on Paris: it had more than once been proposed to place New Caledonia administratively within the regional Gouvernement-générale de l'Indo-Chine and thus link its development more closely with that of the Asian empire. But the 'Calédoniens' felt closer affinity with the neighbouring white populations in Australia and New Zealand, with whom they traded, and among whom they frequently visited. Like the Australians and New Zealanders, they had not shared the debilitating malaise of western Europe in the face of resurgent German nationalism, and old jingoistic and naive ideas of *lutte à l'outrance* lingered in this remote region a generation after they had faded from Europe. Together, these forces aroused massive opposition to the Vichyist military in Nouméa, and on 19 September a motley army of Calédoniens – *les broussards* – with a number of Melanesians assembled outside the city and marched in. Their entry coincided with the arrival of an Australian cruiser bearing the French Commissioner in the New Hebrides, Henri Sautot, who was installed in a few hours as governor.

Subsequent events confirmed the opposition of New Caledonia toward metropolitan control. De Gaulle's London Committee knew nothing of Sautot as a person, and when the Japanese threat became more ominous in 1941, determined to place over him a 'safe' de Gaulle man, who would assume the authority of High Commissioner for all French Pacific territories. The Commissioner, d'Argenlieu, shared his leader's well-founded distrust of American intentions toward de Gaulle vis-à-vis the Vichy authorities, and actively sustained his own authority and independence of action when American forces began to arrive early in 1942. The Americans found it easier to negotiate with Sautot, who gave them unstinted cooperation, and tension mounted between Sautot and d'Argenlieu, who informed London that the governor was proving disloyal to de Gaulle and sought his dismissal. Confident of local support, Sautot resisted, and in May 1942 was arrested together with some members of the Conseil Général and put on board a warship. In the next few days, at the very time when the Japanese navy made its one major effort to debouch into the Coral Sea, there was a general strike in Nouméa, d'Argenlieu was kidnapped and held by *broussards* in a country hotel, and there was a new assemblage of pro-Sautot forces outside Nouméa. The American commander intervened to secure the release and reinstatement of d'Argenlieu, who was thenceforth more pliable. Sautot ended the war in equatorial Africa, but returned to become elected major of Nouméa. D'Argenlieu went on to Saigon, where his continued attitudes toward local independence movements played some part in creating the situation which led to the first and second Vietnam wars. When he died in 1964 the SLN-controlled daily paper in Nouméa, *La France Australe*, reported the event without eulogy or comment. And ambivalence toward de Gaulle and his party remained a force in New Caledonian politics right through into the 1970s.

THE JAPANESE IRRUPTION

Late in 1941 token Australian garrisons were placed in Rabaul and a few other towns in New Guinea, and in the New Hebrides, but there was little expectation that Australia's island screen could be defended without American aid. The Japanese had no great forces in Micronesia, nor much fortification – contrary to popular belief. They had encountered much the same problems with copra and sugar as were encountered in Melanesia during the interwar period, and from 1924 onward had found it necessary to introduce financial subsidies. The arrival of Japanese settlers after 1930 led to economic expansion, but the south Pacific thrust remained secondary in both Japanese commercial and military intentions; these were firmly directed toward southeast Asia.

The strategic aim of driving a wedge between North America and Australia was entrusted mainly to Japanese naval forces, with very limited army support. Ports in northern New Guinea were occupied either without opposition or against only light resistance early in 1942, but subsequent progress was slow. Tulagi, capital of the Solomon Islands, was undefended but was not occupied until May. A more serious naval move against Port Moresby, also in May, was thwarted by the US Pacific fleet in the Battle of the Coral Sea, and only then were ground forces more heavily committed in two overland moves. The Japanese sent too few troops too late: though they came within forty miles of Port Moresby they were turned back, and at Milne Bay were repulsed. They never penetrated the Solomon Islands east of Guadalcanal, and in Malaita, for example, the war consisted of no more than a single landing by a Japanese party at Auki in mid-1942. The British officials withdrew into the bush while the Japanese had lunch, then returned after the visitors had departed. In New Guinea, Japanese forces made no attempt to occupy the interior until early 1943; they were repulsed in the Morobe goldfields, and only one patrol ever entered the central highlands in the Australian territory. Only in the far west of West New Guinea did their occupation extend to the south coast, and more than half the whole area of the island remained under allied control throughout the war. No firm plans for Japanese colonial administration were evolved, though the Native Pacification Unit seems to have provided an acceptable administration in some parts of the country. Elsewhere, however, and especially in New Britain, their rule proved extremely onerous.

THE RECONQUEST OF MELANESIA

Destruction of Japanese naval supremacy at Midway in June 1942 did not immediately shift the balance of power in favour of the Americans, but it changed the whole nature of the Pacific war. Deprived of their dominance of the ocean, the Japanese now sought to retain and develop their island screen by the establishment of well-defended air bases on land. An early move in this direction was the construction of an airfield complex in Guadalcanal, from whence the New Hebrides and northern New Caledonia could be attacked and hopefully neutralized. The Americans had meanwhile built up strong bases in Nouméa, and in the New Hebrides on Efaté and in southeast Santo: they determined to blunt this new threat, and on 7 August 1942 landings were effected on Guadalcanal and at Tulagi. The next night the American landing fleet was almost destroyed by a Japanese naval attack, and the first of many hard-fought land battles in the island war was joined.

The details of the complex land, sea and air operations in and around Guadalcanal do not concern us: they are described minutely and with empathy in the most outstanding volume of Morison's brilliant eight-volume survey of US naval history in the war. Gradually the Americans established ascendancy, and in February 1943 the Japanese suddenly withdrew to bases in New Georgia and Bougainville, which were in turn assaulted and seized in June and November 1943. Meanwhile in New Guinea the Japanese had been driven out of northern Papua, and an onslaught on bases around the Vitiaz Strait between New Guinea and New Britain was launched in September. The 'breaking of the Bismarcks barrier' took most of a year: it was accomplished through a strategy of isolating the main base at Rabaul, which was never subjected to ground assault, and leaping forward, leaving the isolated Japanese bases to wither on the vine. American supremacy on the sea and in the air grew steadily and made possible penetration of the network of island bases and the establishment of new forward bases between and beyond the remaining Japanese strongholds. In 1944 the war swept through and beyond the northwest of Melanesia with the seizure of Hollandia, Biak and Ponape; the assault then moved on to the Philippines, leaving behind large numbers of Japanese. The Australians, once in the front line, were also left behind or diverted to Borneo, and the final battles of the war in Melanesia were the 'mopping-up' assaults of Australian forces against the remaining Japanese. One wonders at the necessity of these destructive battles in a wider strategy; some of them were major operations, especially the reconquest of the inland Sepik District in mid-1945. The remaining Japanese garrisons were included in the general surrender in August 1945. Among these was Rabaul, which had by then been totally destroyed under air bombardment.

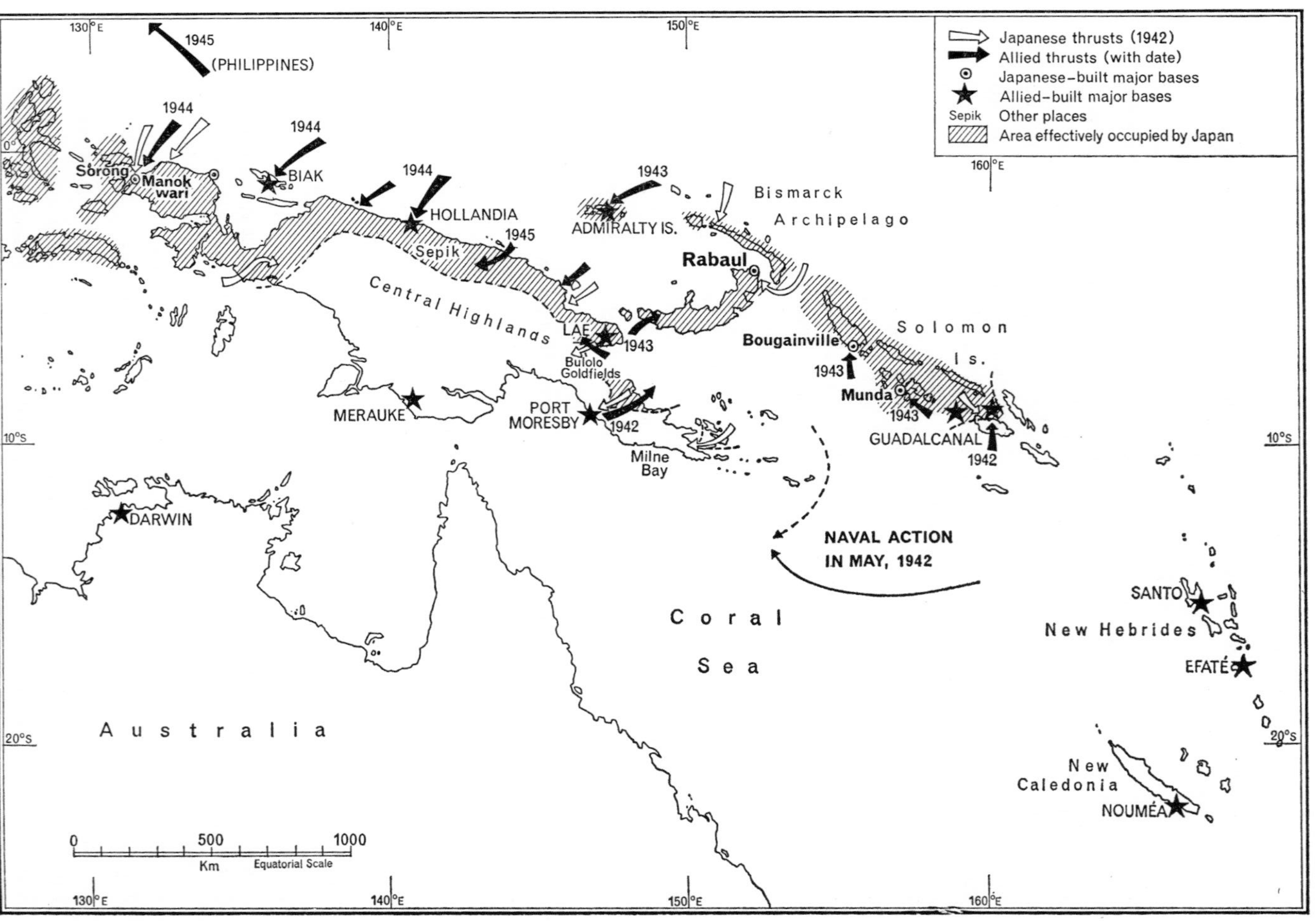

Figure 4. The impact of war, 1942–5

THE MELANESIAN EXPERIENCE OF WAR

Thus far the war from the perspective of military history. We know well enough what it was like for its participants from numerous first-hand accounts, much film and fiction, and the better-balanced collection of half-truths in Michener's *Tales of the South Pacific*. But this was the war as seen by the moving armies. For Melanesians of all colours and cultures it was a traumatic experience in every sense. First was the speed with which it all occurred. The Japanese came in with little violence, and the Europeans fled before them – or were taken, and sometimes butchered if they failed to get away. When war came back it came massively, swiftly and with great destruction. Material goods and men were hurled into the fray in unbelievable quantity and with seemingly reckless abandon. This second aspect was perhaps the most important. The war offered a vision of an undreamed-of world of plenty. The very numbers of men were startling. In 1941, the whole European population of Melanesia was not more than 30,000, half of these in New Caledonia. By the end of 1943 the USA had some 500,000 troops, probably more, deployed in Melanesia. Australian and New Zealand forces, and a small but very effective Fijian force, were additional. Never before had a fraction of the number of ships been seen in the ports, and the congestion was evidence of enormous material power.

Though the war spread in its later stages as Japanese dispersed into the bush and were pursued by Australian troops, its direct impact was very patchy. Many people only a few miles from the fighting saw nothing of it other than aircraft flying overhead, and refugees who moved away from the battle areas. Only an unfortunate minority, principal among whom were the Tolai of northern New Britain, were unable to escape and had to endure the full rigours of war with and from the soldiers. The Tolai population fell by perhaps a third between 1941 and 1946.

Military forces were recruited in Fiji, and auxiliaries were raised among the Melanesians in the Solomon Islands and by the Japanese in New Guinea. Melanesians also joined the French army in New Caledonia, but the Bataillon du Pacifique fought only against the Germans, distinguishing themselves especially in the Libyan desert. The mass of the Melanesians were militarily neutral in the conflict, but their loyalty was actively sought, and they were used extensively as labourers, carriers, guides and informers by both sides. The concept of competing loyalties was almost wholly new in this context, and it is remarkable that so few Melanesians turned from their pre-war allegiance to give willing aid to the Japanese. Some few such were executed by the returning Australians, but not without protests at home. A number of Melanesians became war heroes both in allied eyes and in the eyes of their own people, by refusing to give information under torture, and guiding and aiding allied soldiers at great personal risk. In the main, however, the Melanesians were expected only to give service as demanded, and very arduous service was demanded, especially in New Guinea.

Civil administration in the Australian territory was suspended in February 1942, and its place taken by a military administrative unit (ANGAU), the first function of which was to provide army support among the indigenous population. Recruitment of carriers and labourers was at first easy, since almost all plantations had ceased operation, but the value of these workers, as demonstrated in the land battle for Port Moresby, created an insatiable demand among the military. Numbers mounted from 8,000 in late 1942 to more than 40,000 (55,000 at the peak according to one authority), in the latter years of the war. This labour force was drawn from a relatively small population, and recruitment was scarcely voluntary: virtually the whole able-bodied male population above the presumed age of fourteen years was taken from some villages. Pay was either 50c or $1.00 a month, and ration scales were for a long time so poor that deficiency symptoms were widespread. The principle that the Army's demands came ahead of civil considerations was applied almost throughout the war. Later in the war increasing numbers of labourers were applied to plantations by the Production Control Board, which assumed full control of the whole plantation industry in 1942 and was run by the military government. The impact was heavy, and even in the central highlands there was a first experience with labour recruiting – though only for work within the highlands – at this time.

One aspect of the war that may have softened this impact, however, was the sharp contrast in racial attitudes between the soldiers and the pre-war Europeans, most of whom had left the country in 1942. Despite the blatant exploitation, the more friendly and less domineering attitudes, especially of the enlisted men, were both noted and appreciated by the Melanesians. This applied even more to the American troops, among whom were considerable numbers of black soldiers. In the Solomon Islands, where the American army handled employment directly, wage scales were also very greatly above pre-war levels, and there were numerous opportunities to earn additional money, or to receive or remove material goods which passed out of the well-stocked bases in very great quantity. The reimposition of pre-war employment conditions in this group led to serious trouble in 1946.

Civil administration was totally suspended only in New Guinea. Though all economic activity also came to a halt in the Solomon Islands, the British administration and many private Europeans remained – some of these undertaking the highly dangerous spy work of the Coastwatchers organization, as also in Australian New Guinea. The British administration retreated to Auki when Tulagi was seized, and later was re-established in the American bases on Guadalcanal. In the other territories, there was no dislocation of civil administration or of production, though Government became essentially subordinate to the military authorities in both the New Hebrides and – after May 1942 – in New Caledonia. The populations of these territories had large opportunities to supply and serve the military and the war was a period of unparalleled prosperity. Only one major group was seriously disadvantaged. Vietnamese and Javanese contract workers in New Caledonia and the New Hebrides were not augmented, and labour contracts mostly ran out during the war. Rural workers were allowed to leave the plantations, and made good use of the opportunities for entrepreneurship. But the Vietnamese in the nickel mines could neither be dispensed with nor replaced. They were held at work, on existing pay and conditions, beyond the expiry of their contracts, and attempts at resistance were suppressed by the American forces, as well as by the French.

THE LEGACY OF THE ARMIES

Both physical destruction and physical construction, both economic dislocation and economic stimulus, were left to Melanesia in 1945. Several whole towns were destroyed, most notably the former capital of the mandated territory of New Guinea, and others were badly damaged. Perhaps a quarter of the plantation area in New Guinea and the Solomon Islands was devastated, and many plantations were deeply overgrown after four or more years of neglect. Except in New Britain, comparatively few Melanesian villages were destroyed, but many people had moved out of the battle areas and the base areas and were living either among kin and affines, or in wholly new settlements.

On the other hand, the armies left behind them a huge quantity of material, and a great number of fixed installations, including roads, wharves, and whole base complexes which now provided the facilities for new towns. A widely-spread network of good airfields had been created, and this whole new system of infrastructure was now employed selectively to create a new pattern of circulation and towns. Two colonial capitals, Hollandia in West New Guinea and Honiara in the Solomon Islands, were set up in the abandoned army bases, and other new towns included Santo, second town and port of the New Hebrides. Everywhere, bridges, roads, steel piping and especially the ubiquitous Marston matting, were put into use: one sometimes wonders how New Guinea and the Solomon Islands can ever have existed without the latter, which for two decades provided bridge-decking, fencing and airfield surfacing throughout great areas of these countries. Jeeps were salvaged, and – gradually reduced in numbers by cannibalization – were often still on the roads as late as 1960. Many wartime Quonsett huts are still in use today. For a few years after the war, the business of scrap metal collection, redistribution and sale was a major activity in the old battle and base areas, and enterprising entrepreneurs, and missionaries too, were often able to re-establish themselves quickly with the aid of salvaged material.

Economic dislocation was severe, and not only as a result of the destruction. Expanded demand for vegetables and other comestibles had been met by extensive new planting, which was often without a market once the armies had gone. In New Caledonia the market-garden industry was completely dislocated, first by internment of the Japanese, then by the entry of numerous Europeans into the business, creating a condition of over-supply that was not rationalized for more than fifteen years. Cattle herds were everywhere decimated, both by slaughter for meat and by the destruction of fences, which permitted livestock to run wild. But on the other hand new and solid marketing arrangements had been established by means of contracts with the British Ministry of Food and other buyers, and when these were terminated the advantages of centralized marketing and price stabilization were not again surrendered.

The most fundamental changes, however, were social and political. The war had created new leaders among the Melanesians, sometimes directly encouraged by Government in the search for satraps who would facilitate the swift reimposition of control. Many people had learned new avenues of entrepreneurship, unfettered by the restrictive constraints of the commercial system. The army model of organization was seen by many Melanesians as a road to progress, and authoritarianism, rather than democracy, received a considerable boost. There was a widespread disinclination to return to pre-war conditions of employment, and attempts to reimpose such conditions generated both overt and covert unrest. The pre-war colonial authorities were no longer seen as the only possible form of government, and new patterns of race relations, briefly glimpsed, were not forgotten.

All this might, however, have faded away but for changes in the ethos of the metropolitan powers. There was a new awareness of the rights of colonial peoples, and a new concern over their underdeveloped condition. The idea of public intervention to secure progress had become firmly rooted. Furthermore, it now became an ultimate objective of colonialism to move toward the independence of colonial territories, however far this might lie in the future. Henceforth the opposition was rather between gradualism and speed, than between exploitation and a more humanitarian view of the 'white man's burden'. This trend was given an irreversible boost by the establishment of the United Nations, and by the competition for the minds and hearts of the people of the 'Third World' which quickly evolved out of the world-wide confrontation between East and West. Though another generation still separated Melanesia from an emergence of nationalism such as now swept Asia and West Africa, the form of colonialism which returned to Melanesia in the wake of the armies was already radically different from that which still lingered in 1941.

REFERENCES AND SOURCES

There is a voluminous literature on World War II in the Pacific. Of particular interest for the operations discussed here are Morison (1950), Milner (1957), McCarthy (1959) and Morton (1962). Oliver (1951) and Stanner (1953) are also valuable on the general background of war and its impact. Sautot (1949) provides an intensely personal interpretation of the 1940–2 events in New Caledonia. A large number of useful articles has appeared since the war in such periodicals as *Pacific Islands Monthly* and there are three invaluable papers on the war in relation to the indigenous population of Australian New Guinea in Waigani Seminars (1969). For the view of a critical outside observer of the scene immediately after the war, see Mair (1948).

CHAPTER 9

THE HASLUCK PERIOD AND THE NEW COLONIALISM

During the 1950s the pacesetter in Melanesia was undoubtedly Australian New Guinea, and the unquestioned master of Australian New Guinea in these years was Paul Hasluck, Minister for Territories in Menzies' Government from 1951 until 1963. These were years of gradualism and enlightened paternalism in political affairs, coupled with rapid economic expansion that shifted more and more firmly toward emphasis on the indigenous population. The policies of this period have been greatly criticized, but they need to be seen against what went before, as well as what came after. Other territories took their lead from Australian New Guinea: differences in policy, such as emerged in West New Guinea, played their part in bringing gradualism to an end, but Hasluck's contribution remains despite the failure of some aspects of his work. For the first time, a comprehensive and integrated policy was not only evolved but implemented in Melanesia. It had its weaknesses, but it produced some striking results.

UNIFORM DEVELOPMENT IN AUSTRALIAN NEW GUINEA

Australian New Guinea, with more than half the total population of Melanesia, undertook two major tasks in the aftermath of World War II. The first was the rehabilitation of the economy, and conversion of the static pre-war system into one with dynamic and continuing growth. The second was the integration of the still-undeveloped and primitive interior with the whole emergent national economy without allowing this interior to become a mere labour reservoir for the more advanced coastal regions.

There were strong forces leading in the latter direction in the late 1940s. Rehabilitation of the gold mines in Morobe, and of the rubber plantations of central Papua, were both beset very severely by shortage of labour. The plantations of the Bismarck archipelago were able to call on labour from the Sepik District, and did so in large quantity, but in the country as a whole the supply of capital exceeded that of labour for the first time in many years, and the gold and rubber enterprises suffered particularly severely. As early as

1947 it was proposed to recruit workers from the central highlands for the goldfields, and though medical and other protectionist objections were persuasive, limited recruitment began in 1949 and was formalized in the Highland Labour Scheme in 1950. Under this scheme, Government itself undertook recruitment and transportation; there was strict regulation of the terms of recruiting, and medical prophylaxis against malaria and TB were compulsory. Among a population which had now some two decades of contact, an awareness of the utility of money and a keen curiosity about the outside world, there was a high potential for migration and the response was good. Within two or three years a strong flow of recruits was established, coming mainly from the most densely peopled areas of the central highlands, and the supply of cheap, unskilled labour in large quantities was an enabling factor in the rapid growth of rubber, coconut and cocoa plantations in the coastlands. Other areas, including the Sepik and western Papua, were also being heavily recruited, and all conditions were present for a concentration of both capital and labour into a few areas, leading to backwash effects over the larger part of the country.

This is the context in which the conflict between equity and efficiency was presented to policy makers, and in which the doctrine of 'uniform development' was evolved. In a major review in the middle of his term, Hasluck (1958) expressed his views in clear terms. The following extracts are taken out of context, but I do not believe that they represent his ideas unfairly:

> During the period in which I have had the portfolio of Territories precise directions have been given about land administration; the establishment of law and order; health; education; the development of native agriculture; *the uniformity of development in all parts of the Territory and consequently decentralization of control and spreading of expenditure over the whole Territory* (76)...the advancement of a primitive people is gradual and is necessarily surrounded by some hesitations and many unforeseen complications (80)...Unless there is a society with its own values, its own cohesion, its own standards of conduct and its own loyalties, the indigenous people will never be able to take over from the trustee those responsibilities in regard to just treatment and power (81)...*We need to have much more wisdom and understanding in the next 30 years than we were required to have in the last 30 years and to make a far greater effort* (84)...It is evident from what I have said that I envisage a future time when the people of Papua and New Guinea will seek self-government and some measure of independence. It will also be clear that I think precipitate moves toward that day could prove to be to the disadvantage of the people (85) [my italics].

Thus a policy for regional distribution of development meshed in with the well-established view, advanced by Lord Hailey and many others, that it was a duty of the colonial power to hold back self-government until the politically aware in the population reached a critical mass: otherwise an activist minority might gain control, and exercise power in its own interests. Such a view was certainly not unique to Melanesia: it guided British policy in many parts of the world for more than a generation. It has only retrospectively been realized that the activist minority often constitutes the true leaders of society, and may be at least as disinterested as any group of political leaders in western countries, and more so than many. In Australian New Guinea, however, the policy had a second edge: it was also necessary even to retard economic and social progress in the more advanced parts of the country in order to accelerate progress in the hinterland. Thus a major part of Government effort in these years went first into completing the establishment of control in the interior, then into providing infrastructure and services, and initiating development in hinterland areas.

Resources available to Government expanded fairly rapidly, as annual metropolitan subsidies mounted swiftly to exceed $40 million annually before the end of the Hasluck period. There was a great enlargement of staff, and a major instrument of policy was the strong and professionally competent Extension Service set up in the Department of Agriculture under W. L. Conroy. But resources were at no stage equal to needs, and some very thin stretching resulted, with much waste of effort and finance due to inadequate or insufficiently sustained input. Even so, much was achieved, most especially in the central highlands where European-owned coffee plantations were set up early in the 1950s on land alienated only with considerable care, and this undercapitalized enterprise was then followed swiftly by the introduction of coffee as an indigenous cash crop in the same region: quite unparalleled, and indeed unexpected, success attended the latter innovation, and by the early 1960s coffee was already nudging cocoa from second place among exports, while more than half of the coffee production was grown by the residentiary population on its own land. *Per capita* incomes in the coffee belt in the highlands exceeded those in all but the most advanced of the coastal areas by the mid-1960s. Efforts in other areas were less rewarding, but there was major expansion in social services, especially health, in all reasonably accessible parts of the country. A consequence of these policies was diminution in labour available for the plantations from all areas which evolved adequate local income sources. Although large populations still remain beyond the reach of viable cash cropping, serious labour shortage has re-emerged since 1965, this time with no means of relief except by improving the attractions of wage employment.

Significant restructuring of Government was also involved in the implementation of these policies. It was felt necessary to concentrate power in the minister's hands, and hence through the Department of [External]

Territories in Canberra. Thus the Administrator of the newly united Territory of Papua and New Guinea was much less than a governor; his department much less than a secretariat. He was by-passed in much communication between Canberra and the administrative departments. The same applied at District level, where District Commissioners coordinated but did not control the work of specialist departments, and continued down to the most local level. When a system of Local Government Councils was set up it was not meshed into the District system, and the only ultimate focus of decision-making was in Canberra itself.

This system was not popular, but it made possible the translation of central policy to local implementation without coordinated obstruction. It required a strong hand at the top, and it had this until 1963. But it was hardly a democratic system: perhaps it was never stripped down to its essentials better than by a former indigenous local official, who explained it to his people in these terms:

> The Queen tells Number One in Canberra what to do; he tells Number One in Port Moresby what to do. Number One in Port Moresby tells the District Commissioner what to do, and he tells the Number One Kiap [the local Assistant District Officer] what to do. The Number One Kiap tells me what to do, and I tell you what to do. So you had better do it (Field notes, translated).

Such was the new colonialism, as seen by its recipients.

EQUITY VS. EFFICIENCY ELSEWHERE IN MELANESIA

The same problem was faced elsewhere, most especially in West New Guinea, where the Dutch re-established administration in 1944, over a year before they resumed control elsewhere in Indonesia. Until 1949 comparatively little was done, but in that year a Federal United States of Indonesia was created excluding West New Guinea, where the Dutch retained colonial power. In the following year the cumbersome Indonesian federal system was swept away in favour of a unitary constitution, and from this time on the Netherlands Government determined to retain control of the rump of their former East Indian empire.

The reasons for the Dutch decision will probably not become clear until the archives are opened to research, but it seems likely that interested and disinterested motives became hopelessly intertwined. In 1950 it was still hoped that West New Guinea would become a major oil producer, and it was also expected that the territory would become a home for Eurasians displaced from Java, who might otherwise migrate to the Netherlands – which most in fact did. But there was also awareness that New Guinea was radically different culturally and in state of development from the rest of Indonesia, and an honest desire to retrieve a lost colonial reputation by success in this *tabula rasa*. As early as 1947 the Netherlands adhered to the newly-formed South Pacific Commission on behalf of West New Guinea alone – a step which suggests that the decision to hold on was premeditated. From 1950 until 1953, however, little in the way of policy was evolved, and it was only in the later 1950s that a development programme was firmly implemented. Metropolitan subsidy did not exceed the small local revenues until 1955, but thereafter mounted to reach a level of $35 per head of the estimated population in 1962, being then much higher in proportion to population than the metropolitan subsidies of the time in Australian New Guinea.

The Dutch authorities eschewed development through expatriate enterprise, especially after the failure of hopes of large Eurasian settlement. Major efforts were made to establish cash cropping in settled areas, and at the same time to extend control and initiate development in the very large interior and southern areas that were still totally uncontrolled in 1950. Penetration of the interior, by missions and Government, was some twenty years behind the penetration of central Australian New Guinea, and though progress was rapid after 1955, it was carried out in a very different political climate. For external reasons to be discussed below, the Dutch found it necessary to abandon a wholly authoritarian principle of government after 1957, and to proceed rapidly toward the creation of representative institutions, while at the same time accelerating the pace of localization of the administration, already begun. To do these things, they had to rely on the emergent élite of the few developed coastal areas, but as soon as these people achieved a voice in Government they campaigned for a concentration of effort on those areas where results could quickly be achieved, and abandonment of the dispersal of effort in the interior. These pressures were resisted by the Dutch, who continued to be overtly guided by the Australian model, but when the Indonesians assumed control in 1963 they soon sought to adopt a more restricted development policy. During the years 1963–7 the economy of West New Guinea ran steeply downhill, with greatly diminished metropolitan input, and when in 1967–8 the Indonesian Government sought United Nations Development Programme aid, they proposed a concentration on the coastal areas, opting realistically to apply limited resources in the most 'efficient' manner. The United Nations mission accepted this in principle, but insisted on a partial incorporation of equity principles in the programme finally adopted, and being implemented in 1971. The compromise is unsatisfactory, and the issue is by no means resolved.

A different sort of problem faced the British administration in the Solomon Islands after World War II. The pre-war economy, such as it had been, had entirely ceased operation; the only employment and buying in the country was by the remaining American forces, and by Government itself. Britain refused to make war-damage payments in the Solomon Islands, and the two main Australian trading companies thereupon declined to resume their enterprises: Government itself had to set up its own import-export company to replace them. Even Lever's did not fully return until 1950, but a number of smaller planters and other employers did resume activity in 1946.

Attempts to restore pre-war employment conditions met a swift and hostile response from Melanesians on Guadalcanal, and especially Malaita – the most populous island and traditional labour source. Men had grown accustomed to work at much higher wartime wages. A self-help movement aiming at communal development, modelled on army forms of organization, sprang up, and quickly grew out of hand so far as Government was concerned. It was suppressed in the late 1940s, and a decision was then taken to try to kill the source of discontent by 'spreading' development, especially on to Malaita which was almost totally without local cash income or local employment. Thus was initiated the ill-fated Solomon Islands cocoa scheme, still continued with a main concentration on Malaita even after its second beginning in 1958, and unfortunate in that it was initiated without proper experimental work, on a too-widely dispersed basis, and with little attempt to apply economic principles. The scheme was finally abandoned in 1968, after repeated failures to achieve even more than a fraction of production targets. Rather more success attended semi-spontaneous efforts to restore and develop enterprise in the New Georgia area, but here too a local self-help movement developed in the late 1960s, opposed to Government. On Guadalcanal itself, where the new capital at Honiara grew rapidly, failure to extend aid to the development efforts of the local population, and over-reliance on expatriate enterprise, led to some serious problems in an area where conditions for success should have been greatest. But in the territory as a whole, a wider policy of wage improvement was followed, and this did much to ease the substantial failures of an equity-based policy. However Malaita, with about a third of the total population, remains little developed and is a continuing area of discontent.

In Fiji the equity vs efficiency problem presented itself in an ethnic rather than an areal dimension. By 1946 the Indo-Fijian population had grown larger than the Melanesian-Fijian population, and this latter, still protected within the cocoon of the Fijian Regulations, had only limited participation in the cash economy except as landlords of Indian tenants, as mineworkers in the gold mines, and as banana growers – an activity taken over from European planters. The gold mines were in financial difficulties, and ultimately needed subsidy to continue in production, and bananas have been a source of continued disappointment, especially since 1963 when disease problems became serious. Efforts were made to improve Fijian participation in the cash economy, and advice was sought from a whole series of experts – whose almost unanimous view that the Fijian Regulations were outmoded and, together with the land tenure system, required drastic modification or abrogation, continued to be resisted until the late 1960s. Thus Fiji achieved independence in 1970 with Government firmly in Melanesian hands, supported by a mainly Melanesian-Fijian army and police, but with such part of economic wealth as was not controlled by expatriate enterprise being yielded mainly by Indo-Fijian producers and entrepreneurs. In the total taxation revenue of the country in the last years of political colonialism, only a very minute proportion was derived directly from Melanesian-Fijian taxpayers.

New Caledonia, with the most highly commercialized economy in all Melanesia, faced an equity vs efficiency problem of a very different kind, but none the less serious. In 1945 the political economy of the country was transformed by the almost simultaneous abrogation of all Vietnamese labour contracts, and of discriminatory legislation against the Melanesians. These latter had become significant producers of coffee and some other cash crops since 1930, and were now to enter urban and other employment freely at wage rates which multiplied several times in the course of a few years. The initial problem in the country was the reconstruction of the mining industry to cope with the ending of cheap Asian labour. A heavily capitalized programme of mechanization was instituted, and was quickly achieved: with large-scale use of machinery in the mines, and of automation in the metallurgical industry, the productivity of labour increased more than tenfold, as the work force became mainly European and Melanesian and virtually lost its Asian component. But the expansion of the nickel industry, and of Nouméa, quickly absorbed the labour resources of the country in spite of these changes. Rapidly rising costs first threatened all forms of rural production with bankruptcy, then eliminated all mining activities other than nickel. In the north of New Caledonia, the almost simultaneous closure of a large chrome mine and a meatworks removed a major part of local employment almost at a stroke. In agricultural production generally, holdings had to be subdivided among tenants and *métayers* in order to continue, while the pastoral industry suffered severely from rising costs and an inefficient system of production inherited from earlier times without significant new innovation or investment.

Government intervened in many ways, by divers forms of direct and indirect aid to farmers and pastoralists, and by direct employment, so that in the north of New Caledonia it was estimated that over a third of regional income was derived from Government by the mid-1960s. A series of inquiries into the state of rural New Caledonia was undertaken, but meanwhile the mining industry and Nouméa have continued to grow, at a rate which has accelerated consistently, and very rapidly since 1967. Despite all efforts, and despite large immigration from Europe, Polynesia and latterly also the New Hebrides, the prospect that New Caledonia will become 'Nouméa et le désert Calédonien' is perhaps more threatening now than ever before. And it is not impossible that 'le désert Calédonien' will include parts of the New Hebrides also if present employment trends continue. By the nature of its political system, the latter territory has been unable to follow any consistent policy of development and meanwhile has fallen increasingly into the economic orbit of New Caledonia.

THE STRATEGY OF POST-WAR DEVELOPMENT

The volume of export trade *per capita* in the Melanesian territories shows the most enormous variety in 1970, from almost $1,000 in New Caledonia to not much more than $1.00 in West New Guinea. The contemporary economy of Melanesia has been described in detail in another book (Brookfield with Hart, 1971), both in terms of areas of production and of economic sectors: to recount even the bare bones of this discussion here would be tedious, but certain basic facts are presented in the statistical appendix. The essential fact is that every territory depends overwhelmingly on from one to four export staples; except in Fiji, there is only very limited development of internal supply for the local market on a national or even regional scale.

The strategy of post-war economic development has been to increase exports by all means possible, so as to enhance the foreign-exchange earning capacity of the economy and hence assist in paying for a rising volume of imported goods and services. The drive to export has grown more frenetic as the gap between imports and exports has grown wider, financed by external grants and loans which have reached levels higher than $50 per head of a whole territorial population. This drive has made the policy conflict between equity and efficiency especially acute, and had led since 1960 to partial abandonment of the equity principle. Quick and large returns have become more and more imperative, and there has been eager grasping at opportunities to exploit resources of limited time duration, such as forests and mineral deposits that are generally exploited on the basis of a 25- or 30-year operational life.

Few would question that the basic motives of post-war colonial policy differed from those of pre-war policy in Melanesia. E. W. Ward, Australian Minister for External Territories before Hasluck, was constantly insistent on the paramountcy of indigenous interests, and though planters were encouraged to return and spread their enterprises right through into the 1960s in several territories, there was a steady shift in emphasis toward indigenous cash production. Welfare and advancement were not merely rhetorical aims; their achievement became the main purpose of the enormous increases in public sector metropolitan spending. Grants mounted to over one hundred times pre-war levels by the early 1950s in the New Guinea territories and the Solomon Islands. Yet the acceleration led to a continuation and even intensification of a truly 'colonial' condition of economic dependency right into modern times, and right into political independence.

We will examine this assertion much more closely in a later chapter, but a basic cause is obvious. Emphasis on exports has retarded the growth of internal marketing, has guided the evolution of the communications and central place network, has created a mentality of dependence on remote and powerful buyers. Yet the emphasis has been unavoidable. Between 1951 and 1966, the import bill of Australian New Guinea mounted from $26 millions to $126 millions, and while exports were roughly in balance with imports in the former year, in the latter they reached only $53 millions. Without the mining windfalls, it might have taken until the later 1970s before an export value of $100 millions could have been attained, and meanwhile the import bill has continued to grow at a higher rate, paid for by metropolitan budgetary support, investment and loans. The gap is less terrifyingly wide in the other territories, especially in Fiji and New Caledonia, but the problem is a general one.

The strategy of post-war development has been to lay heavy emphasis on the growth of services and latterly also of infrastructure. Administration, health and later also education services have been expanded enormously under a policy aimed at welfare and advancement. The central aim of policy became the maximization of welfare for the greatest number of people. Economic policy was subordinate to this aim, in the sense that spending toward the principal aim ran far ahead of national income. In so far as the indigenous populations were concerned, the economic policy of spreading access to cash income was essentially also subordinate to the welfare aim: it enabled the Melanesian population to improve access to goods and services by enhancing the utility of welfare. But the main economic objective became simply the total expansion of commerce and industry so as to increase the total national income, and thus defray as much of the costs of welfare as was possible. Expansion of welfare far ahead of capacity to pay has demanded that questions of finance have dominated the whole construction of the development programmes.

The result of this condition has been a set of unresolved conflicts in development policy. The equity vs efficiency conflict is only one such, though in many ways it is fundamental. The capitalist ethos which has required a strategy of encouraging private enterprise, rather than State enterprise, has made it very hard to sustain the equity principle, since this latter would almost always require selection of alternatives offering less than the best benefit/cost ratio in the short- and middle-term. We may also see unresolved conflict in the sort of encouragement to enterprise that has been offered the indigenous population. It would generally be agreed that incentives to produce or seek employment necessarily depend on the utility of money, and that measures to enhance this utility should thus be fundamental to success. In modern times, as in the past, taxation has been seen as a means of enforcing a demand for money, but with the modern variant that taxes paid to local bodies, and used for local purposes, yield a demonstrative result that should lead to voluntary increases in taxation levels. This has conveniently been combined with a need to defray the costs of welfare by urging local councils to absorb part of the cost of welfare services, such as schools and medical aid posts, or to assist essentially non-commercial enterprises concerned with nutrition and human comfort. Only limited success has been achieved by this policy, and there has been mounting resistance to local taxation in many areas: it might be suggested that the attempt to push welfare as a direct incentive has sought to leap necessary intermediate stages, which should include sustained encouragement of the demand for consumption goods. But this would demand state intervention in the 'proper' field of private enterprise.

The strategy of post-war development has been incomplete. It has combined massive state intervention in some areas of activity with virtual *laissez-faire* in others. It has been more concerned with obtaining a total increase in national incomes than with obtaining a proper distribution of participation and benefits. The equity principle has been applied most effectively in welfare, much less successfully in distributing economic activity. In its turn, this partial failure has arisen from concentration on exports, which has led to under-exploitation of the possibilities of internal differentiation and integration. Equity policies in the economic field have also been constrained by state reluctance to enter production and commerce, except as regulator; where the governments have entered the economic field they have generally done so with the intention of withdrawing once the pump has been primed. Reluctantly, the governments have been drawn more into direct participation in the economy, but only now is this rôle coming to be accepted and incorporated into State policy.

THE END OF GRADUALISM

When Mr Hasluck, in the 1958 statement quoted above, mentioned a thirty-year period remaining for colonialism in New Guinea, this was already a concession to a changing environment of policy. As late as the mid-1950s there was still little consideration given anywhere in Melanesia to the possibility that political independence might come within the lifetime of the existing generation of colonial civil servants. Such possibilities were voiced by academics, and by a few political commentators, but it still seemed to almost everyone that there remained ample time to develop and implement new policies with 'all deliberate speed'. Only in West New Guinea were there serious doubts, arising from the sharp escalation in anti-Dutch action by the Indonesians in 1957, when Dutch enterprises were nationalized and Dutch nationals expelled from the Republic.

By 1960 it was clear to the Netherland Government that the only hope of defeating the Indonesian 'confrontation' lay in an appeal to a higher court. They bid for the support of other Afro-Asian countries by pressing forward vigorously with plans for independence, which was unofficially bruited for 1970. In 1961 they created an elected Nieuw-Guinea Raad (Parliament) with an elected majority among twenty-eight members, encouraged the formation of political parties, and acceded readily to demands for a flag and an anthem. The territory was renamed Papua Barat, and a small military corps was formed to be the foundation of an army. The new policy failed in its international objective, but enjoyed great internal success. In Australian New Guinea there was great interest in the rapid progress west of the border, though this was mingled with scepticism. Demands for an acceleration in political progress and the creation of élites became more vociferous. A series of further events impelled Australian policy away from gradualism. The Congo débàcle of 1960 made a deep impression in the south Pacific, where the parallel of a country without an established élite was inescapably obvious. A 'crash programme' to remedy defects in primary and secondary education was instituted, followed in 1963 by the setting up of a commission of inquiry into the whole question of higher education. In 1960 the Australian Prime Minister received a rough handling at the Commonwealth Prime Ministers' meeting in London for his 'reactionary' colonial policy; returning in a chastened mood he declared that he now believed it better to grant independence too soon than too late. In 1962 came the collapse of Dutch resistance in West New Guinea, and also the report of the most distinguished United Nations mission ever to visit Australian New Guinea. This mission to the Trust Territory vigorously criticized gradualism, sought more power for local representative councils, higher wages and better communications, citizenship and a flag, and a parliament of 100 members elected by adult suffrage on a common roll.

It was the end for gradualism in Australian New Guinea, though a rearguard action continued for another decade. Hasluck was promoted to the Department of External Affairs in 1963, and strong direction vanished.

Australian colonial policy was henceforward much more open to pressures from various directions. Foremost among these pressures until the 1965 coup in Djakarta was the fear of Indonesia. This fear was also communicated much deeper into the Pacific, and it provided just the additional impetus needed to set off a far-reaching train of constitutional changes in the Solomon Islands, and some small but significant changes even in the New Hebrides. Fiji had gone through its own crises, with a cane-growers' strike and race riots in 1959–60. Here two strongly worded reports, by Spate and the Burns Commission in 1959 and 1960, disturbed complacency and initiated changes in both economic and political fields. From about 1962 onward, all roads began to lead toward independence.

REFERENCES AND SOURCES

The volume of post-1945 literature, both official and unofficial, exceeds that of the pre-war period by many times. Annual reports of governments and departments, ministerial and other official statements, well-informed academic and journalistic commentaries ranging from whole books to mere ephemeral newspaper articles, and scattered references to events and policies throughout the literature together provide an enormous mass of source material for this period.

'Stock-taking' discussions and reports perhaps provide the most useful references. On Australian New Guinea there is Wilkes (1958), International Bank for Reconstruction and Development (1965), Fisk (1964), and the papers of the successive Waigani Seminars (1967–71). Also valuable is Howlett (1967). On Fiji there is the comprehensive report of Burns, Watson and Peacock (1960) preceded by that of Spate (1959) on the Fijian people. More recent is the economic review of Fisk (1970). The modern review literature on New Caledonia is far more scattered and some of the most interesting items are not very accessible; a great deal of 'reading between the lines' is often necessary. Much background material may be obtained from surveys by the Service des Affaires Economiques (1957, 1959) and by Pisier (1962), but the major source is perhaps the files of the weekly *Bulletin du Commerce*; much else, and many additional references, are to be found in Doumenge (1966) and Brookfield with Hart (1971). There is little of a comprehensive nature on the New Hebrides beyond a single economic survey by Wilson (1966), and even less on the Solomon Islands where the most penetrating single inquiry is perhaps that of Lasaqa (1972) on northern Guadalcanal. For West New Guinea, Groenewegen and Van de Kaa (1964) and United Nations Development Programme (1968) provide essential background data. Brookfield (1961b) summarises the situation toward the end of the Dutch period, and the course of events leading to the change of sovereignty is most concisely presented by De Iongh (1967), and Lijphart (1966).

In addition to these sources there is invaluable commentary in Stanner (1953), Legge (1956) and Rowley (1965).

CHAPTER 10

THE ADVANCE TOWARD POLITICAL INDEPENDENCE

During the early 1960s the island region of the western Pacific swiftly became isolated as the world's last block of contiguous territories – if this term may be applied – under direct external rule. By 1970 only two of the once numerous group of trust territories remained in the world – the Australian Trust Territory of New Guinea and the US Trust Territory of the Pacific Islands. Eastward in Polynesia varying forms of political independence came to the New Zealand territories in the later 1960s, though local autonomy continues to be denied in French Polynesia. After a prolonged wrangle Nauru became independent in 1968, and in 1969 the formal dependent status of West Irian was terminated, without the achievement of any independence that would be recognized as such by most of the world's people. Then in 1970 came Fiji, and all indications are that by the mid-1970s at least major progress toward independence will have been achieved in both Australian New Guinea and the Solomon Islands. One can hardly envisage the present form of government in the New Hebrides surviving to 1980, nor does it seem very credible that the existing constitutional relationship of the French Pacific territories to France will endure this long.

This acceleration is accompanied by another change. The early phases of constitutional advance toward independence in the Melanesian territories – except New Caledonia – were achieved with minimal enthusiasm on the part of the resident populations. Melanesia did not seek its own decolonization. Only since 1968, even 1970, have there been clear signs of the emergence of a vocal political nationalism, and over a large part of Melanesia the voices now calling for independence remain a minority. But the change is rapid, and reluctance to lose the certainties of external rule is being replaced by a growing impatience to be rid of the colonial masters.

From this point forward we are concerned essentially with contemporary Melanesia, and its interpretation. This chapter outlines the political framework of change, and in the next we consider the economic framework. The social context occupies two further chapters, but in each of these discussions we are inevitably in the presence of all the others.

THE COLONIAL ADMINISTRATIVE SYSTEMS COMPARED

Melanesia is among those regions where the administrative systems that future independent states will inherit represent a much higher order of territorial organization than anything which preceded them in pre-colonial times. The small federations of local communities were at best ephemeral, and language created no political solidarity: except where there is now ethnic pluralism, the context of both regional and national consciousness is provided only by the colonial administrative systems, and by the economic regions also created by colonialism. The administrative structure of each territory has remained rather stable through major modern changes in the legislative and executive levels of territorial government, and thus provides an important element of continuity.

To compare the colonial administrative systems is thus also to compare the basic internal structure of the future states. This is not an easy task to achieve in a few pages, for there are radical differences both in administrative hierarchy and in concepts of government. A broad comparison of the systems in the late 1950s is rather tentatively essayed in Figure 5. The degree and clarity with which the systems are tiered differs greatly, ranging from a near-absence of significant lower tiers in the French system to the multiplicity and overlap of tiers in the Australian. Local differences and also national colonial policies are reflected in these contrasts.

In the French system, centralization and uniformity are virtues. New Caledonia was a very minor territory in the former French empire, though it has gained more absolute as well as relative significance today. From 1856 until 1946 there were separate administrations for Melanesians and expatriates. The Régime de l'Indigènat had complete authority over the Melanesians, who were subject to a range of laws not applicable to the rest of the population, and were under the control of the Gendarmerie Nationale. This system was abrogated in 1946, but the appointed indigenous officials were retained.

All other administration was and is concentrated in Nouméa. Until the 1950s the civil service was staffed overwhelmingly by European Calédoniens, except that the highest positions were generally filled by metropolitan French. There was some nepotism within this tight society, and it has been noted that numerous kin and affinal links were to be found within departments, and between such departments as the Service Topographique and the land-holding families. Latterly an increasing number of outsiders has been appointed, and some measures have been taken to employ Melanesians at clerical and higher levels.

The British system has always shown greater variety in principle than the French, though perhaps not much more variety in practice. Each territory in

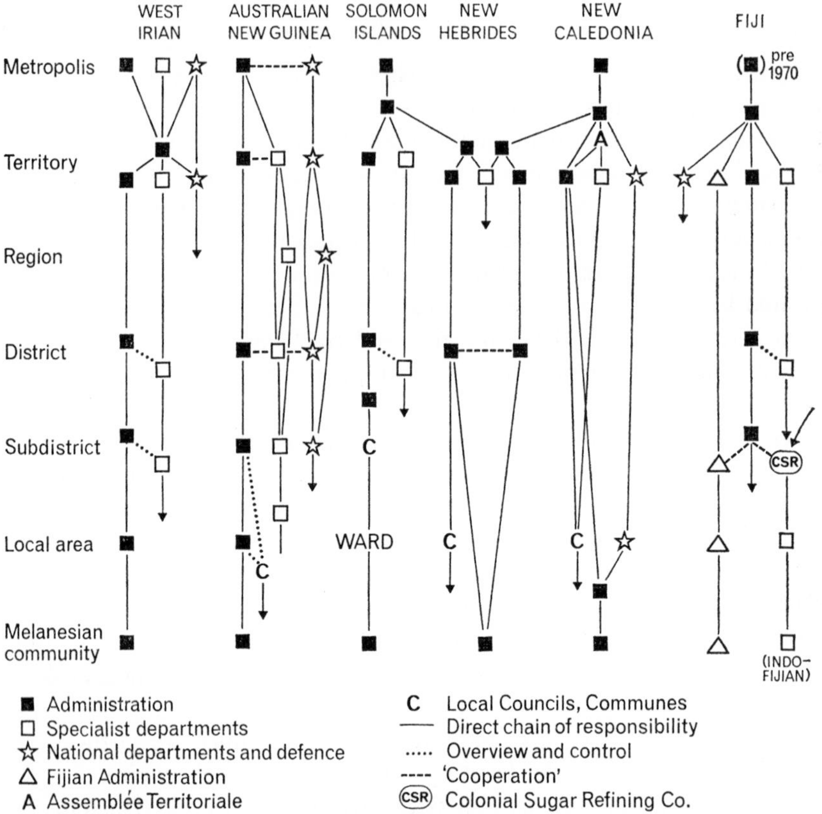

Figure 5. A diagrammatic representation of the colonial administrative systems in the mid-1950s

the former British empire was a separate fiscal and legislative entity, responsible through the Governor to the Colonial Office in London, but able to act with a fair measure of independence. Certain general principles, however, were widely applied: among these were indirect rule through indigenous institutions wherever practicable and coordination of all branches of administration, through a Secretariat headed by the Colonial Secretary, who was assisted by a Financial Secretary. District organization was generally strong, and consistently applied.

In the western Pacific there is also an unusual form of regional organization, comparable in some respects with the Gouvernement-génerale system of the French in Africa and Indo-China. From 1877 on the Governor of Fiji was also responsible for matters affecting British interests in the then ungoverned parts of the region, as well as for relations with Tonga. After the establishment of land-based government in the Solomons, New Hebrides and Gilbert and Ellice Islands he became, as High Commissioner for the Western Pacific, responsible for the British administrations in these groups. In 1952 the headquarters of the High Commission were removed to Honiara, Solomon Islands, and the Secretariat there is responsible not only for Solomon Island affairs, but also for overview and coordination of the activities of the British administration in the New Hebrides, and of the Gilbert and Ellice Islands Government. But there has been no further move toward fusion, nor any attempt to parallel this administrative structure with any legislative federation.

In both the Solomon Islands and Fiji there has been considerable simplification of the internal District system since World War II. The 8 Solomon Island Districts were reduced to 4, and in Fiji 18 pre-war Districts have been regrouped into only 4 Divisions. The Fijian system is, however, complicated by the presence of what has virtually been a dual system of administration, the Fijian Affairs Department having its own budget, administrative hierarchy and territorial system of government. The general government staff at District level were responsible for 'coordination' with the Fijian Affairs authorities, but were specifically discouraged from direct interference.

The Dutch system was based on that of the former Nederlands-Indië, and it has been taken over by the Indonesians with little change, except in titles. The country was divided into six *Afdelingen* (divisions), now increased to eight, and the Resident of each *Afdeling* had substantial autonomy in day-to-day affairs. This principle of local responsibility extended down to the *Onderafdeling* (subdivision) where the *Hoofd van Plaatselijk Bestuur* (head of local administration) had more freedom of decision than his counterparts at this level in other systems. Most junior officers were already Melanesians by 1963, and the local proportion of the staff has since been increased to a level higher than in any territory but Fiji.

The curious constitution of the Australian system has already been discussed: it is characterized by a striking absence of intermediate integration, even in the colonial capital. The size and population of Districts is also more than usually varied. Until certain large Districts were divided in the late 1960s the populations ranged from 16,000 to over 300,000. It has frequently been suggested that the three or four major groups of Districts in the Australian territory should be organized as Regions for purposes of both administration and representation: such a change would, however, have imperilled the deliberately created direct communication between Canberra and the field, would have made the goal of uniformity much harder to achieve, and would now have provided the basis for either a federal form of future government, or for dissolution of the country into three or four states.

The advance toward political independence

The administrative organization of the New Hebrides is written into the international agreement which forms the basis of government. The Condominium system has undergone only minor structural change since 1922, when a second tier of administration was created by division of the group into four Districts, each with a District Agent from each power. In former times these officers often worked without much relation to each other, but more recently they have been rehoused side by side, and liaison is much closer. The Condominium department and their staffs are responsible to both Resident Commissioners, and this system is supported by a complicated budgetary arrangement involving backward and forward subsidization in three currencies. All significant, and many insignificant, decisions must be taken jointly, and the two administrations often give the superficial impression of being diplomatic missions to each other, as much as a 'joint' government. Three or four times a month announcements are posted on important matters; these range from major pieces of legislation, such as a 1971 move to control land speculation which is already a model for other territories, down to the declaration of dog-licence areas and the appointment of a new member to the board of the Cultural-Centre-Culturel in Vila/Port Vila. Severe delays sometimes result, as in the institution of a code of labour legislation, but in general decisions get taken and translated into action with about as much speed – or lack of it – as in other territories. Perhaps there is a lesson here: government is only one of a number of forces operating in a colonial territory, and it need not be heavy-handed to be effective.

GRASS-ROOTS DEMOCRACY: LOCAL GOVERNMENT

Long before it came to be regarded as an 'education in democracy', indigenous local government was widely used to spread the net of control, and make use of local ability. Appointed officials were established in the villages of every territory, sometimes with a hierarchical order. A few such individuals were able to exercise despotic power for long periods, but in other areas villagers were asked for nominations and a rudimentary electoral system was thus created. By far the most complex system was that of Fiji, which had a four-tiered structure until 1968. Each village had an elected headman (*turaga-ni-koro*) in somewhat doubtful relationship to the hereditary chief. Villages were grouped into 76 *tikina*, and these in turn into 14 Provinces, headed by a *roko* and an elected council. These in turn meshed into the Fijian Affairs Board, advised by the Council of Chiefs. The system had a symmetry which was appealing, but the use of traditional leadership both to preserve the 'ancient' order and to carry out the development policies of government was often self-defeating. Proposals were made to convert the system into a multi-racial form of local government, as by the Burns Commission in 1960, but these foundered on the rock of Fijian conservatism. In 1968 however the intermediate *tikina* level was made obsolete as a step on the road to modernization.

Local government was also set up at an early date in New Caledonia, where rural Communes were formed in the 1870s, and Nouméa became a Commune de Pleine Exercise, run by an elected council with a mayor as chief executive. Until 1946, however, the system applied only to Europeans, and its conversion to a multi-racial basis is still not complete.

The first local councils were set up in the Solomon Islands before 1940, and between 1948 and 1956 the whole Protectorate was divided into indigenous council areas which became the effective subdistricts for purposes of administration. This close linkage with central government was thus described in a White Paper issued in 1962:

> Local authorities are the basis on which all modern democratic systems of government are built...it is the central Government and the local Councils together which are chiefly responsible for looking after the things which affect people's daily lives.

Law-keeping and the operation of native courts were entrusted to Councils, and these local bodies also undertook an important share of public works; sometimes they received direct grants from central Government. There was no attempt to obtain uniformity in size, and Councils were set up for an entire island. Given a more expanding economy, the system might have achieved better results.

The system in Australian New Guinea, on the other hand, took many years to become settled in form and is still not properly meshed with the District administrative structure. The initial object seems to have been to provide education in democratic processes, though since each Council was placed under an administration officer who guided proceedings and sometimes spoke for about 60 per cent of the time at meetings, the educative value was somewhat doubtful. Only limited progress was achieved between 1950 and 1957, when there were still only 19 Councils serving about 100,000 people. Subsequent progress has been rapid and over 80 per cent of the population is now incorporated. Meanwhile the small initial Councils have been combined into larger bodies, thus economizing on use of supervisory staff, who now take a less active rôle in business; only since 1967 has any attempt been made to convert some Councils into multi-racial bodies with powers over all inhabitants in their areas.

A partial comparison of the revenues of the local government systems in Australian New Guinea, the Solomon Islands and Fiji may be illuminating. On a *per capita* basis, the comparative revenues in the late 1960s worked out at around \$1.00 in Australian New Guinea, \$1.10 in the Solomon Islands and \$3.10 in the Fijian administration: there was wide variation around these means. The greater financial potential in Fiji would seem to offer scope for using local government as a vehicle of development, but despite some moderate successes the general results of such efforts have been disappointing. This may in part follow from the costly load of administrative staff carried by the Fijian system, but the basic problem lies in the inappropriateness of a communal type of organization as a vehicle for development where progress depends on achieving sustained consensus over goals and means, and sustained mobilization of inputs in competition with other and individual demands. The experience of council-sponsored schemes in Australian New Guinea, where there was very heavy reliance on voluntary self-help, leads to a parallel conclusion: short term concentration of effort has been mobilized fairly readily, but continuity has been very hard indeed to achieve.

Throughout Melanesia, the relationship of local authorities to the executive branch of government is of greater significance than their relationship to the territorial legislatures, since the two first-named forms of organization operate in the same field. Except in West Irian, there is only limited meshing of local representative institutions into national legislative bodies. Yet with a tiered administrative structure so widely developed, it is perhaps surprising that so few attempts have been made to set up a tiered system of representative bodies within the same territorial framework. Further, whatever the merits or demerits of this approach to self-government, it is surely remarkable that there has been so little discussion of the theory of local government in relation to national political developments.

THE ADVANCES IN NATIONAL CONSTITUTIONS

In both British and Australian territories action was taken soon after World War II to either create or reconstruct a characteristic legislative council/executive council system, following the British Crown Colony model. The Dutch embodied provisions for a similar construction in the Act which established the separate administration of West New Guinea in 1949, but did not implement such a structure for several years. In New Caledonia the franchise was greatly widened in 1946, when the Melanesians became citizens of France and New Caledonia came to be represented in the legislative bodies of metropolitan France. Other changes were minor, and the old Conseil Général continued for several more years. In the New Hebrides there was even a reduction in representation, in that a pre-war unofficial advisory council of planters and businessmen on the French side was not reconstituted. In all territories but New Caledonia, the new Legislative Councils continued to be dominated by official representatives and had few Melanesian members.

In each territory there is a critical year for constitutional change, when there was an abrupt transition in the direction of responsible government. In New Caledonia the year is 1958, in West New Guinea 1961, though in both these territories there was subsequent retrogression. In Australian New Guinea the critical event should have been the creation of a House of Assembly with a Melanesian elected majority in 1964, but the initial results of this 'instant democracy' were disappointing. In Fiji the critical year is 1966, when a new constitution established the basis for self-government. In the Solomon Islands it has been 1970, and in the New Hebrides the year of critical change is still not in sight.

We have already noted the constitutional changes that took place in West New Guinea in 1961, and the success which they achieved. The Indonesian Government recognized the danger which this Dutch move presented to their claims, and early in 1962 began to land armed parties by sea and air in the western and southern coastal districts. Though it achieved very little military success, this offensive brought the West New Guinea issue into the focus of 'cold war' politics, for the Indonesians had been successful in gaining Russian and Chinese support. The United States intervened to force the Dutch into surrender hoping perhaps to halt the drift of the Sukarno Government into the 'eastern' constellation. Perhaps the United States also hinted a wish for neutrality to its Australian client; certainly the Australian Government made no move whatever throughout the crisis, withdrew its support from the Dutch, and remained totally quiet on an issue which concerned its New Guinea subjects very closely – and even imperilled its own security if the pre-crisis statements of Australian politicians were to be taken at face value! The result was Dutch handover to an interim United Nations administration, which in turn handed the territory over to Indonesia in 1963. The Nieuw-Guinea Raad was dissolved, and its place taken by a 'temporary provincial parliament' of appointed members, which was surprisingly effective in exerting pressure in a number of fields. Following the Act of Free Choice which confirmed West Irian's adherence to Indonesia in 1969, the normal constitution of a Province in the unitary state of Indonesia is being applied, with an elected provincial parliament.

Notwithstanding official disclaimers, there can be little question but that progress in Australian New Guinea was linked to events in the west. Until 1960 only small changes were made in the composition of the Legislative Council, but in that year an unofficial majority was introduced, though only 12 of the 22 unofficial members were elected, and only 6 of these – but also some of the appointed members – were Melanesian. This modest change created a very useful Council, but further developments followed quickly. New proposals put forward in February 1963 fell short of the United Nations mission's design for a 100-member elected parliament, but created a House of Assembly of 64 members, of whom 54 would be elected, 44 of them by members of any race representing 'open' electorates. Haste was important, and the whole design of electorates was completed – with some striking anomalies – in a few months, leading to an election in February 1964. A fair number of Europeans was elected, and about two-thirds of Melanesian members had experience with the local government councils, but more than half had no formal education and two-thirds little or no ability to read. The majority language of the House became Pidgin English, and since there was little concession to this fact in the formal procedures of the Assembly – despite a simultaneous translation system – the effectiveness of the body was greatly reduced by widespread lack of comprehension.

In 1968 a larger house of 94 members was elected, retaining the ten 'official' members but increasing the 'open' electorates to 69, while the number of 'regional' electorates, representatives for which needed certain educational qualifications, was raised from 10 to 15. Provision was also made for the appointment of 'Ministerial Members', who represented Departments in the House of Assembly. In 1970 these members assumed ministerial responsibility for the policy of their Departments, and in a reconstituted Administrator's Council acted collectively as an embryonic cabinet. A greater measure of responsibility also passed to the House, including control over the locally-raised portion of the territorial budget. But up to 1972 the vital control over the major part of the budget and other sensitive matters remained with Canberra.

By 1970, however, the lead rôle in Melanesian political advance had passed to Fiji, where as late as 1960 it had been possible for the Burns Commission to observe that they discerned no popular demand for constitutional change. When in 1961 the Governor announced that the Legislative Council would be reconstituted and steps taken toward a ministerial system of government, there was surprise, coupled with widespread alarm among the Fijians and expatriates. In 1963 the Legislative Council was increased in size to 37 members, with an official majority of only 1. In place of the 5 members formerly representing each ethnic group there were now 6, but all but 2 of the Fijians were elected. Universal suffrage was introduced, but with separate rolls for each communal group. In 1964 there was a further advance in the creation of the 'Member' system, whereby 6 unofficial members were brought into the Executive Council.

London was determined to move quickly, and in 1965 a constitutional conference was called, attended by all the Legislative Council, because of deep and irreconcilable differences between the Indo-Fijians, who sought a common roll, and the Melanesian-Fijians and Europeans, who insisted on communal representation. The British authorities essentially accepted the latter position in an unsatisfactory compromise which led to deep political troubles in the Colony. A new Council of 40 members had only 4 'officials'; most seats were filled on communal rolls, the Europeans and Chinese receiving 7, the Fijians 11, and the Indo-Fijians 9. In addition there were nine 'cross-voting' seats, filled communally in three groups, but elected by the whole population. Davidson (1966, 167–8) commented:

In so far as the Constitutional Conference has been a success, it has thus been so in terms of short-term political management, not in relation to the resolution of fundamental political problems...there is no easy solution to the problem of constitution-making in a plural society; but in Fiji the task of seriously seeking a solution is one that still has to be faced.

In effect, the 1965 constitution determined the ethnic composition of the new Legislative Council in advance: excluding the four 'officials', it became virtually certain that there would be 10 Europeans or Chinese, 14 Fijians, and only 12 Indo-Fijians to represent the largest group in the population. A full ministerial system was introduced in 1967, and shortly afterward there was a challenge to the constitution from the mainly Indo-Fijian opposition party, which withdrew from the Council. A new election confirmed the stalemate, but in 1969 a new Indo-Fijian leadership, coupled with a statement of British determination to proceed quickly toward independence, ushered in a new spirit of compromise. A further constitutional conference held in 1970 resolved on a new pattern of representation, reducing the communal element and also the disproportionately large group of European, Chinese or mixed-blood members, and providing equality between Fijians and Indo-Fijians. 27 members are to be elected on communal rolls, 25 on a common roll but with ethnic composition of members determined in advance. The lower house will thus have 22 Fijian members, 22 Indo-Fijians and 8 'general' members. An upper house will be similarly predetermined.

The first election under the new system did not take place until 1972, but on the basis of the agreement reached, full independence was proclaimed in October 1970. Fiji became a Dominion with a newly militant Fijian leadership firmly in control, and with a remarkable spirit of cooperation and compromise between the two main ethnic groups which flourished right through 1971: how long it can endure is another matter.

British determination to be rid of its colonial image faces a far more difficult problem in the Solomon Islands, where the economy is small and weak and the level of education far lower than in Fiji or even the New Hebrides. Until 1960 there was only an appointed Advisory Council, but in that year the standard British Legislative Council and Executive Council were introduced, the membership still being wholly nominated. Elections for a few Legislative Council members were introduced for the first time in 1965, and in 1967 this Council was replaced by a new body in which there were 15 appointed members – including *ex-officio* members – and 14 elected members. There was little comprehension of the electoral process on the part of the public, and the results of this innovation of democracy were very disappointing. As early as 1969, however, a further stage was announced, with significant departures from former practice.

Both Legislative and Executive Councils are abolished, and their place taken by a single Governing Council having 17 elected and 9 appointed or *ex-officio* members. The whole membership is grouped into overlapping Committees, each with responsibility over a defined field and a measure of executive power: the four committee chairmen are, to all intents and purposes, ministers. The intention is to achieve government by consensus in the supposedly characteristic Melanesian pattern, rather than by majority vote. The election in 1970 generated more interest than its predecessors, and the first few sessions of the Governing Council were regarded as successful by most participants and observers, though with some dissenting voices. The experiment is interesting, but it is not easy to see how it could readily be translated to the government of a larger country.

The long-term future of the Solomon Islands remains unclear at the time of writing. A goal of economic viability by 1980 has been stated, but unofficial forecasting indicates much earlier achievement of responsible government, perhaps soon after the next election in 1973 or 1974. Current thinking at the official level seems directed toward a solution comparable with that adopted for the 'associated states' of the eastern Caribbean, leaving foreign affairs and defence to the British Government while all other matters, including regional affairs, are determined locally. But it remains to be seen if this would long be acceptable in the absence of any strong cultural and historical links with Britain such as characterize the eastern Caribbean states, and while full political independence seems to be the goal of all the immediate neighbours of the Solomon Islands. New Zealand has this sort of relationship with its former Pacific territories, and such a relationship is the current goal of at least some French Polynesians with France, and some Micronesians with the United States. But in each of these cases the cultural or economic links with the metropole are firmer than in this Melanesian island group that has for so long been administered by Britain, but developed by Australian – and now also Japanese – entrepreneurs and companies.

There remains for Britain the New Hebrides. In this territory the inflexibility of the Protocol demands that any advance should await agreement between two administering powers with radically different approaches to the question of decolonization, and with completely different current interests in the group. The only major change that has yet proved possible in the absence of such legal agreement is the introduction and improvement of an Advisory Council that has no legislative or executive powers, but which is none the less acquiring more and more influence on the course of affairs. Franco-British discussions on the future of the Condominium have been held, but in a most desultory fashion, and progress seems to be minimal up to 1972.

To the British the problem is simply one of decolonization in as short a time as is possible. Preference has been expressed for the well-tried road leading from Legislative Council to ministerial system to self-government to independence, perhaps with variations now to incorporate the faster methods of the Solomons experiment. But Britain is unable to take even the first steps along this road without the consent of France. The French have a preference for a presidential system, and for continued association with the metropole. Moreover, they have larger local interests to preserve, and these are closely linked with New Caledonia, which they regard as French territory in perpetuity. Much the greater part of French commercial and landed interests in the New Hebrides operates under control of parent organizations in Nouméa, and since 1969 the New Hebrides have again become an important source of labour for New Caledonia, especially for the construction industry in that territory. As many as 3,500 New Hebrideans are estimated to be in Nouméa, mostly as short-term migrants, and their remittances, and the money taken back home with them, may be worth as much as $2,500,000 a year to the New Hebrides – making this migration the second most important foreign-exchange earning activity of the group. Wages in Nouméa are so much higher than at home that the road to New Caledonia has become the brightest prospect to many a New Hebridean: leaders and employers on the other hand view this exodus as a severe drain on the limited labour resources available for development of the New Hebrides themselves. Thus this issue has simultaneously highlighted the growing satellite condition of the Condominium toward New Caledonia, and sharpened the emergence of nationalism in the New Hebrides themselves. Hostility toward the absorptive nature of the French approach toward constitutional development in the group has grown in conflict with a willing acceptance of the new road to wealth.

As late as 1965 nationalism was as weakly developed in the New Hebrides as in any part of the Pacific. By 1972 a demand for self-rule leading to full independence is heard more and more widely. The tone of Advisory Council debates has undergone a sea-change and it seems even possible that in this one Melanesian territory the laggardly hand of metropolitan governments will be forced, sometime later in the 1970s, by the vocal emergence of a xenophobic nationalism.

In New Caledonia itself the Melanesians are in a minority in the population, only slightly more numerous than the European population: a very heterogeneous group of migrants from Polynesia and Asia makes up almost all the balance. In the last years of the Fourth Republic, New Caledonia shared with the rest of the French empire in moves toward liberalization and decentralization. It is perhaps surprising, in view of the population composition, that this territory did not follow the French Antilles, Cayenne and Réunion, and become a Département d'Outre-mer of France in 1946. However, this does not seem to have been seriously proposed, and so New Caledonia was included in the Loi Cadre legislation of 1956, which was adopted by referendum in the territory in 1957. The old Conseil Général was replaced by a new Assemblée Territoriale of 30 members with wide powers over the local budget, and elected by adult suffrage on a common roll. Members of any race are elected for four-year terms from four multiple-member divisions, weighting rural representation and especially that of the mainly-European rural west coast. Here 8 members represented 11,000 people at the 1963 census, against 5 for 15,000 in the Loyalty Islands and 10 for 43,000 in Nouméa and the Ile des Pins. The Assemblée sends one *delègue* and one *sénateur* to Paris, and from its ranks was drawn a local Conseil de Gouvernement with ministerial responsibilities. A substantial measure of self-government seemed to be achieved, although the Governor retained direct control of the French national departments, and of the Gendarmerie Nationale.

Implementation of these changes did not go smoothly, being delayed until 1959 by political troubles reflecting the larger troubles in France and Algeria. In 1963 the ministerial system was abolished for reasons to be discussed in a later chapter, and curbs were placed on the development of local autonomy. Renewed agitation in 1968 reflected similar and more powerful agitation in Tahiti, but Government took clear steps to indicate that no further relaxation was in prospect. 'Nous sommes ici la France' remained and remains the doctrine. From 1969 onward the announcement of successive new plans for major expansion of the nickel-mining and metallurgical industry merely reinforced French determination, and a national claim to a large share of the profits was justified on the grounds of big metropolitan subventions to New Caledonia in the past. Substantial new immigration promised to make the European population an actual majority within a few years, but the pace of expansion has been far slower than was anticipated, and in 1971 a prolonged strike in the nickel industry – with the support of all local political groups but the Gaullists – put the whole prospects of expansion in jeopardy. Conflict is now mainly in the economic field, but the underlying political conflict between the metropole and the local advocates of self-determination is sharpening. As in Tahiti, French ability to retain control is not in doubt, but the will to do so may be eroded by persistent local pressures.

REGIONALISM: THE SOUTH PACIFIC COMMISSION

The interplay of trends in different territories emerges as a growing force in the story recounted above, and may be expected to become much more significant in the future. Suggestions have been made by outsiders that at least some of the Melanesian territories should federate, but although the Dutch, and some West New Guinea leaders, became seriously interested in such ideas after 1959, they commanded no wide support among either governments or people. Local particularism in the development of national identity is a characteristic of island regions, and although not carried in the Pacific to the extremes that have bedevilled all attempts at integration and cooperation in the West Indies, such particularism is a strong force in Melanesia.

There has, none the less, been something of a surge of interest in regional activities such as the periodic South Pacific Games, and in the South Pacific Commission, first set up as an agency for technical cooperation between colonial governments in the late 1940s. The genesis of the Commission perhaps lay in the reluctance of Australia, France and the United States to admit United Nations agencies into their dependent territories; even this much association with other powers was only reluctantly accepted by France, and only when it was agreed to set up the head-quarters in Nouméa. Britain, New Zealand and formerly the Netherlands also joined on behalf of their Pacific territories.

The Commission thus evolved as an inter-colonial organization in the fields of health, agricultural advice, housing, census taking, some village industry and minor technical assistance. Attempts to set up large-scale programmes dealing with such thorny questions as urbanization have had only transitory success, and lack of continuity in programmes annually budgeted by contributions from several governments has bedevilled the work of the Commission almost from the outset. Much of the technical work has been very good, but the advantages of centralized research, technical advice and data collection have been only sparingly exploited by the participant governments. More significant politically have been the biennial conferences, attended by island representatives. For many years the subject matter of these meetings was confined mainly to the activities of the Commission itself, but in 1965 the Fijian delegate – the present Prime Minister of Fiji – launched a move to convert the meetings into something like a regional parliament, where political and other issues of wide span might be discussed. Some significant changes followed, although they had little impact on the work of the Commission. Regional economic cooperation has evolved – so far as it has done so at all – more outside the aegis of the existing body than within it. But at least such regular meetings, now normally held away from Nouméa, provide a framework from which something like the Organization of African States might evolve following the wider extension of political independence.

We shall return to the question of regionalism more than once in the following chapters. The advantages both of formal meetings and of *ad hoc* collaboration and interchange are very widely appreciated, and conferences of regional scope in technical fields – or more politically orientated meetings such as the Waigani Seminars held annually at Port Moresby – arouse widespread interest. The improvement in regional communication by air during the 1960s has been accompanied by a greatly increased inter-territorial movement of officials, technical officers, politicians or just men with grievances. Quite apart from the substantial movement of West Irian refugees into Australian New Guinea, which still continues and includes political leaders, there is growing contact between emerging politicians throughout the Pacific. But while this may presage greater coordination of political activity and greater mutual awareness of problems and attitudes, there is no indication that any move toward closer political association is likely to follow.

THE SANCTITY OF COLONIAL BOUNDARIES

A remarkable feature of decolonization throughout the world has been strong adhesion to arbitrary boundaries inherited from colonial rule. Notwithstanding the fact that many originated as mere lines on maps in European capitals, wars have now been fought to retain them intact and to hold united the political entities which they contain. The central argument of Indonesia in the West New Guinea dispute rested on the necessary wholeness of the former Nederlands Indië, and if it seemed surprising to outsiders that Sukarno's Indonesia made no moves to seize Portuguese Timor, this was entirely consistent with the legal position adopted over New Guinea. Fears of dispute over the position of the unmarked border between West Irian and Australian New Guinea have also proved largely groundless, even though it was only in the final months of Dutch rule that a number of deep penetrations by Dutch administration, into territory that was by treaty Australian, were rather hastily surveyed and taken over by Australian officials and police. A number of minor border incidents notwithstanding, there has been no conflict at government level. Some difficult issues have been posed by the refugees, some of whom have certainly been sent back by the Australian authorities in the greater interest of keeping relations with Indonesia sweet: others have been admitted, but mostly housed in isolation on Manus island. The number who have penetrated the several barriers to reach the principal towns of the country, especially Port Moresby, is unknown, but it is not inconsiderable.

But if the one land border in Melanesia is relatively quiescent, other borders seem likely to create difficulty as political independence approaches. The boundary of Queensland against Papua in Torres Strait is a relic of Queensland's attempt to annex eastern New Guinea in the 1870s: the Imperial Government permitted annexation of all islands up to the Papuan coast, but not of the mainland itself. The bounds of Australia thus reach within a kilometre of the Papuan shore, and the 5,000 Torres Strait Islanders are Melanesians, closely intermarried and still in trading connexion with Papuan coastal people. Since the 1880s many observers have pointed to the inequity of this boundary, and irredentist statements have latterly been made by Papuan politicians.

Much more serious is the issue of Bougainville island, as large as Jamaica, and now the site of the largest single mining development not merely in Melanesia but in the whole Pacific and east Asian island region. Bougainville is part of the Solomons chain, somewhat isolated from the rest of Australian New Guinea; the people of southern Bougainville are closely connected with Solomon Islanders as far south as New Georgia. After the Anglo-German settlement of 1889 Bougainville was the only one of the Solomons group left in German hands, and the opportunity of 1919 to link it with the British Solomons was allowed to pass by. Remoteness encouraged prolonged neglect by the Australian administration, and also by the trading companies; in the 1964 House of Assembly election this island formed only one electorate – with almost twice the average electorate population. Bougainvilleans, who are mostly of unusually dark skin, call other New Guineans 'redskins', and think of themselves as a different people. Once it became clear that the copper explorations by Conzinc Rio Tinto in the Crown Prince Range were going to lead to establishment of a mine that from 1972 will alone provide some two-thirds of the export income of all Australian New Guinea, active demands for either separation, or for 'reunification' with the British Solomons, were heard loudly and persistently. Not only Australia, but also the political leaders in Australian New Guinea, oppose these demands, while Solomon Island leaders are interested but tactfully quiet. The issue is not going to die away easily, and presents a major problem to a future independent government of eastern New Guinea.

There are breakaway movements elsewhere in Australian New Guinea, of which the strongest is among the sophisticated and economically advanced people of the Gazelle peninsula of New Britain, where anti-government agitation centred on land has already erupted in both riot and murder. The future perils of this country are clearly underlined by reports that when, for a time, most of the police in the country were concentrated in this area to put down a feared rising, there was danger of a resumption of tribal warfare in parts of inland New Guinea long thought to be under firm control. No comparable localized movements are yet apparent among the more widely-separated island groups of eastern Melanesia, but certain islands are remote from the centres of government and participate little in the territorial economies: their people are unlikely to feel so willing to follow the instructions of relatively weak independent governments as they now are to obey the dictates of colonial powers.

REFERENCES AND SOURCES

Published sources covering the material of this chapter are closely similar to those given for Chapter 9, but a great range of more ephemeral sources now becomes significant. Of particular value among these are the *Newsletters* published by the colonial governments: for this and several subsequent chapters this body of source material was consulted *in extenso*. *Pacific Islands Monthly* is also a continuing mine of information and opinion. In addition, *Pacific Viewpoint* and the *Journal of Pacific History* have made a practice of including sections on the contemporary Pacific, consisting mainly of notes and short articles often on constitutional and political matters. Certain papers in Waigani Seminars (1969) and more especially Waigani Seminars (1970b) are of major and more lasting value.

Important on specific constitutional developments in New Guinea and the attendant politics are Bettison, Hughes and Van der Veur (1965) and Parker (1966). Davidson (1966) provides very effective comment on the Fijian constitutional issues, while developments in the later 1960s are reported and briefly evaluated by Haas (1970). On the question of boundaries, the outstanding source is Van der Veur (1966).

Since completion of this book, an important additional article has appeared by Davidson (1971), outlining recent political and constitutional development from a privileged position of participation in much that is described.

CHAPTER 11

THE DEEPENING COMMERCIAL COLONIZATION OF MELANESIA

It has been an argument of this book from the first chapter that political control by an external power is only one phase of the total phenomenon of colonialism. Political independence by itself does not end colonialism while the territories remain dependent on the colonial commercial system to maintain their economies. Such dependence can well increase as independent former colonies are deprived of direct budgetary support and grants: such deprivation is stated British policy, and implied Australian intention, and the British authorities have advised both Fiji and the Solomon Islands that direct grants will have to be replaced by interest-bearing loans. Loans require to be serviced, and such servicing can absorb a substantial share of national budgets. Dependence on private capital inflow may increase.

As in other parts of the world, such capital inflows are drawn increasingly from the resources of great multinational corporations. The operations of such corporations lead to increases in national income and revenue, and generate employment on a substantial scale; they are therefore desired by governments seeking rapid development of national economies, whether these be ex-colonies, still-dependent territories, or highly-developed countries of the western world. Certain of these recipient countries have revolted at the price in true autonomy that has to be paid for such development; in others a major debate rages on this increasingly live issue. For countries such as those of Melanesia, whose expectation levels have been inflated by a period of easy subsidy under late colonialism, the dilemma is especially acute. This dilemma is likely to provide one of the major issues of the 1970s, and it warrants close examination.

A SET OF SMALL, OPEN, SATELLITE ECONOMIES

Fifteen years ago Hoselitz (1955, 420) drew a polar contrast between 'dominant' and 'satellite' economies in these terms:

The ideal case of a dominant pattern would be exhibited by a country with a fully closed economy, with no need to resort to foreign borrowing for purposes of capital accumulation, and without exports. At the other extreme we would have a society which draws all its capital for development from abroad and which develops only those branches of production whose output is entirely exported. If we further stipulate that all or the bulk of capital imports come from one source and that all or the bulk of exports go to one destination, we have the ideal typical case of a country with a satellitic pattern of growth.

There is no difficulty in determining where the Melanesian countries would lie along such a continuum. Very little capital is locally generated, and until recent times the whole development effort has been put into export commodities. Capital sources have become more diversified in late years, but Australia, Britain and France were the overwhelmingly dominant suppliers until after 1960, since when they have been joined very substantially by Japan and the United States. The bulk of regional exports also go to the same group of countries.

The satellitic condition is further displayed in the financial system. The currencies of Fiji and New Caledonia are respectively linked to those of Britain and France. Australian New Guinea, the Solomon Islands and the New Hebrides use Australian currency, and while in the New Hebrides the Pacific franc circulates alongside the Australian dollar, it is separated from the New Caledonian franc and tied to the Australian exchange standard. West Irian formerly used Dutch currency; after 1963 a special Irian Barat *rupiah* was created and held separate from the Indonesian *rupiah*, but was convertible only through Indonesia; now the two currencies are being brought to par. The attempt to protect West Irian from the hyperinflation of the Indonesian currency was only partly successful; New Caledonian currency was devalued with that of France in 1969, and Fiji's currency with that of Britain in 1967. In the latter case an unnecessary measure of automatic devaluation was quickly corrected by striking a new rate almost, but not exactly, at par with the Australian dollar.

Except in West Irian, trading-bank services have until recently been provided entirely by Australian and French banks, plus one bank each from India and New Zealand in Fiji. Savings can thus readily be transferred out of the territories, and except in the case of the deeply-involved Banque de l'Indo-Chine, the ratio of loans and local investment to deposits has seldom exceeded 50 per cent and has been reported as low as 20 per cent. Even in Fiji, where the performance of the trading banks has been better than in most territories, balances due from banks abroad still equalled about one-third of the total assets in 1969. No territory yet has a central bank, except in so far as the Banque de l'Indo-Chine was monopoly banker with the right of note issue in New Caledonia until 1969. There has been a large increase in the number of branch banks since 1950, coupled with the entry of new banks at a rising rate. The First National City Bank of New York set up a branch in Fiji in 1970 with the object of assisting mainly American investment and other business 'conforming to free-enterprise principles', and in 1971 Barclays DCO entered the region, joining with three Australian banks in a sudden surge of entry into the New Hebrides, which has recently been 'discovered' as a tax haven for company registration. In the main, however, the greatly increased entry of trading banks reflects a major surge in direct investment from abroad, especially from Australia.

In Hoselitz' sense, the whole economic history of Melanesia has been the conversion of closed economies, without foreign transactions, into satellitic economies. The island trading companies that grew up in the late nineteenth century were for long the principal agency of transformation, directly or indirectly financing a very wide range of production, trade and transport operations with the goal of long-term balanced growth of the companies themselves. They provided invaluable service to the island economies, but the integrated growth of the territorial economies was not their aim, and their operations did much to prevent it. In particular, they created and still sustain a heavy dependence on imported produce, mainly from Australia and France, which has the effect of constraining local marketing and production. Through these companies, and now also through banks and through more recently-arrived finance companies offering hire-purchase facilities, credit for the import of consumption goods has always been the easiest and most widespread form of credit made available. Until recent years it has gone mainly to Europeans, or to Indo-Fijians, but this has often been for the retailing or further supply of imported produce among the residentiary population. Credit has also been offered to producers of export goods, overwhelmingly Europeans, but often on terms which have obligated the borrowers to buy from the lending houses. In more recent years, with the larger-scale entry of trading banks, credit has also become more widely available to entrepreneurs producing goods for import substitution, but again, the bulk of such credit has gone to expatriates. This has also been the pattern of the development banks, set up by governments in Fiji and Australian New Guinea, and of the multiply-linked loan funds of New Caledonia: a numerical majority of loans has gone to members of the indigenous population, but until 1971 most of the money has been lent to expatriates.

A COMPARISON OF INVESTMENT BY FIELDS OF ENTERPRISE

Data on investment in the Melanesian territories are inadequate for most territories and totally lacking for some: adequate data on the operations of banks are collected and published only in Fiji, and in the Australian currency area as a whole there is the further difficulty that many private accounts are kept in Australia, though this would apply to few companies owing to the tax advantages of local registration. The New Hebrides, having no income tax, has many registered companies that do no business in the territory.

Published sources of data yield certain information. In Australian New Guinea private overseas investment totalled $26.4 million in 1967–8, $22.5 million of this coming from Australia: a steep increase has followed due to the new mining developments. The total capital formation in this territory was estimated at $86.8 million in 1965–6, most coming from public sources, and it is unclear how much of the $29.2 million attributed to the private sector represents retained profits and depreciation allowances of overseas firms; domestic capital formation represented just under 27 per cent of gross monetary sector expenditure. In Fiji capital formation represented 21 per cent of gross domestic product at market prices in 1967. Fijian data do not specify increases in private long-term assets, but record an item of 'unidentified capital inflow' which has ranged between $2 million and $7 million in recent years, and is generally exceeded by a net outflow of 'investment income' of between $3 million and $6 million. New Caledonian data show 'investment credits' from outside New Caledonia rising from $14 million to $31 million between 1963 and 1967. On a *per capita* basis this is much the highest level of inflow.

There is great variation between different fields of enterprise. Agriculture generally receives only small infusions of capital, and the level of profit retention is also low. New plantation industries growing cocoa, coffee, oil palm and tea have been set up since World War II in Australian New Guinea, and there has been extensive coconut planting, but it is notable that some coffee estates have changed hands at a small loss in the late 1960s, while a major coconut planting proposal in the Solomon Islands was scratched because of a very poor benefit/cost ratio obtained under close examination. Loans and government subsidies have been quite important in the agricultural area, and in the last few years such loans have also begun to flow to indigenous growers, through the medium of the development banks. In the main, however, the large expansions of cash-crop areas in the residentiary systems have been achieved without benefit of any credit from external sources.

There has been rather more substantial investment in forestry and fishing, with a large proportionate contribution from Japan. Unexpectedly low profitability in forestry has reduced the rate of investment in this area, but the low rate of return seems to have been due mainly to undercapitalization in some early enterprises; large-scale operations appear to be doing well enough. Local forestry enterprise, whether expatriate or indigenous, seems to be relegated largely to very small operations producing mainly for the local market. A plan evolved in West Irian for a blending of small indigenous operations within a larger scheme has not yet been put to the test.

Much the most important area of investment today is in mining. Though there remains a small fringe of miners without capital, including some Melanesians, this has become a business favouring operation on a massive scale, and open only to large international companies. Excluding New Caledonia, well over $150 million has now been spent on prospecting alone in Melanesia, and activity continues at a rising rate, with search for oil and non-ferrous minerals. Over $50 million has been spent on the search for oil, over a 50-year period, but only the limited and unprofitable West Irian operation has yet resulted. However, substantial gas reserves in Papua have at last reached the stage of attracting prospective buyers. The oil search in Australian New Guinea began with small Australian companies, but these are now backed by international interests, and non-ferrous mineral prospecting is a field of enterprise in which a wide range of American, French, British, Canadian, Japanese and Australian companies is engaged. Since 1967 mining has come to dwarf all other fields of investment in Melanesia as a whole, and this activity is now leading to the conversion of Melanesia into a nickel and copper mining region of world significance, at an investment cost substantially in excess of $1,000 million over a five-year period from 1969.

The largest announced developments are in New Caledonia, where three new nickel companies have been formed, two of them by consortia in association with the established Société le Nickel, the third by International Nickel of Canada in association with a group of other French companies and the government-financed Bureau des Recherches Géologiques et Minières. In each case agreement stipulates that control will remain in French hands, even though the bulk of capital is non-French. These plans prompted France to restrict exports of crude ore to Japan, a business mainly in the hands of a number of small New Caledonian companies and sub-contracting entrepreneurs. But except for the expansion plans of Société le Nickel itself, which, but for a major labour dispute, would have reached an output of 60,000 tons metal content in 1971, the announced growth is already far behind schedule. Late in 1971 even the International Nickel group is still only in the stage of detailed exploration of its low-grade reserves on the southern plateaux. Delays have resulted partly from labour shortage, from unexpectedly high development costs, and reportedly also from difficulties experienced by the French partners in raising sufficient capital from national sources. Meanwhile a forecast world oversupply of nickel is coming about three or four years ahead of expectation, and the future of the ambitious plans announced between 1968 and 1970 is in doubt. It was stated inability to pay wages awarded by arbitration that led to the strike against Société le Nickel in 1971. From the long-term point of view of New Caledonia this is not necessarily to be regretted: the plans amounted in effect to conversion of this beautiful island into an industrial site for the benefit of French industry and its European and North American partners. Calédonien entrepreneurs and farmers, to say nothing of the Melanesians, look for something of a breathing space in which to adjust to an overwhelming change in their environment.

The other large developments are in the New Guinea area, on Bougainville and in the Ertsberg mountains of West Irian. Among a series of copper-bearing deposits spread through the New Guinea-Solomons chain, these, together with one other close to the international border which is still being explored, have been identified as the most promising. The Bougainville development, which came into production early in 1972, will yield an initial output of some 160,000 tons of copper per year, together with significant gold and silver. Development costs may have exceeded $400 million, and other private and public investment is expected to have cost at least $100 million. Banks and trading companies which have neglected Bougainville for years are now setting up branches there, even though the mining company intends to develop a full range of its own services. The government of Australian New Guinea holds 20 per cent of the equity, and a further block of shares has been offered to Bougainvilleans and other New Guineans at par. Some 14 per cent of materials used in construction have been supplied from within the country.

The mine will be the principal contributor to territorial revenue, and an important employer and buyer of produce, but the multiplier effect of its operations will be constrained by isolation, and also by the low labour co-efficient in modern mining. The training will be invaluable, and wages excellent by local standards, but comparatively few will benefit directly. The central treasury will gain, but a decline in the Australian grant is very likely to offset this advantage. The Bougainvilleans have very mixed reactions, even though they will gain significantly, and although the company is making every effort to employ them and buy from them, and to encourage indigenous entrepreneurs by loans and assistance.

For all its difficulties, and the hostility which its explorations have generated, the Bougainville operation offers more to the Melanesians than anything else now in prospect. The Ertsberg operation is in an unpopulated area, and labour is being recruited largely in Java. The possible third operation near the international border is also in a remote area with few and only primitive people. The other major current enterprise, a Japanese bauxite mining operation on Rennell island in the Solomons group, is on a very isolated island and, whatever the policy of the company, spread effects will inevitably be small.

Investment in air transport and in tourism are so closely linked that they must be reviewed in close relation to one another. During the 1960s the expansion in regional air transport has been impressive indeed. There has been large public investment in airport construction and improvement, and the nationally-financed airlines of Australia and France have both greatly increased their services, keeping pace with a rising market. But perhaps the most significant development is the absorption of a considerable number of small companies by the major airlines, so that much the greater part of the network is now under metropolitan control.

The most striking instance is in Australian New Guinea, where the Australian overseas airline, Qantas, operated main-line services until 1960, and a dozen or so small companies ran extensive charter services, often with very ancient aircraft, but with surprisingly good safety records in view of their practice of normally overloading aircraft and operating under weather conditions that would keep most companies firmly on the ground. In 1960 the two main Australian domestic airlines, one government and one private, took over the Qantas services, and the Australian 'two-airline policy' of avoiding competition by maintaining equality in all things was extended to New Guinea. But the airlines could compete by taking over the charter companies, and this they did until road improvements late in the 1960s deprived them of the most profitable sectors of the cargo business. They then decided to withdraw to the main lines, and permit the charter operators – such as were left – to resume. The possibility of developing a viable national New Guinea company in the 1960s was aborted.

In the New Hebrides two small companies, one with only a single aircraft, began operations at the end of the 1950s. After repeated breakdowns, frequent damage due to landing on execrable airstrips, and one disastrous accident, the two went into a consortium termed Air Melanesiae, which continued to suffer from the same weaknesses until in 1969–70 it was taken over by a combination of Qantas, with BOAC participation necessary under contractual agreement, and UTA. The airline is re-equipped, operated wholly by Qantas staff, and only a single local member remains on the board. With the backing of a major international airline, the Condominium authorities have now been persuaded to improve the airfields. Greater efficiency certainly results, but other means of achieving this might have been possible without airline colonialism.

The only exception to this trend is the growth of Fiji Airways, which began as a small internal company in Fiji, and with the joint backing of the Fijian, Tongan and Western Pacific High Commission Governments, and of Qantas and BOAC, has grown rapidly into a highly efficient regional airline. Extending further in 1970 by taking over the Samoan-based Polynesian Airlines and developing services as far as Port Moresby in the west, the company has been further reorganized with stronger backing from the several territorial governments, and has changed its name to Air Pacific. Further expansion, including the initiation of extra-regional services, is now in prospect with a view to the explosive growth of tourism that is anticipated. Here is a model of cooperation between several governments and the main international carrier of the region that might have been followed with advantage elsewhere.

Investment in tourism has become a major activity since 1965, when real expansion began in Fiji and to a lesser extent in New Caledonia. Minor investments were made elsewhere, but they had to await improvement in air services to become viable. In Fiji, where Nadi airport remains a focal point for trans-Pacific traffic, the number of hotel beds rose from a few hundred in the early 1960s to almost 4,000 by 1971, and further hotels were then under construction. Some investment has been local, but the largest sources of capital have been Australia and now also the United States. Expansion in New Caledonia has been similar, but smaller, and since 1968 there has also been the beginnings of a boom in hotel construction in Australian New Guinea. The boom reached the New Hebrides in 1970–1, and 'packaged tours' are now bringing large numbers of both summer and winter tourists from Australia and North America. A major extension in these, coupled with some cost reductions for such bookings in 1971, is believed to presage a much greater boom in this industry. The short-term multiplier effect has been substantial, especially in construction, taxi and car hire business, retailing of 'duty-free' goods, and the sale of curios and some local foodstuffs. But few are taking note of warnings coming from the West Indies, where modern studies are showing that not more than about 30 per cent of tourist expenditure remains in the country, that the long-term multiplier effect is far smaller than was optimistically estimated, that there are both serious economic disadvantages to the host country through rising living costs and inflation in the price of land, and also most pernicious social drawbacks. Prominent among these is a grave deterioration of race relations prompted by the brutal contrast in wealth, and resentment at the behaviour of a significant minority of the visitors. As yet certain wider effects of tourism in the West Indies have not appeared in Melanesia. These include the emergence of a chronic shortage of agricultural labour as potential workers drift away to the tourist areas either to work or in the hope of finding jobs, a devaluation of agricultural work in the minds of the people because of its smaller and slower return, and the emergence of a parasitic population, both male and female, who seek a living by exploiting the vices and vanities of the visitors. In certain West Indian islands there has been an enormous decline in agriculture from these and related causes, and all forms of other activity are finding it difficult to get reliable labour. At the same time the entry of a large new foreign-controlled and -operated sector of the economy is seen by many as replicating the pattern of the plantation, an enterprise in which the local population can participate only in a peripheral, and mainly servile, capacity.

Nor is this all. Already in certain Pacific territories there has been an enormous surge in land speculation, due not so much to tourism itself as to the gullibility of ultimate buyers, who believe they are securing a tropical residence to which to retire in idyllic ease, further softened by low taxation. This began with the sale of some plantations and small islands to wealthy professional men genuinely interested in productively developing their properties, then to others who planned to build 'private pleasure kingdoms' for the rich on their properties. This first generation was quickly followed by others who bought plantations, subdivided them on paper, then sold the subdivisions to buyers resident overseas who often resold in turn on a rising market. One such company operating in the New Hebrides began in 1968 with a single plantation located far up the east coast of Espiritu Santo – a malarial area also affected by a major land dispute between a French company and Melanesian squatters. Advertising the properties for sale in Hawaii, they enjoyed great success, and on this and other land in the area sold some 4,000 subdivisions to non-resident buyers, none of whom had visited the site, or checked the rather remarkable advertising claims. The company went on to buy land in other islands, and the price of suitably-located plantation land rose fivefold and more in two or three years as planters hoped to sell out at a large profit and retire. In 1971 the New Hebridean authorities finally acted by introducing heavy retroactive taxation on subdivisions, imposing conditions regarding the reservation of land for public purposes, and strengthening the immigration ordinance to make it difficult or impossible for a buyer to obtain permanent residence rights. A month later in Hawaii it was announced that the company had halted all sales. The three-pronged pattern of legislation was also being studied urgently in Fiji, where a very similar surge of land speculation has also arisen since 1969. Such measures are strongly opposed by European landholders, but enjoy solid support among Melanesians, to whom land alienation is everywhere a matter of deep and increasingly bitter concern.

Although few other investment areas have the same set of complex economic, political and moral issues as investment in tourism, similar questions arise in all fields. The fundamental question is the degree of Melanesian participation, and the nature and extent of Melanesian benefit. Perhaps the problem is most sharply delineated in the fields of surface transport, construction and especially manufacturing. These are areas of enterprise in which the small size and lack of integration of the island markets restrict the expansion of enterprises. This is a constraint which should cut two ways: in the first place the inability fully to utilize economies of large scale limits profitability; in the second place this consideration should reduce attractiveness to external capital, while providing openings for local capital, and for exploitation of economies of very small scale.

In fact, the place of locally-based entrepreneurship is strongest in surface transport, second in construction, and weakest in manufacturing, but the growing scale of the island economies is favouring external enterprise in all three areas. In Fiji and New Caledonia local Indian and European entrepreneurs control most of surface transport. In the Solomon Islands, Government set up the initial network, but it is more and more in the hands of local entrepreneurs who are still more often Asian than Melanesian. In the New Hebrides there has been a recent increase in the share of local shipping handled by companies and expatriate entrepreneurs. In Australian New Guinea a mix of European and Melanesian entrepreneurs handle most road transport, but the rising scale of activity has tempted large Australian freight-forwarding companies into the business.

There is a similar pattern in construction and contracting. Local expatriate, Indo-Fijian and some Melanesian entrepreneurs handle quite a large share of this business, and local Melanesian councils in New Guinea have often set up successful construction units which have benefited from Government patronage. But the larger-scale business of road construction, harbour development and heavy engineering has drawn in not only locally-based firms capitalized from abroad, but also international companies, of which much the most prominent is the huge Dillingham Corporation of Honolulu.

Manufacturing is perhaps the most active field of investment after mining and tourism at the time of writing. There is a fairly substantial group of Indo-Fijian establishments in Fiji, and some Chinese-owned manufacturing enterprises in Australian New Guinea and the Solomon Islands. But there are few Melanesian-owned plants, other than primary-produce processing and marketing organizations run by the various Cooperative Society associations, under Government aegis. Especially in Australian New Guinea, vigorous efforts are being made to foster small Melanesian manufacturing businesses, with heavy inputs not only of loan finance, but also of supervision and even facilities. Efforts are also being made to sponsor joint ventures between local expatriate entrepreneurs and Melanesians, with some success. But the net result of all this pales into insignificance alongside the 'branch-plant economy' being established mainly by wholly-owned local subsidiaries of overseas firms, sometimes singly, sometimes in partnerships that may involve the island companies. Except for the agricultural-processing and timber-using industries, the majority of these plants depend heavily on imported raw materials, usually obtained through the channels of the parent organization.

Manufacturing is rather highly localized. Nouméa, Suva, Port Moresby and Lae have at least half the establishments, and probably much more than half the value of output, numbers employed, power used and other unavailable indices. Other places with some significant manufacturing other than primary processing include the Nadi-Lautoka area in Fiji, and Rabaul and Madang in New Guinea. There is a very little in Vila, in Honiara, in Djajapura and some other New Guinea towns, but the size of businesses is very small. Much the largest plant, in a class by itself, is the SLN metallurgical plant at Nouméa, but this apart, the main fields of activity are in engineering, including vehicle repairs, in food, drink and tobacco manufacture, including bakeries, breweries and cigarette factories, in sawmilling, plywood manufacture and joinery, and in sundry fields such as cement manufacture, textiles, printing and manufacture of packaging. Fiji and Australian New Guinea produce most of their own beer and cigarettes, almost all territories are self-sufficient in soft drinks, but even such industries as motor repairs still depend largely on costly airfreighting of parts from Australia; the need for expansion in the engineering field is acute.

Not only small size and population, but also the poverty in good internal communications, demand that industry be restricted to fields in which the threshold size of an economic plant is small. There is a measure of protection due to high freight rates, especially in Australian New Guinea, and a tariff structure is emerging. But there is no doubt that many branch-plants are being set up rather in terms of long-term expectation than of short-term profit. The five-year tax holidays and other incentives seem to be effective mainly in inducing firms to set up 'too soon' in a rising market, perhaps in the expectation that it may be easier to market products after independence if a local subsidiary is already established.

Except in New Caledonia, a very high proportion of the factories being set up are branch-plants of Australian companies, and the slow reduction in the Australian share of total imports to the Melanesian territories needs to be viewed against this fact. There are some Japanese interests, but it is clear that Japanese capital is generally welcome only on certain terms: the French, for example, have for years resisted a Japanese proposal to establish a consulate in Nouméa. Japanese cars are now dominating the market, but the first car-maker will be an Australian-owned New Guinea company, now distributing British vehicles.

There is no share market anywhere in Melanesia. Most locally-owned companies are private concerns, and shares in the companies with significant Melanesian capital are not traded. Locally-registered public companies that are not wholly-owned subsidiaries of overseas concerns are listed on the Australian and sometimes the British stock exchanges. Even in New Caledonia, where a much higher proportion of enterprise is locally-financed than in other territories, many local capitalists also have significant investments in Australia. There is a small New Zealand share, but long-lasting restrictions on the export of capital by New Zealanders have led to their interests in the islands west of Samoa being swamped by Australians. The present pattern of investment has one curious effect: Melanesian residents, indigenous or otherwise, with capital to spare, will often invest this money in Australia for want of worthwhile local outlets. In recent years Australian investment companies have begun to make efforts to tap this supply by advertising, and have enjoyed considerable success. Thus not only do banks, marketing boards and cooperative societies often invest abroad substantial sums of locally-derived funds, but there is also direct export of capital by private individuals. At the same time, the growing points of the economy are being financed overwhelmingly from abroad.

INVESTMENT, GROWTH AND DEVELOPMENT

The combined rate of savings and investment, together with capital imports from abroad, seems to have been rising for some years in Melanesia, and now stands at levels well above the 10 per cent regarded as critical for 'take-off' by Rostow (1960). There is evidence to suggest that high savings and investment rates are also characteristic of significant groups among the residentiary Melanesian populations. But the 'social and institutional framework which exploits the impulses for expansion in the modern sector', and so converts such a situation into 'sustained growth' seems to be absent, and we perhaps have here what Rostow terms 'enclave economies' in which the indices of total growth seem excellent, but true 'development' is not being achieved.

The indices of growth are indeed impressive, as the following figures on gross domestic product at factor cost in three territories indicate. The data are not wholly comparable in construction, and include a variable contribution from 'subsistence production', but expansion comes mainly from the monetary sectors and is as shown in the table on p. 139. Though there are great differences in scale, and in *per capita* levels (not reproduced here because year-to-year population estimates are unreliable except in Fiji), growth rates are steady and significant, and in all cases well ahead of the estimated rate of population increase.

These are not poor countries by Third World standards, and within them few people are in genuine need. Yet the growth of the GDP is a poor indicator

	Australian New Guinea ($ million)	Solomon Islands ($ million)	Fiji ($ million)
	288·2		
1963		17·7	108·5
	304·7		
1964		19·1	115·1
	328·8		
1965		20·0	119·9
	351·8		
1966		20·8	124·5
1967		22·8	132·4
1968		—	145·4
Estimated population in last year of series	2,185,000	146,000	512,000

Official sources: (*See discussion at p. 138.*)

of true development, as is any index which treats a colonial economy as though it were a single unit in which simple maximization of national income is the path to progress for the whole population. Fisk puts this point very clearly in the case of Fiji, and his comments have wider validity:

The picture that emerges is roughly that of a 3-tier society in which the European/Chinese group manages and operates the large corporations and institutions, often on behalf of foreign owners, the Indians own and operate most of the medium to small-scale enterprises, including most of the commercial farming, whilst the Fijians own most of the land and are still heavily engaged in a non-monetary, but affluent, subsistence sector (Fisk, 1970, 42).

and elsewhere: 'the main economic problem requiring massive and urgent government intervention in Fiji is *not* the size of the national income but its distribution, and this requires recognition at all levels' (*ibid.*, 59).

The essential point is that which has underlain the whole interpretation presented in this book. The colonial commercial system inevitably operates mainly for its own benefit, and while its trading requirements have led to rather intermittent encouragement of residentiary participation other than as labour, there has also been conflict of interests between residentiary 'development' and the demands of expatriate producers. When it has been possible for the commerical system to import labour, and to operate a whole economic system from which the residentiary population is effectively excluded, this has been done. Fisk adds the point that the very 'primitive affluence' of the residentiary population has operated to deter them from long-term commitment to participation in the wider economy. Then in modern times, governments have inherited and developed the traditional view that growth generates the diffusion of growth, and though they have ceased to rely on *laissez-faire* to obtain such diffusion, their efforts have been guided by the priority goal of maximizing national income. During the Hasluck period, when time did not seem to be a scarce factor, there was some downgrading of this goal in favour of maximizing equity, but such policies were never adequately developed and implemented, and have tended to be submerged under the perceived urgency of accelerating total growth that has come to dominate in the 1960s. Thus while equity-orientated policies have continued to prevail in the more slowly-growing agricultural sector, they have received little more than token concern in the drive to build up the newer and more rapidly-growing forestry, mining, tourism and industrial sectors of the territorial economies.

The effect has been to reinforce the colonial economic structure inherited from an earlier and overtly exploitative period. Quite insufficient attention has been paid to the need to transform this whole structure, including that of the residentiary systems, in harmony with the changing political and social objectives. Perhaps we may here draw insights from thinking outside the Pacific, in the Caribbean, where Demas (1965), following and developing from Kindleberger (1958), has argued that the true criterion of development or underdevelopment in a country is the degree to which it has achieved transformation of the structure of production. This transformation includes unification of the national market for goods and services, capacity to absorb innovations and adapt to changing external situations, facility for ready shifting of the factors of production between sectors and geographical areas, forging of links to obtain a greater degree of interdependence among domestic industries and activities, changes in an expanding foreign trade pattern away from import of consumer goods toward intermediate and capital goods, and away from export of raw materials toward export of part-manufactures and finished products, and reduction in the disparity between returns to factors of production within the economy which is the mark of dualism. It will be evident that progress in these directions in the Melanesian territories is thus far rather limited, and that although there are definite advances in some areas, achievement in others remains minimal.

Narrowing his discussion to the problems of small countries, Demas goes on to discuss the limits of import substitution in such economies, due to the limitations of the local market; as the economies of scale become greater due to technical and organizational innovation in the large, developed countries, so the terms of trade against size-constrained import-substitution industries in small, underdeveloped countries steadily worsen. He might have gone on to add that such disadvantages can to some degree be offset by the organizational economies possible in branch-plant operation, thus investing such enterprises with competitive advantage over wholly-local concerns of comparable size within the small, underdeveloped country. He thus argues in favour of economic integration between groups of small countries, implying the construction of an interconnected regional transport system, the adjustment and lowering or elimination of tariffs between cooperating countries, and conscious intergovernmental action to allocate manufacturing growth points within the 'common market' so formed. Here too is a field in which little progress has yet been achieved in the south Pacific, although Fiji has taken the initiative in discussions in this area – having perhaps the most to gain. Such allocation of growth points does not, however, imply simply the widening of a market for the most developed members of the group: the model of such a situation is already visible in the growing New Caledonian economic colonialism in the New Hebrides.

On the situation within a single national economy, Demas and Fisk seem to be wholly in accord. Both argue that it is necessary to divert resources from the growth points in order to improve productivity in the backward sectors and areas, and that the cost of doing this in terms of a slowing down of total growth rates is much less than the long-term cost of allowing a major part of the economy to stagnate. This argument too applies at the interterritorial regional level, and indeed at the world level, but it is one demanding a massive programme of public education, since it runs counter to the short-term interests of those who hold economic power.

SIZE AND DEPENDENCY

All Melanesian economies are small, but some are smaller than others. All are essentially satellitic economies, with strongly skewed patterns of resource endowment and domestic production. The export industries of all are to a great degree enclave economies, supported by heavy foreign investment. All depend on foreign funds, public and private, for growth. Not only is there lack of integration between territorial economies, but also within them. Significant parts of all territories are economically stagnant or suffering from backwash effects. So much are the growth centres and new industries in the hands of foreign enterprise that no less a person than the Prime Minister of Fiji has observed that if the nation's capital and chief industrial centre, Suva, were burned to the ground, the Melanesian-Fijians would lose nothing but the records of their debts.

There seems to be an inevitability about this condition, and if so little but masochistic pleasure is to be gained from deploring it. If both growth and development require foreign investment, and if the available local resources in these small countries are inevitably insufficient to support either true transformation or maintenance of welfare at present and desired levels, then there is no alternative to dependency but stagnation and retrogression. Independence may give a nation self-respect, as the same Fijian Prime Minister retorted to a questioning journalist, but it is a self-respect that must be severely constrained by awareness that the power of economic decision-making is greatly limited. To maximize self-respect is not accordant with maximization of either income or welfare: many countries much larger and richer than the Melanesian territories are learning this, and deciding either to compromise or to forgo self-respect.

There are still further dimensions to this problem that must be briefly explored. Few of the companies which ultimately absorb and market the export produce of Melanesia are wholly dependent on Melanesian sources; the position of the Société le Nickel is exceptional. The larger island trading companies have substantial, if not dominant, interests in Australia and elsewhere; most mining companies have operations in many countries; even the larger forestry companies are territorially diversified. The buyers of Melanesian agricultural produce draw from many sources, and they often have the further advantage that they blend produce from different sources to prepare the marketed product. The branch-plant industrialists seldom have any major share of their operations in the islands, and except in New Caledonia there is indeed only a minor sector of the whole foreign-controlled economy which could not write off its Melanesian operations without insupportable loss. Even the Bougainville copper development, which is the largest single current enterprise of the Rio-Tinto group, could probably be liquidated without doing irreparable harm to the parent company.

It follows that the condition of dependency is not mutual: taking the foreign-controlled sector as a whole, it operates in only one direction. If all the Melanesian Governments were simultaneously to seize all foreign enterprises in the group they might wreck a few Australian companies, and one or two French and other foreign corporations, but their own losses would be far more severe since no comparable marketing outlets and capital sources could be re-established in a sufficiently short term to avoid economic collapse. Their small size, and satellitic condition toward Australia and France, deprive them of even the measure of flexibility which enabled Indonesia just to survive the years of aggressive anti-colonial nationalism between 1957 and 1966, and they lack the international strategic significance which has enabled Cuba to survive.

This is not to say that opportunities to acquire control of foreign enterprises will not arise. A clear illustration of a pattern that may be repeated occurred in Fiji in 1970. We recall that after the end of the plantation system in sugar production, the monopoly Colonial Sugar Refining Company of Sydney retained control of the milling, but contracted for almost all the cane supply with growers who were mostly tenants either on company land or on Fijian land. Following the strike of growers in 1959, an inquiry led to new cane contracts in 1962 on terms which never satisfied the growers. These contracts terminated in 1970, and in 1969 a new inquiry was instituted. This time the growers were in a stronger position because of improved world prices under a new International Sugar Agreement, and because competition for their votes led both Government and Opposition parties to espouse their cause and present evidence in their favour. The new award was much more favourable to the growers than the old, including provision for a minimum price and a more equitable share of profits from final sales. CSR, however, determined that they could not be sufficiently certain of making a profit under the new award, maintaining that the company would have lost money under it through the period of low prices between 1964 and 1969. After six weeks' ominous silence, CSR announced that they would crush the 1970, 1971 and 1972 crops, then withdraw entirely from Fiji, disposing of their properties and interests there. The company, industrially diversified and based mainly in Australia, could afford to do this without serious loss. The decision was final, made in no spirit of bargaining.

The Fiji Government cannot afford to lose the sugar industry, even though problems will certainly increase despite the favourable terms negotiated by Britain with its future partners in the European Common Market: Fiji is included among the territories whose sugar will be admitted on preferential terms. Fiji, however, depends also on the North American market for a large part of its sales, and this cannot be regarded as secure. The government had two alternatives: either to invite a new company, or to operate the industry as a national or semi-public corporation. The latter course has been adopted. Negotiations over the CSR freehold land were still proceeding in 1971, but there were disturbing indications that this Indo-Fijian occupied land might be distributed mainly for the benefit of Fijian landholders.

There are wider issues. It has long been known that with more intensive methods the Fiji sugar crop could be produced on less land, thus facilitating diversification. It is hoped that plans will include such action, so as to reduce Fiji's dependence on a crop in a chronic condition of world over-production. There are also prospects of regional marketing that have been little explored. At the very same time as the CSR announcement, it was also declared that Australian New Guinea will probably initiate sugar production, to replace its present imports from Australia, as soon as the local market improves sufficiently to support a mill of minimum economic size with an output of 30,000 tons a year. Such is the present state of regional economic cooperation that the coincidence passed almost without remark.

Small size, political compartmentalization and fragmentation of territories into many islands all accentuate dependency on both foreign governments and foreign corporations. As in the West Indies, each territory is a world to itself, and the problems of neighbours seem remote and irrelevant in relation to one's own. Possibly nothing can be done in the short term to alleviate the vice-like grip in which the New Caledonian economy is held, although the pain is alleviated by high living standards for a large part of the population, and the disadvantaged and angry Calédonien entrepreneurs have found it hard to raise much sympathy. West Irian is now firmly inside Indonesia, and while United Nations aid and advice may lead to some limited development, the remote position of the territory within Indonesia militates against anything but a peripheral rôle. Development of any sort of internal viability in the Solomon Islands depends on the chance of mineral exploitation, at least in the short term, while the New Hebrides has its particular problem of satellitism toward New Caledonia. But in Australian New Guinea and Fiji at least there is considerable scope for internal integration, reallocation of the factors of production, and emergence of a public sector. The central parts of these two territories, together with Nouméa, constitute potential 'growth poles' whose full value can only be realized if there is greater regional economic integration.

But present trends do not run this way. Most territories continue to experience widening gaps in the balance of payments on current account, and with an end in sight to liberal external grants look more and more to investment in mining and tourism to rectify these trends. Projections made for planning purposes show such private investment as rising continuously through the coming decade. With economies as small and weak as those of Melanesia it is hardly possible to eliminate a condition of dependency, and even massive action to increase flows within the internal and regional economies, demanding decisive intervention to plan the allocation of resources and create new linkages, can scarcely have more than a palliative effect in the foreseeable future. But action to create something more like a mixed economy in these territories is possible, and it seems certain that failure to proceed in this direction will lead to persistence and further deepening of the present satellitic condition. This is especially likely if simple maximization of total income continues to be the goal of governments. And in this not unlikely event, political independence will be deprived of a very large part of its meaning.

REFERENCES AND SOURCES

References already cited in Chapter 1 are again a principal source here. Some of the evidence is already presented in Brookfield with Hart (1971), but the form of comment reflects subsequent reading of writers such as Furtado (1964), Demas (1965), Frank (1967), Levitt and Best (1969) and Levitt (1970), and close contact with Caribbean economic thinking since 1970. For a balanced and well-presented review of the relationship between political independence and commercial and cultural dependence in this area, see especially Lewis (1968). Factual sources include government reports and surveys, and the statistical publications of the Papua-New Guinea Bureau of Statistics, the Fiji Bureau of Statistics and the Service des Affaires Economiques in New Caledonia. Fisk (1970) also provides both data and corroborating comment on Fiji. In this chapter there is also an important contribution of 'personal communications' from administrators in the islands and from economists at work in the area.

CHAPTER 12

THE FACE OF PLURALISM IN MELANESIA

In the sense that Melanesia is populated by a multitude of groups differentiated culturally by such learned attributes as language, religion, diet and taboo, ethnically by skin colour, hair form and build, and socially by differing institutions governing marriage and property, this region with its small population of only some four millions is among the most diverse on the surface of the earth. There can be no place on earth where Talcott Parsons' conditions for a society, requiring shared, symbolic means of communication and shared understandings, goals and norms, are less met than in the political units of Melanesia: indeed the alternative of the 'war of all against all' was perhaps as closely approximated in pre-colonial Melanesia as anywhere in the world. Yet there are also senses in which we can speak of only three groups in Melanesia: the Europeans, the Asians and the Melanesians, and still another sense in which we can – in parts of Melanesia – discern the emergence of a stratification based on achievement rather than ascription. It can perhaps be suggested that colonialism has tended to weld the Melanesian complex into a plural society, by introducing or creating solidary groups differentiated by rôle, ascribed status and privilege, while the needs of living together under independence in small societies are introducing tendencies toward a stratification that is not ascribed. This is gross simplification but we are dealing with an area in which there are few applicable guidelines, and which remains, in Melanesia, a near-virgin field for social inquiry.

Yet the relevance of these concepts is already evident from the discussion of the previous two chapters. We speak constantly of 'ethnic groups', and where we speak of 'monetary' and 'non-monetary' sectors, this is often hardly more than a euphemism for 'expatriate' and 'indigenous'. Political constitutions recognize the existence of such groups, and their importance. What we still lack, however, is any profound inquiry into their nature and meaning in society, polity and economy. We have public stereotypes, and we have the insights of many academic writers and some journalists who explore behind the stereotypes, but in a haphazard fashion. A small number of academic papers and monographs treat of pluralism in particular communities, with varying success, or else treat of single ethnic communities in adaptation to a plural setting. Among these one of the most widely informative is provided by an M.A. thesis in geography at Sydney University, written by a Fiji-Chinese on the Fiji-Chinese population (Wong, 1963). But for attempts to apply or generate theoretical models we must look outside Melanesia.

In his stimulating discussion of the plural society of the Commonwealth West Indies – on which my use of 'cultural pluralism' in this chapter is largely based – M. G. Smith (1965) finds it possible to identify a single embracing 'West Indian culture' based on the dominant Creole-European tradition. We cannot parallel this in Melanesia, though there are tenuous elements of a common Pacific islands culture shared a little ostentatiously by a growing number of both Melanesians and Europeans, and based on what is believed to be Polynesian tradition. But this is weak, as also is a sense of territorial identity among members of different plural groups living in the same country. Thus New Guinea Europeans may be 'New Guineans' when in the presence of foreign Europeans, but self-consciousness is stretched toward absurdity when they make the same claim among Melanesian New Guineans, to whom they are inevitably Australians. Only in New Caledonia is a significant European population truly 'landed' and able to join credibly with Melanesians in opposition to outsiders, however sharp may be the internal cleavage within the territory.

We thus have a cultural plurality of particularly stark form. Groups are differentiated in multiple ways, culturally, ethnically, economically and in social system; there is no common scale of values or normative consensus; incompatible institutional systems coexist in a single economic and political bond. There are gross discontinuities in the continuum of status positions, and these are determined by different modes in the several sections. Within major sections there may be subdivisions across which there is some continuum of status, consensus about goals, and common scale of values: such sub-cleavages would separate metropolitan Europeans from South Pacific Europeans; Europeans from Métis; caste, religious and language groups among the Indo-Fijians; descendants of indentured workers from those of free migrants among the same section; regional and language groups among migrant Melanesians, and so on: the sub-cleavages are of almost infinite number, depending on the scale of examination.

Pluralism is unifying as well as divisive, and indeed among populations of varied origins fusion into defined plural groups may be a fundamentally unifying process within a whole emergent society. Unfortunately such a process contains forces which inhibit, and may prevent further unification into a single society: these may include emergence of a single goal for which the groups are in conflict, or are perceived to be in conflict, which has the same effect. Or social order may be achieved and sustained without common values, and without further move toward unification. Fear may come to constitute an immovable block to further change. But the emergence of common interests, or common opposition of two groups against a third or an external force, or a realization that the number of significant differences has diminished, may presage a new move toward unification. The argument of this chapter is that the group of dichotomies contained, *inter alia*, in the master/servant tradition, in the exploiter/exploited relationship, in the resident/newcomer distinction and in the civilized/uncivilized contrast form a set of oppositions whose presence, real or perceived – and it is no matter which – is inherent in the colonial process. Such oppositions fuse people into groups whose mutual behaviour is governed by public stereotypes, and we recognize this state of affairs as a cultural plurality. A change in the ambient conditions will remove, re-sort and change the significance of the dichotomies, or may give rise to new dichotomies. Pluralism may not vanish, but its nature will inevitably change.

MASTERS, EXPLOITERS, NEWCOMERS, CIVILIZED MEN – THE EUROPEANS

The European and European-Métis resident in Melanesia number about 100,000, and can be readily placed in terms of each of the dichotomies stated in the preceding paragraph. Melanesians see them as the 'masters', and most of them still think of themselves in these terms, though they would be less ready also to accept the soubriquet of 'exploiters' with which they are also endowed. Even though individuals and many of the Calédoniens may have no home outside Melanesia, as groups they do have other countries with which they retain close contact, and they are all 'newcomers' as seen by the indigenous population and even many of the Asians, who lack opportunities for migration. They identify themselves as 'civilized men' in opposition to all others, and there are still comparatively few among the indigenous population who would not concede them a measure of cultural advantage. Yet there are many cleavages, both sharp and graduated, within the European communities.

Such cleavages are partly defined by rôle: government servants, missionaries, planters, businessmen, artisans and working men are distinct in outlook. There is also class stratification partly overlapping the rôle distinction. But the most fundamental cleavage is perhaps that between the sojourners, who expect to remain only a limited time in the islands, and the true residents who expect to work there all their lives and perhaps die in Melanesia. The latter tend to be patronising, even actively hostile in some cases, toward the former, though they are often ready enough to provide instruction in the formation of stereotypes suitable for island behaviour, instruction which many sojourners are ready to receive and adopt. Resident Europeans in all rôles often tend to authoritarianism and are frankly dubious – often colourfully so – of the ability of Melanesians to do a job properly or run their own affairs. Their voice is the island press, and the Sydney magazine *Pacific Islands Monthly* which has shifted greatly from its former illiberalism, but still has an occasional lapse and remains loud in praise of its European readers. The efficient running of the economy – or what passes for efficiency – depends on the Europeans: they know this well, and tend to be arrogant in this knowledge. Their view that the islands cannot do without them has only recently been challenged among the residentiary population; many regard themselves as the true leaders of Melanesian society, and some have indeed been accepted in this rôle in certain contexts. But they are now subject to rather violent swings between confidence and extreme anxiety over their future position, even in New Caledonia where they are surely secure enough. Though this has led to some modification of attitudes, it has also encouraged some *après nous le déluge* behaviour which is as depressing as it is short-sighted.

INDO-FIJIANS AND ASIANS

Asians are settled in all Melanesian territories. Most are the descendants of contract workers, but there has also been significant free immigration in Fiji and West Irian. People of Indian origin form half the population of Fiji, and on the two main islands constitute 90 per cent and more of the population over quite large tracts of country. They also dominate in the towns. Suva, with its mixture of Indo-Fijian, European, Chinese and Fijian population, has the aspect of a miniature Durban, South Africa.

But the Indo-Fijians are not a single group by origin. Contract workers were drawn from many parts of India, and though the majority natal language is Hindi, of several dialects, there are also substantial numbers of Tamil, Urdu, Telugu and Gujerati speakers; most are Hindus, but there is a Muslim minority and a small number of Christians; most Hindu migrants of higher caste tended to form a population section distinct from the contract migrants, and also sought political and economic leadership in Indo-Fijian society as a whole. Mayer (1963) has emphasized that during the immigration period the Indo-Fijians were defined as a 'community' only by their rôle and status in the colony; they were not organized and were essentially atomistic. Most were under thirty years of age at time of arrival, and their fusion into a plural group drew as much on experience as on tradition.

Today the Indo-Fijians constitute the closest approach to a fully-stratified society within one population section to be found in Melanesia. The largest group still live on independent farms, and although some family members may work for wages, the family units remain on the land, mostly in relation to the sugar corporation as buyer and overseer, and to the corporation or a Fijian land-holding group as landlord. The cane sectors are the effective local groups, and the cane growers' unions major organs of wider solidarity. A second major group lives in the towns as employees, often in conditions of severe residential overcrowding. Where they belong to trade unions, these are only sometimes specifically communal, but communal factions have developed. Common opposition to the colonial commercial system has, however, given joint economic cause to both Indo-Fijian and Fijian workers. There is a large class of small businessmen and in the field of small entrepreneurship Indo-Fijians are overwhelmingly dominant, often having displaced Chinese and Europeans who filled this niche in an earlier period: there is as yet only a very small number of true Fijian entrepreneurs in the Schumpeterian innovation-adopting, risk-taking sense. Among Indo-Fijian entrepreneurs there is a stratification based mainly on achievement, and dominated by some capitalists of significant scale. Alongside this group is an Indo-Fijian professional class, similarly stratified, and including most of the political leaders. But a majority of the higher strata are descendants of free migrants, and the Gujerati-speaking group is well represented, as also among the traders and moneylenders of the rural areas. This has been a source of internal friction of some significance.

The main unifying forces have been external: relegation to second-class status as newcomers, under-representation in the political field; grave limitations in access to land; distrust and dislike among the dominant expatriates, and fear among the Fijians. But there has also been a sense of Indo-Fijian resentment as being disfavoured by comparison with the 'less civilized' Fijians. These pressures have led to the creation of Indo-Fijian institutions, especially in education, and the widespread use of Hindustani as a common language, which have done much to cement a sense of community consciousness and soften the impact of strong divisive forces within the population section. Yet these divisive forces have continued to operate, encouraging cross-community links as among the urban trade unions, and having important political consequences in the 1960s.

Except in West Irian, where the information required for an adequate discussion is lacking, other Asian communities are only small minorities. The Javanese in New Caledonia preserve a high degree of detachment from the surrounding scene, and often have little or no knowledge of political events. Dewey (1964) shows them to be self-identified as sojourners, even when residence has lasted more than twenty years. Only among a younger generation is there closer involvement. Vietnamese in New Caledonia and the New Hebrides have had an unusual history. Most of the 8,000 remaining in 1945 were either contract workers of the post-1932 period or their children; there were comparatively few survivors of the 1920s migration. The adults came from a Vietnam in which there was already strong anti-French feeling, polarized around Ho Chih Minh, and they took a keen interest in the proclamation of a Democratic Republic of Vietnam in 1945, and in the subsequent efforts first of the British then of the returning French to restore colonial rule. A few were repatriated to Tonkin in 1946–7, but these ex-miners and ex-plantation workers nourished a deep hatred for their former French employers, and immediately joined the Viet Minh forces. Repatriation was halted and not resumed until 1960.

During this long period most Vietnamese became urban and peri-urban dwellers, acquired a large share in the available employment for skilled artisans, and participated actively in market gardening and trade. Younger women, all born in the Pacific, found employment in offices and shops, and were much sought after by European men. The economic status of many Vietnamese improved rapidly, but a large number continued to live in tight ethnic communities, where their allegiance to North Vietnam was kept alive by Viet-Nam-Hon news-sheets, political meetings and rigid discipline, tolerated by the authorities so long as it remained confined to the segregated camps. Pressures toward cultural integration led to persistent erosion, especially but not only among the Catholics: a breakaway group, who sometimes call themselves Anciens Communistes, became almost equivalent to Europeans in economic opportunity, but socially remained at a little distance. Most of the 'hard core' were repatriated between 1960 and 1964, together with a number of waverers and some often very unwilling young people. The balance includes some elderly people, mostly Catholic, and young people who now find it easier to assimilate among the increasingly cosmopolitan society of Nouméa and Vila.

Chinese mostly entered the Pacific as free migrants, and are engaged overwhelmingly in trade. They often replaced European traders, as the latter raised their satisfaction levels and were eliminated, and in turn the Chinese rural traders are now being replaced by Melanesians. The present Chinese population of the region is overwhelmingly urban, with the largest concentrations in Rabaul and Suva: their relative economic importance, however, is perhaps greatest in the Solomon Islands. Separation of the Chinese as a group is partly due to external attitudes, but partly by design: business and social contacts are often maintained with Hong Kong and Singapore, and many children are sent there to school. But among the younger generation there is growing adoption of European values and social norms, and substantial mingling. And as the Chinese community is becoming fearful of maintaining its specialized place in the economic system, so a number of individuals are cautiously seeking entry into politics, generally in a central position in the spectrum.

MELANESIANS IN A PLURALISTIC RELATION

The main discussion of Melanesian reactions to colonialism is deferred to the next chapter: here comment is confined to a review of the local relations of Melanesians with other groups in the rural and urban contexts. Except in the cane country of Fiji, some parts of rural New Caledonia, and a few coastal areas in southern West Irian, Melanesians massively outnumber all other ethnic groups in all rural parts of the region. Their relationship with members of other groups is that of the ruled toward the ruler, worker toward employer, customer toward seller, seller toward buyer. Its main dimensions are political and economic, and social intercourse is negligible – unless the prostitution that is quite rife in some areas can be regarded as a social relation. Much the more significant social relationship in the rural areas is that between residentiary and migrant Melanesians. The latter sometimes occupy specialized rôles in government and other employment and hence have a superior relation toward residentiary Melanesians. More often, however, the migrants are unskilled workers living in labour compounds.

Considerable hostility has sometimes arisen in these situations, and there are quite numerous instances of attacks on individual migrant Melanesians, with fewer instances of mass conflict. The most common immediate issues are conflict arising in economic relations, resentment at relations with local women, fear of the potential implantation of alien groups. Despite the widespread use of *lingues franches* – Pidgin English in its several forms, Police Motu, Pasar Malay, French, English and Bauan Fijian – sharp linguistic differences alone restrict intercourse between residentiary people and migrants, and facilitate misunderstandings. But there are many instances where migrants, mostly as individuals, have become settled in residentiary communities, have married and become absorbed. There are many other instances in which migrant individuals and small groups have been allowed to settle because they provide useful labour: such people are essentially tenants-at-will, and it is not expected that many will remain permanently. Though there is a strong sense of cultural differentiation between people of different areas, values and norms have close similarity. These conflicts arise between people distinguished more by place than by cultural characteristics.

Melanesians may find themselves in close contact with rural Asians frequently in the future, if further Indonesian migrants are brought to join the few hundred families settled in West Irian between 1963 and 1969, and the descendants of an earlier settlement made in 1905–10. At present this sort of pluralistic situation is developed principally in Fiji. Studying a Fijian community among the Indo-Fijian farmers of the cane country, where many Indo-Fijians held their land on lease from the Fijian villagers, Watters (1969, 171–2) noted first the unusual commercialism of the Fijian village, and the superficially friendly and harmonious relations between the communities:

> Thus Fijian villagers provide business to the five Indian stores in the locality, as well as to the numerous Indian shops in near-by Nadi Township. Villagers also hire tractors and other equipment from local Indians for ploughing their land and the charges were generally reasonable. Though there was segregation in the Nadi-Sorolevu bus the two peoples mingled in the Nadi market, restaurants and hotel bar, and together enjoyed many social occasions. But closer acquaintanceship with the Fijians revealed that beneath their superficial friendliness lay a deep suspicion and uneasy mistrust...

The Indo-Fijian neighbours perhaps had more to fear, as they were by law to be evicted from their land on the expiry of the current leases. In Fiji as a whole there is negligible intermarriage, there are almost no business partnerships, and social intercourse is limited in the main to 'neutral' ground. Mutual intolerance and contempt widely underlie the necessary superficial cooperation.

PLURALISM IN THE TOWNS

The towns of Melanesia are places owned mainly by Europeans or the governments, and to a lesser extent by the Asians, in which large numbers of Melanesians come to work and to experience a new sort of life. In stereotype, the Melanesian is a sojourner in town, which is thus a place in which European value systems can be prescribed as normative, and be supported by sanctions. Asians cannot be expected to be sojourners, but they can be relegated to particular parts of towns. This is the sort of framework in which Melanesian towns have come into being, and developed until the most recent years. Intermittent, but at times very serious, efforts have been made to control the 'influx' of Melanesians into these alien places, so as to hold numbers to levels which the urban system is able to utilize without strain. Residential segregation has rarely been legally institutionalized, but it has been enforced by a variety of measures, both public and private.

In fact, Europeans are today at least as much 'sojourners' in town as are the Melanesians: the permanent residential population of both groups is small, and the majority are fairly recent arrivals. Furthermore, the trend in this matter is against the Europeans. The true adult resident urban populations may even be dominantly Asian at the present stage, but it is true of most urban dwellers, of whatever group, that their links with fellow group members in other and distant environments are socially more significant than cross-group linkages within the town. Economic linkages structure the urban systems of Melanesia far more exclusively than in towns in most countries. Rapid growth in modern times, at rates commonly as high as 10 per cent per annum, leads to the persistence of this condition, and hence to the persistence of cultural plurality. Yet it is also in the towns that the most hopeful breaks in the present pattern of cleavage can be discerned.

Such breaks arise mainly among the educated, and especially among the young. Cross-group social gatherings, friendships and marriages are far more common than a few years ago. Such change has been facilitated by the legally enforced ending of segregation in such places as hotels and restaurants, but it is symptomatic also of emergence of common ground among the educated, among professionals, and even among businessmen of different groups. A decade ago I wrote of Port Moresby that 'race relations are better described as non-existent than as good or bad'. Today such a statement would be absurd. A developing cross-group stratification based on achievement and the adoption of common values is emerging at certain levels; at the same time, however, race relations between the mass of both white and black communities can now very definitely be described as bad. But they are bad largely because the true European sojourners have withdrawn even more strongly into in-group patterns as the present régime approaches its end, while the Melanesian sojourners, especially those living in the twenty to thirty shanty settlements scattered around the city, are coming to demand a greater share in the benefits of a place which they now regard as part of their own country.

Trends are not wholly in one direction, however. When a town is small, and offers only a limited number of age-mates within each group for formation of friendships, selection tends to extend across the cleavages. This was the case in Vila in 1965. By 1969, a substantial influx of Europeans had occurred, mainly from New Caledonia, and social life had become more, rather than less, group structured. And in New Caledonia itself, where some progress toward greater integration has been achieved during the 1960s, substantial new immigration from various source areas is likely to lead to some retrogression toward more segregated patterns.

PLURALISM IN POLITICS: NEW CALEDONIA AND FIJI

Contrasted though they are in many ways, the two southeastern Melanesian territories have in common the presence of immigrant groups that collectively form more than half the territorial populations. The comparison ends there, since the dominant group in New Caledonia is European, even though it is slightly smaller than the Melanesian group, while in Fiji the largest population group has hitherto been the least powerful politically. In both countries the Melanesians were for a long time excluded from participation in the export economy, but whereas the New Caledonian Melanesians hold only 8 per cent of the land on the main island, the Fijians hold 84 per cent of Fiji, though they contribute little except through their labour to the export economy.

Universal suffrage has brought pluralism strongly to the fore in the politics of both countries, but its expression has been radically different. In New Caledonia, French constitution makers imposed a common roll from the outset; in Fiji, pressures for the 'protection' afforded by communal rolls has been allowed to prevail. While party politics have developed in both countries, the New Caledonian parties are formed around common issues, but in Fiji mainly communal issues have prevailed.

There were some tentative moves toward the formation of communal parties in New Caledonia after certain Melanesians were enfranchised in 1946, but these vanished after the formation of the Mouvement de l'Union Calédonienne in 1953, uniting Melanesian interests with those of the European small businessmen, farmers, graziers, subcontract miners and workers, against the commercial and mining oligarchy. The UC has won every election from 1953 to this day, despite strong opposition from Société le Nickel, which has effective control of the news media and the ear of Government. In the early 1960s some very positive efforts were made to suppress the UC. The ministerial system was suspended and at a critical moment the UC leader was arrested and convicted of complicity in a bomb attempt on his own headquarters; certain other UC leaders were removed from New Caledonia. But metropolitan attempts to supplant territorial control in some branches of Government increased UC popular support. The opposition attempted to rally under the Gaullist banner, a doubtful issue in New Caledonia since 1942, but even though de Gaulle was rapturously received on a visit in 1966, the 1967 election increased the UC majority and eliminated the last SLN-backed representatives from the Assemblée Territoriale. Renewed agitation for local self-government followed, and for a break in the SLN monopoly. At one stage a force of French paratroops conveniently visited Nouméa.

The UC successes carried their own dangers, for the wide support rested on common opposition to external forces rather than on unification of communal goals. A series of breakaway movements in 1970–1 removed part of both European and Melanesian support, and left this still multi-racial party in a minority in the Assemblée, though still the largest party at the end of 1971. The new political environment is creating new alignments, and with self-government a seemingly unattainable goal, local divisive issues seem again to be coming to the fore.

Common issues are also present in Fiji, but they have long been overlain by communal issues. When fully-representative political institutions were created in the early 1960s, parties were formed which accurately reflected the balance of power. The Fijian leadership combined with members of the European community to form an Alliance Party; the Indo-Fijian leadership formed a Federation Party in opposition, and campaigned vigorously for a common roll. The Alliance Party carried its view at the 1965 constitutional conference, and thus inevitably formed the Government. A Federation walkout in 1968 was followed by new elections in the vacant seats, but as all Federation candidates were returned it at first seemed that a stalemate had resulted. However, an Indo-Fijian proposal for equal Fijian and Indo-Fijian representation, coupled with much reduced European representation, opened the way for a new compromise, the independence constitution, and perhaps a new and less communal phase in Fijian politics.

Underlying common issues were never lost from sight, even in the most overtly communal phase of Fiji politics from 1965 to 1969. The Federation Party sought wider support by campaigning in opposition to the colonial commercial system, thus exposing the weakness of the Alliance position, which was its dependence on European support. Some success was also achieved among Fijian commoners by pointing to the chiefly dominance of the Alliance Party. The Alliance, in its turn, sought to exploit differences among the Indo-Fijians, especially low-caste resentment against the Gujerati and high-caste leadership, and to argue that Indo-Fijians could prosper only by recognizing Fijian priority in land. Both sides gained support and membership among the opposite communal group. The Alliance leadership was unhappy at its dependence on colonialism: there have long been Fijians who resented the Europeans as much as the Indo-Fijians, and despite trends toward communalism, urban workers have demonstrated ability to act together in the pursuit of common goals. The Prime Minister himself supported Fijian moves toward economic nationalism from the time he assumed office, and in 1969 took the lead in this area by accelerating localization in the civil service, introducing moves to require licensing of the employment of foreigners, and speaking in much more strongly nationalist terms than hitherto. His cool reaction to the CSR withdrawal, noting that it would reduce Australian control of the Fiji economy, was in line with this trend of policy.

Fiji thus entered independence with the formation of a broad common goal between the two parties, and a most healthy Fijian determination to abandon the dependent syndrome. It will not be easy, and the contrasted economic condition of the two groups will inevitably make the Alliance a conservative party, while the Federation can more freely espouse socialist solutions. But on such a basis, the communal identification of the two parties could well be further eroded. Whether or not this will occur is another matter. A great deal will depend on the handling of the CSR withdrawal in 1973. The 1972 election returned the Alliance to power with a reduced majority.

It has often been said that the unwavering loyalty of most Fijians to the British flag represented a wish to be within a stable social system, whose institutions would defend them from 'external' dangers. Yet the British not only introduced the Indians, but also permitted Australian corporations to gain a dominant interest in the economy. Once it became clear that British protection would be withdrawn, a large number of Fijians seemed to lose their passivity in face of change, and one of the most remarkable aspects of the years 1969–70 in Fiji was the sudden and massive emergence of nationalism in the country. Independent Fiji inherits enormous problems, both economic and communal, which could easily rend the present harmony. But it is none the less true that the spirit in which independence has been taken is one that no observer foresaw, even a year before the event. There is a lesson here for our observation of other Melanesian territories in which there seems great reluctance to take independence. It is a lesson that Fijians themselves are teaching, as I saw myself in overhearing a conversation between two strongly-political friends, one Fijian and one New Guinean, in Port Moresby in 1970.

REFERENCES AND SOURCES

Though it is not overtly discussed, the treatment of pluralism in this chapter is underlain by a large volume of controversy among sociologists on the utility of Furnivall's (1939, 1945, 1948) 'plural society' model. It is often argued that pluralism is merely a form of stratification, and that the approach initiated by Parsons (1952) provides a more coherent and valid method for understanding society; it is, indeed, sometimes maintained that, far from being held together by colonial rule, the divisive plural society is in fact the creation of colonialism. A partial selection of the theoretical-empirical literature, which has minimal reference to the Pacific and draws mainly on the Caribbean, Africa and Mauritius, would include Benedict (1962), Rubin (1962), Smith (1965), Kuper and Smith (1969) and Plotnicov and Tuden (1970).

The face of pluralism in Melanesia

Specific discussions of pluralism in Melanesia are few, but include Mayer (1961, 1963), Wong (1963), Dewey (1964) and a paper on Vila by Glick in Plotnicov and Tuden (1970). *Inter alia*, however, there is much material of value in Spate (1959), Burns, Watson and Peacock (1960), Watters (1963), Doumenge (1966), Davidson (1966), Lasaqa (1972) and specifically on towns in Brookfield with Hart (1971).

CHAPTER 13

MELANESIAN REACTION

It can fairly be said that no expatriate observer is qualified to write on the subject of this chapter. Whatever insights we gain from observation, whatever we deduce from first principles, the result can only be partial. But the attempt must be made, for 'to see as through a glass, darkly' is better than remaining totally blind. And if I misinterpret, and offend, this is surely better than offending by simply ignoring.

The writer is a geographer, not an anthropologist or sociologist whose business it is to comprehend social interaction. Nor is he an island resident European, who 'understands the Native, and knows how to manage the Native for his own good'. He does not claim to be a candid friend, nor an essayist who can skilfully build up a picture of the Melanesian mind from the pitifully few literary productions of Melanesians themselves. He is simply a social scientist whose bread-and-butter has for a decade been provided by the Melanesians and the academic problems that their action and reaction present. The tactic adopted here, then, is to make certain assumptions about Melanesian behaviour, and to attempt an interpretation of economic and political activity in the light of these assumptions, and of the wider interpretation of colonialism presented in earlier chapters. But the interpretation is personal, and the style adopted in this chapter seeks to reflect this fact.

My assumption is that Melanesians are what we term 'boundedly rational' men, fully rational within the bounds of their perceived world, and in accordance with perceived needs and values. I also assume that they seek to order their environment in terms of comprehensible categories, so as to bring the system within which they operate into seemingly-managed order, reducing uncertainties and minimizing risk. I further assume that their aspirations may include power. To say all this is to say that they are like any other men, except that their 'world' has properties unique to themselves. It is a world compounded of an old pre-contact society being transformed in a manner that is hard to comprehend, by forces over which they find it difficult to obtain any sort of control. The transformation necessitates a great widening in the scale of 'world', and of the structures which compose it. It entails establishing relationships on terms quite different from those governing relationships within the old, local world, and thus also requires that people be classified in new ways. And it entails a struggle to find a viable place in this wider world, and an identity that has dignity. This is not easy, for the parallels most obviously available are the African and West Indian Negro, whose identity is often defined by bitterness:

> I am fuck-
> in' negro,
> man, hole
> in my head,
> brains in my belly...
>
> Edward Brathwaite, *Rights of Passage*

Most Melanesians do not have this bitterness, yet something very similar has flared up from time to time, and in their response to external attitudes the Melanesian reaction differs only in degree, and not in kind, from that of the West Indians. The difference in degree reflects differences in length and intensity of remembered colonial history; the similarity in kind reflects comparable reaction to comparable forces.

I begin this discussion by facing a major difficulty. Melanesia is the *locus classicus* of that most seemingly irrational of behavioural patterns, the so-called 'cargo cult' or millennarian movement, in which it is believed that the 'cargo' – the material wealth of the Europeans – can be obtained by some short-cut method. I propose to join the argument that these are wholly rational movements, within the concept of bounded rationality. This done, I then go on to discuss economic behaviour in a wider sense, and then political behaviour. But the 'cargo cults', which have both economic and political facets, are the right point of entry for an outsider into the system of Melanesian reactions.

THE 'CARGO CULTS'

The first cargo cults were observed in Melanesia during the nineteenth century, and until the most recent times such movements have emerged like a chronic skin complaint, now here, now there, all over the body of the region. They have attracted immense scientific interest, though much of this has entailed mere description, and writing has been loaded down by the idiosyncratic peculiarities of individual movements. But though there is now an enormous literature on the subject, it is still not wholly clear how 'cargo cults' are to be defined precisely.

There is really a set of attributes that is used to define 'cargo cults'. Not all are present in any given instance, and some attributes also characterize movements that are not cargo cults, but some are clearly diagnostic. There is always prophecy that great material benefits will flow to the followers of the movement, and this prophecy is almost always the dictum of some charismatic leader. Most movements involve rejection of European advice, and the adoption of some ritual or magic that will bring the cargo. Many have the additional feature that the cargo originates from ancestors or spirit people, and is designed for the indigenous population, but is being intercepted and put to use by the Europeans. Commonly it is believed that no physical work is needed to secure the cargo; given the prescribed ritual or other means, all good things will come and the people can live at ease.

The objective irrationality of many of these beliefs is the characteristic used by many to distinguish cults from other movements. Yet the beliefs differ only in degree from those characterizing such movements as the enthusiastic adoption and adaptation of European advice, such as that sometimes provided by agricultural extension officers. Often, too, eager reception of the doctrines of the Christian missions has a strong material motivation. Some movements have both leadership and prophecy, but there is no rejection of external advice and the doctrine is progress through work or business enterprise. I would agree with anthropologists such as Brown (1964), who has argued that to distinguish between 'cults' and movements such as these is to cripple the power of explanation. There is one single common characteristic of paramount importance: all these several types of movement are seeking a road to gain material wealth quickly, by means under the direct control of, and within the understanding of, the indigenous population.

There is one further problem. It would be wrong to suppose that movements always command the unanimous support of the populations involved, though a measure of consensus is usually obtained. Dissidents either remain neutral, or else leave the area. But some movements have been remarkably persistent even through generations, surviving repeated failures of prophecy or programme, and re-emerging in new forms.

It will be helpful to recount the history of two such deep-seated movements. Lawrence (1964) has traced the history of a search for the 'road bilong cargo' on the north coast of New Guinea which, in various forms, has persisted almost a century. Initially a lone European settled, and was regarded as a deity, as were later visitors of less benign intent. In a second phase German entrepreneurs seized land and labour. The idea then emerged that the Europeans were intercepting the cargo and that the deity who controlled and provided the material wealth was black, not white. Revolt was seen as the road to eliminate the interlopers, and there were disastrous risings in 1904 and 1912. Lutheran missionaries came, who taught a way of life leading to redemption of the sins of Ham – the ancestor of the New Guineans in this mythology – which might also lead to social and economic equality with the white man. But obedience to the missionaries yielded neither kind of equality, and in the 1930s people withdrew from the missions and set up independent churches. They hoped for a return of the cargo deity, with rifles to drive out the Europeans. The Japanese invasion in 1942 seemed to answer these hopes, and there was open collaboration. After 1945 came a new period of hope, as a leader with an epic war record, Yali, replaced the discredited pro-Japanese leader. The road now became that of cooperation with the Australians, whose promises Yali believed and whose country he had seen. A movement modelled on the colonial administrative system grew up around Yali, but disillusion led to a new emergence of cargo beliefs. Yali became convinced that he had been deceived by the Australians, and accepted the leadership. This led to his imprisonment, and other action to break up the movement. The new colonialism of the 1950s brought substantial economic growth, and cargo thinking receded, but remained below the surface, ready to re-emerge in face of a new disappointment.

Religious and secular objectives were overtly mingled in the Jon Frum movement on Tanna, in the New Hebrides. Tanna was deeply affected by sandalwood traders, labour recruiters, missionaries and early planters in the nineteenth century, and in 1939 had for years been dominated by a successful association between the British District Agency and the Presbyterian Mission. A numerous population, affluent in terms of basic needs, was grouped in coastal villages around the missions, who provided little education beyond catechism and were able to take disciplinary action against any 'bigheads' who challenged their authoritarian paternalism.

In 1940 it seemed to the missionaries that the Tannese revolted against the rule of Christ and turned to the Devil. A leader emerged, to whom the spirit of Jon Frum appeared, telling the islanders to turn away from the missions, cease to make hard-to-sell copra, and resume living in dispersed settlements in the bush, where they should work in the service of Jon Frum who would bring them the cargo. The Tannese did these things in large numbers, but in a few months failure of the initial prophecy enabled the mission to recapture some of its hold. New prophecies then foretold the coming of the Americans, which eventuated soon afterward; over 1,000 Tannese left the island to work for them. Jon Frum now established communication with his apostles through 'radio'; he himself became a confidant of Jesus, with a message of wealth and salvation for the Tannese. There was violence, quelled by use of troops, but the Tannese continued their withdrawn life in the interior, the fiery red crosses of Jon Frum in every hamlet.

The movement flared up anew in the 1950s. Attempts were made to declare Tannese independence, and an 'Army of the Tanna United States of America' marched across the island with wooden rifles. It died again, and in the late 1960s rested as not much more than a breakaway church. But Tannese have remained in the interior, have made little copra and migrate to work much below normative expectation. They gave only partial cooperation to the 1967 census, and the only recent enterprise that has gained their vigorous support has been the building of an airstrip. The Presbyterian mission has failed to regain influence, and the British and French administrations have finally set up secular schools, over twenty years after the initial outbreak.

Each of these movements has gone through several phases. There have been periods of total rejection of innovations, while at other times there has been both enthusiastic cooperation with some invading element, and modelling of a local organization on that of the invaders. This latter characteristic emerged most clearly in a number of movements following World War II, among which the Marching Rule movement in the Solomon Islands, modelled on military organization as seen in the army camps, is the best known. Other movements have taken the companies as model, and have either had the objective of replacing the island companies by indigenous organization, as in the Viti Company in Fiji, or of bringing 'company' organization to aid development in neglected areas: the Purari Kompani in Papua is the best known of these movements.

All these were recognized as acts of Melanesian initiative, and as such were at times encouraged but more often severely discouraged by the authorities. But numerous other instances in which Melanesian initiative has been a major factor have gone unrecognized, because it was presumed that the whole pace and direction of progress were 'under control'. I witnessed such a movement in the Chimbu District of Australian New Guinea after 1959. A local government council was formed, and there was great initial enthusiasm for this body as a vehicle for speedy attainment of wealth. The dominant and charismatic leader, Kondom, preached constantly the doctrine of hard work and high standards. Many traditional pleasures, such as courting parties, were banned; work was reorganized, and women formed parties to do men's work while the men laboured on the council site, on the enclosure of large new areas of land, and on roads. Dissidents slipped quietly away. At one meeting, a carpenter from near Lae, employed by the council, spoke imaginatively of the military organization of such bodies on the coast, where men were awakened early, stood by their beds for inspection, were imprisoned if they failed to work, and thought of nothing but progress toward wealth: his words were greeted with rapture. Threats were made: backsliders and dissidents were warned of the fate of coastal people who, it was alleged, had been mown down by police rifles for failure to collaborate. Poor results emerged in terms of wealth, and enthusiasm gradually faded, re-vivified from time to time by Kondom and other leaders. Kondom was killed accidentally in 1966, and in the same year the price of coffee, the main hope for success, tumbled. Many then left the District to seek employment in the growing towns, and by 1970 even a record price for coffee failed to restimulate enthusiasm: preparations were being made for a return to old ceremonial patterns, and the drive of a decade before was almost forgotten. There was never a 'cargo' prophecy, unless the promised gain from hard work was such a prophecy, but in 1965 one local leader, himself a notorious gambler, made this appeal to a visiting UN Mission during its brief stopover in the area:

> Children in civilized countries are educated. But look around. These children you see here are not in school...We have talked a great many times but it looks as though nothing will be done to improve education here...I want to be like you. But I have no power to take what you have. I am asking you to give me all that you have in your minds, so that I will become like you...You are masters of everything – money and mind. Give us what you have, to make our lives better (Field notes, translated).

Moments such as this offer insights to the field worker, and this one helped to convince me that the whole of Melanesian reaction to development is to be interpreted subjectively as the search for a rationale to explain the state of underdevelopment and dependency, and for means to command a road out of this condition. The search has been feverishly pursued, and many impatient experiments have been made, each rational within its cognized premises. Some have also appeared rational to outsiders, but ethnocentricism not only among officials but even among some anthropologists has placed blinkers on the perceptual processes of these observers. Each movement, cultist, Christian, rebellious or slavishly cooperative, 'rationally' economic or millenarian, needs to be viewed against the current state of perception of the whole system, internal and external, among the participants. We may not know this perception, but we have, in truth, rarely tried.

MELANESIAN ECONOMIC ACTIVITY AND MOTIVATION

Melanesian reactions to the economic system imposed on them, or offered them as a road to progress, have shown as much variation as have the characteristics of 'cargo cults'. We have the profligacy with which land has often been sold in the early phases of colonial contact, and the tenacity bordering at times on parish-pump obstinacy with which land is retained today. The supply of land has never shown much response to the theory of price. Though modern Melanesians are vociferous in complaint that they or their ancestors were cheated, even high prices often fail to induce new supply in modern times. Melanesians from many areas have recruited willingly as contract workers at low wages, but with experience and growing sophistication they have become far more responsive to variations in the reward of labour in modern times. Yet the labour market remains highly erratic; an increase in wages does not always produce an increase in supply, and even well-paid workers do not necessarily remain long on a job. The elasticity of supply in cash-crop production is also very variable and unpredictable.

There has been quite substantial evidence to suggest that Melanesians have regarded employment and cash-crop production as alternatives, so that a fall in cash-crop prices leads to some increase in labour supply. The evidence rests both on long-term trends during the inter-war period, and on short-term variations at the local level in recent years. I was once tempted to suggest that this relationship could be employed for prediction, in a paper on economic development up to the later 1960s in the Chimbu area of New Guinea. But the pattern of utilities is radically different in the two fields of activity compared, and cash returns are by no means the only important variable. Employment also offers a change of environment, which itself has utility. Cash-cropping offers the opportunity to participate in other local activities, social and ceremonial, which have their own periodicity governed by a range of internal factors. My prediction in Chimbu failed because of an increase in the utility of local social activities, following a delayed peaking in the local ceremonial cycle. In competition for inputs, the requirements of cash-cropping acquired a disutility which outweighed the utility of money gained by this means, so that despite a rise in returns in the later 1960s local cash-crop production did not increase.

Motivation is related to needs, but these are not measured only in material terms. There are also the needs of participation in local social activities, and the attraction of other and especially urban environments. Each has its own scale of utilities, varying between individuals and groups, and through time. Fisk, whose views we discussed in Chapter 1, is undoubtedly right in supposing that awareness of needs is the primary source of motivation for peasant economic development in Melanesian societies, but he disregards the different scales of needs, which are in competition for inputs. Melanesians find security in having their own 'world' to fall back on, but the existence of two worlds, the local and the external, greatly complicates the problem of choice, especially as the choices offered by participation in the external economy are both more enticing and also fraught with much greater risk and uncertainty. The expected utility of such participation may be high, often unwarrantedly high, but the subjective probability of success is low. Hence the search for comprehensible roads which will seem to increase this subjective probability, and transform it into seeming certainty.

The variable supply of land to the invading system provides an especially difficult problem, already touched on briefly in Chapter 3. We have to explain both the early profligacy and also the present tenacity. It is most commonly suggested that in the early contact phase Melanesians offering land to alienators had no conception of the permanence of the transfer, and believed that the trinkets, muskets, tobacco, porpoise teeth and small cash rewards they were offered were merely payment for a sort of temporary occupation licence, comprehensible within the bounds of a system based on face-to-face reciprocity. This has been disputed, and it has alternatively been suggested that the nature of the transaction was understood, for land transfers of a permanent kind are well within Melanesian experience, but that the goods offered in exchange were overvalued in the perception of the recipients. Modern Melanesians, who are often extremely bitter on this subject, normally tend to the latter view and hold that their ancestors were cheated, and that the recipients of the goods were motivated by short-term greed and lacked foresight. It has also been argued that Melanesians were seeking contact with the invading system in order to learn its secrets and obtain its wealth: the land sales were then made with an eye to future benefits which failed to accrue. In this interpretation there was no lack of foresight, but Melanesian perception of their ability to gain from contact was based on a very limited comprehension of the invading system, or on an inadequate realization of the range of contrasts between the new system and their own. In all these interpretations, the result has been disappointment and deprivation, and the present tenacity is seen as an over-reaction.

The present response is wholly rational, given the total system. It is the local complex that provides the base of Melanesian identity and personal security. This personal security is obtained through reciprocal aid, and the basis of personal standing within the system of reciprocal aid is membership of an identifiable, land-holding group. In the absence of any other viable base for identity and security under Melanesian control, land as held by traditional tenure within the local complexes provides this base. It is this social rôle of land that underlies the failure of land to become incorporated in the market-exchange economy, or to acquire realistic and comparative valuation. If land is retained because of its base function in society, it is not surprising that monetary compensation fails to produce a supply: only other land can be equivalent, but because there is also a spatial aspect to the network of interpersonal obligations, land at a distance is intrinsically of lower worth, attractive only if some other utility is much more highly rated than at home. Thus resettlement schemes have rarely drawn whole groups: individuals may move, retaining the option to return home if the expectations of the move are not realized, but whole groups have rarely shifted voluntarily, abandoning altogether their inherited land rights.

But if the present is rational, what of the past? We must presume that concepts of monetary value were far less developed than today, and also that there was only limited comprehension of the purposes for which land was required. Material goods were sought, and the means to acquire them, and it seems likely that the profligacy was motivated in part by immediate greed, in part by hope of future benefits, in part by uncertainty as to how to behave in response to external demands whose nature was understood only in part. These considerations do not apply in the case of forcible alienations, or cases in which deceit was employed, but such represent only a limited part of the whole, except in New Caledonia. The shift to tenacity emerged partly in response to a realization of error, but more as the perceived system came to be restructured in such a way as to restore and even enhance the rôle of land in providing security in face of external uncertainty.

Minimization of risk and the reduction of uncertainty in decision-making are fundamental Melanesian strategies in economic behaviour. They lead to the spread of inputs over a range of activities – not necessarily pursued simultaneously – that characterizes so much of Melanesian participation in the economy. Thus a peasant-farmer living within reach of an urban market might at different times or at the same time be a grower of an export cash-crop, or of more than one such crop, of produce for the local market, and of goods for his own subsistence and for gift to others to whom he is linked by reciprocal relationships. He might work occasionally as a stevedore, and for periods go away to town to live and seek employment. He might invest, with others perhaps, in the operation of a trade store, or a vehicle. He might assist in the enterprises of others, and in turn receive aid in his own activities. It seems a common principle that where choices are available, they are all availed, so that specialization is limited and rarely more than partial. Yet though he gains security, he is rarely satisfied. He may well be prepared to take on new risks, provided he has security to fall back on, and the risks that he takes may disregard the bad experiences of others. And, like the cargo cultists, when he loses, he is not necessarily deterred from trying again. A specific instance will illustrate:

Kawagl is a Chimbu subsistence farmer of moderate means, aged about 40. He is not a leader, and though he has adequate land he is not rich. He can read only simple words and cannot write. His farm – a scatter of dispersed holdings – includes a small but useful area of coffee, and he has participated actively in various coffee-processing enterprises on a cooperative basis for several years. With small savings, and assistance from fellow villagers, he set up a trade store in 1965 and – finding it badly located – he borrowed land adjacent to a main walking track in 1966 and re-located the store. In 1967 he obtained two ovens and began baking bread.

The history of his business can be reconstructed in part from the order slips covering purchases of stock, which he has retained. Buying goods from a number of retailers in the nearby town, but increasingly, as time went on, from one who offers especially favourable terms to local storekeepers, his business showed a turnover of \$302 in 1966, at purchase prices, rising to \$487 in 1967 and \$593 in 1968. At the end of 1968 he decided to embark on a new enterprise, that of purchasing coffee beans locally and selling them in bulk at the factory 10 km distant; for this purpose, again with some aid from fellow villagers, he bought an aged Landrover and hired a driver at a wage which is not recorded. Only a part of the costs of this vehicle can be reconstructed, but in May and June 1969 alone he paid \$131 in time payments, and \$100 on repairs. During this time his trade store business shrank almost to nil.

His operations as middleman took him into a larger scale of business. Buying and selling several hundred kilograms of coffee each month, he grossed from the factory sums ranging from \$199 in December 1968 to \$301 in July 1969. The price he paid for coffee from the local producers is unrecorded, but he was operating on a falling market and it is unlikely that he was adequately aware of this fact. In any event, the costs of operation were eating up his working capital, and when the aged Landrover required a new motor in September 1969 he was unable to meet the cost. The vehicle lies unrepaired behind the Council workshop, and his new business came to an end. Disgusted, Kawagl went away to work for a few months, and on return early in 1970 he resumed his trade store business, but not his breadmaking. In four months his turnover was \$162, and despite his setback – and a taste for beer which gave him a nasty hangover when last seen – he was again casting around in his mind for new areas of enterprise.

This man, and many like him, had ideas, but lacked the ability to judge which enterprises were beyond his range of knowledge and skill. To a man in this position, the security offered by a village economy and by a spread of his inputs are vital. He seeks roads of entry into the new system, and has been able to get aid from friends in order to do so, but both the scale needed for success in this new system and the know-how required to operate in it are beyond him. He feels, not without reason, that he was misled over the Landrover and the price of coffee, and indeed this enterprise channelled much of his savings into an expatriate pocket. He is not responsive so much to a 'market', which he cannot even understand, as to perceived opportunities for finding a road to wealth, but he is cautious enough to hedge his bets in the all-too-likely event of failure.

There are more successful men than Kawagl, even in Chimbu, and many more in other parts of Melanesia. But they stand as isolated individuals from a mass who lack their enterprise and acumen, and whose personal interest in participation in the external economy is limited to the satisfaction of modest needs. Such people, however, are always ready to support some entrepreneur who seeks a road to higher things, largely in the hope that such individuals will lead the masses out of underdevelopment and dependency. Whether in 'cargo cults' or in moves toward economic nationalism, promising leaders are assured of a ready following.

ECONOMIC PROTEST AND POLITICAL PROTEST

Protest movements are inevitable in a colonial situation such as we are describing. Many of the 'cargo cults' constitute such protest, in part, and incidents continually arise in which there is protest either against governments or, more commonly, against private agents of the invading system. It may be helpful here to recount another story:

The President of Kanaka Council in 1962 was Mr Kite [the names in this case are fictitious and owe something to J. Lennon and P. McCartney], who was also a member of the territorial Legislative Council. He had been told in Capital that Europeans who cheated the indigenes would be expelled from the country. Late in one meeting through which most of the Councillors had slept while the Government Officer had harangued them on a range of subjects, Mr Kite left the Chair to speak on his own motion. It concerned Mr Henderson, an Expatriate entrepreneur who employed Kanaka people to run his scattered trade stores; several of these Kanaka people had been prosecuted and gaoled for stealing from Mr Henderson. Mr Kite maintained that they had been framed, and further implied that the Judge had listened only to Mr Henderson's evidence, disregarding all evidence to the contrary. Mr Kite waxed eloquent, maintaining that Mr Henderson had abused the hospitality of the Kanaka people, was screwing them for all he could get, and should be returned to the place in which his mother bore him. He sought a vote from the Councillors which he could take back to Capital, and have Mr Henderson expelled. The Councillors, none of whom had slept during Mr Kite's oration, gave him this vote by acclamation. The only unhappy man present was the young Government Officer, who disregarded the Chair by hastily adjourning the meeting so as to return to Base and seek advice.

Three days of silence ensued from Base, during which Mr Kite visited parts of his constituency advising and exhorting on the condition (bad) of cash-crops. On the third day he was interestingly followed around by a Government Landrover, driven by the police, and this observer waited for the skies to fall. He expected the District Commissioner, Henry the Horse, to come in person, but instead a meeting was summoned for the fourth day, attended by an orator almost as skilled as Mr Kite – Pablo Fanques, the District Officer. In one of his finest performances, Mr Fanques went through the Court records to demonstrate the impartiality of the Judge. He was not concerned with Mr Henderson, he said, but only with the slur on the probity of the authorities.

Mr Kite stood up and acknowledged his error; when he sat down he was trembling violently. Councillor after Councillor then stood up in turn to admit that they too were wrong. And the vote was repealed.

There the matter might have rested, but two years and more later it was being said in Base, and even in Capital, that Mr Kite had turned hostile toward the authorities. Official support for him was notably weakened, and the Kanaka people – who had grown in stature with Mr Kite – suffered accordingly. His political demise was quickly followed by his death.

Mr Henderson remained some time longer in Kanaka District, but after a while moved his enterprises to nearby Bishopsgate, a more central and fast-developing location. Being a man of acumen and energy, he continues to do very well there.

The 'Mr Kite' of this story was in fact one of the most staunch supporters any colonial administration could wish to have, but he was a Melanesian none the less, and – in embryo – an economic nationalist. He was concerned, as are many Melanesians of greater education and experience than he, at the expatriate dominance of the economy, and he fastened on one man who had been particularly successful in his own area to voice his protest. Others, in other times and other places, have turned the edge of protest toward Burns Philp or CSR, Ballande and SLN. Colonial government, as in the affair of Mr Kite, has almost invariably reacted in support of expatriate enterprise.

Protest over labour conditions has been rather more rare. There were some stirrings of modern labour troubles in Fiji in 1920 and in New Guinea in 1929, but the first major labour troubles were in Fiji, mainly in Suva, in 1959. Since that date there has been a slowly rising tide of protest, but organization of viable unions has been tardy. Further, the position of Melanesian labour is so weak, since the local concerns are generally only branch-plants, and Melanesian unskilled workers are readily replaced, that effective strike action is hard to achieve. Much more widely useful is the silent protest of sullen, uncooperative workers, doing the minimum required of them, slowly, and unmindfully. This is a form of protest that unskilled Melanesian workers have developed so highly that many European employers have regarded it as the normal behaviour pattern of their workers. Yet it is protest: Melanesian workers are capable of a very different performance when they wish.

Perhaps the most persistent form of economic protest, however, is that over land. Melanesians fought desperately, perhaps without hope, in defence of their land in nineteenth century New Caledonia, and when French companies sought to develop alienated but hitherto unexploited land on Malekula, New Hebrides, in the 1920s they too met with resistance. Land was responsible for sporadic revolts in German New Guinea, and it was fear of further alienations and oppressions that led Fijians to accept British control in 1874, accompanied as this was by an assurance that Fijian lands would be preserved.

In the late 1960s two land issues came sharply to a head in Melanesia. In the Gazelle Peninsula of northern New Britain, the Tolai people lost much land in German times, and title to individual areas has been challenged more than once. In 1969 a cross-Tolai group called the Mataungan Association was formed to protest against the continued alienation of undeveloped land, and to demand that the tenure of such land be restored to Tolai holders, under their control and allocation. A crisis arose on a land settlement scheme, in which Government proposed to allocate land: the Mataungan Association disputed the Government's right to do so, and put squatters on the land. A force of almost a thousand police was assembled at Rabaul to oust the Mataungan supporters, but they were skilfully led, and a compromise was finally reached on this issue. Mataungan continues active protest, however, and passive resistance to Government demands.

A precisely parallel protest movement has evolved in the New Hebrides since 1967, the only significant difference being in the quality of leadership. There has been a succession of 'cargo cults' and related movements in the Santo area, the latest in 1965–6 being against the companies. Then in 1967 a movement began among Santo bush people who squatted on undeveloped alienated land belonging to the Société Française des Nouvelles-Hébrides or to the French State. This movement gathered adherents from all over the group until it claimed several thousand members, of whom some two thousand were living in the squatter settlement at Vanáfo, in the middle of the disputed land north of Luganville town. The organization, called Na Griamel, posted notices on all the properties it claimed, and sought means to develop some of the land concerned. Until 1969, Government managed officially to ignore it, but it then became necessary to issue 'solemn warnings'. But with only French land affected, and the British unwilling to become involved, it was difficult to put many teeth into the 'solemn warnings': by 1971 it was no longer certain that the tiny police forces of the Condominium, limited in size by Protocol, could control the movement even if the two Governments should jointly so decide. Given a leadership equivalent in quality to that of the Mataungan Association, Na Griamel might quickly become a nationalist force of formidable proportions.

Land, more than anything else, is the plane of conjunction between economics and politics in contemporary Melanesia. It is at the root of the Fijian/Indo-Fijian problem in Fiji and is the weak point in the European-Melanesian coalition that forms the Union Calédonienne. It is the main political issue in the New Hebrides, where the conflict is sharpened by the modern prosperity of an extensive form of commercial land use – cattle raising – that is at last to utilize some of the huge alienated tracts. It is a focus of dissension in the most politically active areas of Australian New Guinea, around Rabaul and on Bougainville. It is the main problem between Government, private enterprise and the Melanesians on the plains of Guadalcanal, Solomon Islands. Control over land implies control of the means of production, and hence access to wealth. To Melanesians still interested, as ever, in material equality with the Europeans, and increasingly aware of their subordinate rôle in the territorial economies, the alienated land is becoming a primary focus of protest.

UNWILLINGLY TO INDEPENDENCE?

The sort of 'normal' anti-colonial behaviour outlined in the previous section has been accompanied by a very abnormal, but very widely stated, preference to continue for some time more under colonial rule, rather than seek independence. In certain instances the objective has been overtly self-protective: the Fijians preferred to rely on British support than to deal with the Indo-Fijian problem themselves; the West New Guineans showed a massive preference for continuation of Dutch rule in 1962 rather than face absorption by Indonesia; New Hebrideans tend sometimes to value the protection which the British presence supposedly gives against the spreading control by New Caledonian interests. These are essentially tactical moves, yet underlying them is a widespread reluctance to dispense with the order and security provided by political colonialism in a region which was quite uniquely politically incoherent and insecure within an almost-remembered past. Of the Fijians, it has been suggested that loyalty toward Britain has satisfied a need to belong to a coherent social system in which traditionalism had great force. The underlying motive of pro-colonialism has probably been similar in New Guinea: the risks and uncertainties of independence are so great, in contrast with the security of colonial rule, that until very recently hardly a political leader could be found to stand for early independence.

A more materialist interpretation is also possible, and there is evidence to give it credence. Though it may seem to smack of the 'brains in my belly' syndrome bitterly lampooned by Brathwaite in the lines cited earlier, it is a view by no means limited to Melanesia. In Québec, for example, both Federal and Provincial Governments seem to believe that provision of funds, work and welfare will damp down separatist agitation and even eliminate it; Robert Browning seems earlier to have had the same idea:

> Irks care the crop-full bird? Frets doubt the maw-crammed beast?

The doctrine has been most specifically enunciated by the Indonesians. Faced with a series of minor outbreaks of resistance, and one major rising in the Vogelkop which endured from 1965 to 1969 despite unrestricted military measures of suppression, the Indonesians diagnosed the trouble as a reaction to the deteriorating economic condition of the country following the handover. They described the movements as 'stomach politics', the result of currency inflation and shortage of goods. They thus sought to remedy the situation first by a 'crash programme' in 1966, then by seeking United Nations aid in 1967–8, after the crash programme had failed to get off the ground.

I was once prepared to put more weight on 'stomach politics' than I am today. It is indicative of the changing situation in Melanesia, and the new dimensions that have become emergent, to quote without change what I wrote in an earlier draft of this material, written in the early months of 1968:

> Whether or not 'stomach politics' have been the driving force of opposition in West New Guinea, there seems little doubt that they were a major force in producing political apathy in a large part of East [Australian] New Guinea after 1964. Early hopes for the development of political cleavages at the national level in the new House of Assembly...proved illusory, and shortly before the rising of this House at the end of 1967, Meller commented:
>
> > Government in Papua-New Guinea has been 'executive' government, and dependence on the *Kiap* (district administrative officer) has now merely been transferred to the legislative scene. The indigenous Member comes to Port Moresby '*to tell the Kiap*', and then he returns home to tell his people what the government said...the processes of government remain alien or incomprehensible to the indigenous member. The Administration has failed to involve him as an integral part of the governmental structure of the country (Meller, 1968, 13).
>
> While this situation might undergo change following the appointment of 'ministerial members' in the new House of 1968, and politics may become more active through the success of the Papua-New Guinea Union Party (*Pangu Pati*) in establishing itself as a mainly indigenous party of opposition, with a programme of limited home rule, the real disease is perhaps more fundamental and more revealing. A vacuity in Australian policy toward the country that persisted for several years was balanced by a seeming dependency complex in East New Guinea that was iterated in some form almost daily. Australia will allow East New Guinea to move, at its own speed, to the destiny of its choice: East New Guinea is grateful for the guidance and the 'vast expenditure' of the Australian people, and does not wish this withdrawn. It is a little like the counterposed sections of a Greek chorus, and seems to have little to do with the often bitter complaints of the urban Papuans, or the more sullen hostility of rural people in many parts of the country.
>
> There is a key: the 'vast expenditure'. Australia is at last sending the cargo, at a rate of some $50 per head per annum...the mass of East New Guinea Melanesians have moved into a position of 'guided cooperation', and were willing to go through whatever ritual might be necessary to sustain the supply...The development of political factions that might rock so well-laden a boat was stifled, and political foes were seen as those external anti-colonialists and internal grumblers who might cut East New Guinea off from the mother that gave so much milk.

Such a view rests too much on the verbal utterances of Melanesian politicians who were speaking as much to an Australian audience as to their own people, though it certainly contains a measure of truth. Melanesians must face the obvious fact that budgetary subsidies and direct grants will not continue at present levels beyond independence, though the cut-off may not be so complete as some Australian and other politicians have led them to believe. Such considerations must be balanced against the 'self-respect' of independence, and it follows from the emphasis on acquisition of 'cargo' throughout Melanesian colonial history that the supply of free cargo will be a weighty consideration.

But this is only a part of the total sense of weakness and uncertainty. It is not so much finance and cargo as a sense of incompetence to cope with independence that underlies the reluctance and the seeming inferiority complex that disturbs so many observers, such as the leader of a visiting United Nations mission with whom I once discussed this issue – in French – to the distress of the watchful Australian official observers. Perhaps an insight may once again be obtained from my late friend Kondom, the illiterate Chimbu leader who addressed the same mission in these terms:

> I am very happy with the Australian Government and with all the laws they brought to New Guinea...I have heard on the radio of the good things you plan for New Guinea. Just one thing you have said makes me unhappy. I have heard you want to give us self-government. I ask you not to give it. *When I feel strong enough I will ask for it*, but I do not want you to force it on me...Before we can have self-government we need six things: pilots and aircraft factories; an arms factory; an ammunition factory; a mint to make our own money; factories to make glass and iron for houses; meat and clothing factories. All the work in these must be done by Papuans and New Guineans. When my people make these things I will know I am ready for self-government (field notes, translated [my italics]).

The list may seem strange, but it is eminently practical. The means to produce needs and maintain power and internal communication must be in indigenous hands and within their total competence. Economic nationalism is more important than political nationalism. Independence without power is of no value. *Mutatis mutandis*, the same might be said by economic nationalists concerned at the penetration of Canada, France or Australia by mainly American multinational corporations. The highly-educated and forceful Prime Minister of Fiji was voicing parallel sentiments in his comment on foreign control of Suva, cited in Chapter 11. But where Kondom erred was in his belief that these things could come under the sort of colonial rule to which Melanesia has been subjected. The counter-argument that political power provides a state with greater ability to secure economic power, notwithstanding the loss of external grants, is one that has gained force and adherents since 1965.

The sudden emergence of a spirit of self-reliance in Fiji, once independence became inevitable, has been noted in Chapter 12, and we have also noted the strong overtones of economic nationalism that have simultaneously arisen. A Fijian Development Corporation, and other bodies designed to develop a commercial system controlled by the Fijian people and parallel to the companies and the Indo-Fijian organizations, have arisen during this same period. In Australian New Guinea the visits of some Melanesian politicians to African countries have led them to argue for independence sooner rather than later, and such statements have not been promptly disavowed by their followers, as others were two or three years ago. Even in the interior, where a more favourable colonial experience coupled with fear of the more advanced coastal people have led to solidly pro-colonial views among a large majority, recent observers have noted a change. The idea of working with Europeans in 'partnership' – a doctrine adopted from the ill-fated Federation of Rhodesia and Nyasaland in its short-lived heyday – is reported to be dying:

> Although the Gorokans, probably because they realize that they have received considerable benefits from their short association with Europeans, are certainly not the most radical of New Guineans, their views on specific local issues are not unlike those of [Melanesian and European critics]...who attack Australian economic planning for favouring European private enterprise and for failing to provide concrete ways and means for New Guineans to increase their share in the country's developing economy. By no means are the Gorokans unwilling to work with Europeans – only now they want to be equal, if not senior, partners in new enterprises (Finney, 1970, 134).

This sort of hostility toward the present economic arrangements, the inequality of which is increasing as large corporations become more and more dominant in the colonial commercial system, is widespread, and it would seem to follow logically from the analysis of Melanesian reaction presented in this chapter. This analysis has argued that perception of economic inequality has underlain a very major part of Melanesian reaction, and that the reaction to this perceived condition has varied through time and between places according to the total perception of the system and of the scope for Melanesian action within it. Also constantly present, in this interpretation, has been the sustained objective of finding a road to lessen the inequality, within Melanesian capabilities and under Melanesian control. The 'cargo cults' reflect a very limited level of accuracy in total perception, leading to attempts to seek a road from within pre-colonial patterns of belief and behaviour. Revolt has entailed a trial of strength, with poor results. Active participation in European-guided enterprises has been motivated in just the same way as the 'cargo cults', reflecting a hope of learning and a measure of somewhat doubting trust. More sophisticated protest, by squatting on vacant alienated land, and employing dispersed forms of organization of a type easy for Melanesians to achieve but hard for Europeans to combat, has provided a promising road in recent years, and there is evidence that the long-lasting Vogelkop revolt in West Irian has employed techniques of guerilla warfare and surprise attack borrowed from elsewhere, though not developed sufficiently to obtain success. Most recently, political independence is being seen as a means of gaining the same economic result, following growing disillusion with the hope that the large 'cargo' inputs under late colonialism would bring the means of securing the desired road to self-controlled progress.

If this analysis were based on sound premises and logic, it would follow that economic nationalism would be a dominant element in Melanesian political nationalism. This is not to say that Melanesian economic nationalism has yet attained much sophistication, but it provides a series of vaguely-defined goals and a probable pattern of responses to be expected in the future, as experience widens: it is not improbable that the literature on post-colonial issues which Melanesians will find most stimulating will include such works as those of Nkrumah (1965), Dumont (1966) and Frank (1967), all of which strongly criticize development through externally-controlled capitalism, and maintain that underdevelopment is a creation of capitalism. There is a real sense in which such a theory of Melanesians' condition of underdevelopment and dependency would be entirely in line with the more primitively-based theories underlying the 'cargo cults'. To say this is not to say that Melanesian economic nationalism will succeed through such realization, but merely that future economic colonialism will encounter a more coordinated and less readily manipulable response.

Melanesian political apathy seems now to be a dying phenomenon. It was never a characteristic of those areas with strongly developed ethnic pluralism, but in the remainder of Melanesia it can now be viewed as symptomatic of a period of uncertainty in the face of a new and financially generous colonial policy leading to decolonization, coincident with a policy of economic colonialism pursued by private interests, enjoying Government support, with greater vigour than at any previous time. Melanesians were uncertain of how to deal with this, and despite much European aid – which was often suspect – in the formation of political parties, such parties did not emerge for want of internally divisive issues of social policy. On economic policy, which is of prime concern to Melanesians, there has been little difference on basic goals, and though differences over tactics have emerged, they have not taken a form readily amenable to organization on party lines. It seems more likely in the near future that a consensus over basic objectives in relation to the external system will provide the integrative force in the politics of independent Melanesia, while regional or ethnic interests will constitute the bases for division. Such is not an uncommon condition in newly emergent countries, and it is a supposition that is of help in attempting to predict the future.

REFERENCES AND SOURCES

The problem of interpreting 'cargo cults' has a major place in the anthropological literature of Melanesia, and there is a very large body of material both describing and analysing particular movements, and attempting to generalize over the whole range of phenomena. The best single account of a movement is perhaps that of Lawrence (1964) on the Rai coast cults, described briefly in this chapter. The Marching Rule movement in the Solomon Islands was described from close at hand by Allan (1951) and also discussed by Belshaw (1947). The Tannese movement is described especially by Guiart (1952, 1956). Other well-known discussions of particular movements of different types include Maher (1958, 1961), Burridge (1960) and Schwartz (1962), all in the New Guinea area. Major contributions to the wider discussion include Stanner (1953), Worsley (1957), Guiart and Worsley (1958), Jarvie (1963, 1964), Brown (1966) and Cochrane (1970), but this is only a small selection from a very large and complex literature. The dispute over interpretation is by no means resolved, and the view presented here would not necessarily command wide acceptance.

On the question of land the literature is much more diffuse. France (1969) presents one of the more important efforts at interpretation through time: close field studies of the rôle of land in society include Brookfield and Brown (1963) and A. L. Epstein (1969), whose work colours the interpretation presented here. The subject is also discussed in the final chapter of Brookfield with Hart (1971).

On politics, most of the sources have been referred to above, but reference should be made particularly to Bettison, Hughes and Van der Veur (1965) and to Waigani Seminars (1970b). Press reports, however, represent the major single body of sources.

CHAPTER 14

A VIEW OF THE THIRD WORLD

The purpose of these final chapters is to carry the analysis forward beyond the present. Prophecy is not my intention, for such an exercise would be demonstrably absurd even before these lines are published, but looking forward is none the less possible by analogy. We have argued that the colonial processes affecting these islands have paralleled processes incident in other colonial areas; using the assumption of equifinality in systems subject to similar forces, we may presume that parallels will continue to be evident. The argument of the preceding chapter is crucial here: that notwithstanding seeming passivity, the Melanesians have been as keen as any people on achieving self-determination – control of their own destiny.

By 1972 the global diffusion of black nationalism had advanced in Melanesia from a primary stage of initial acceptance to the dynamic stage of adoption and rapid dissemination. Throughout the region, even in the 'quiet' New Hebrides, a new sort of voice is heard, anti-colonialist in sentiment, and with signs of that indiscriminate hostility toward whites that characterizes black nationalism in other parts of the world. Though not yet with the force encountered in Africa and the Caribbean, there can be no doubt that the emerging peoples of Melanesia are coming to feel themselves part of the 'Third World'.

A sense of assimilation with Third World countries will introduce a major new force. Hitherto, since the beginning of colonialism, Melanesian perception of the world-wide environment has been refracted through the metropolitan colonial powers. Now this vision is likely to take on wholly new perspectives, and the search for managed order will reach out for new models. In this chapter, we therefore attempt to preview this new vision by calling on some wider Third World comparisons – especially in the Caribbean region, with which I have some recent familiarity. In the final chapter we then turn back to the problems and prospects of Melanesia itself, with benefit of this wider view.

THE ECONOMIC DIMENSION

Melanesia has approached independence saturated in the belief that progress and prosperity demand the continued admission of foreign enterprise, direct investment and aid not only without hindrance, but with every possible encouragement. Paradoxically, this view has not prevailed at the local level where there has often been very strong resistance to external enterprise and demands, but it has dominated thinking at the national level, both in colonial administration and in national politics. Territorial legislatures have passed carefully phrased resolutions assuring investors of a continued welcome, and disclaiming any wish either to nationalize enterprises or to restrict repatriation of capital and profits. The growing doubts of other Third World countries have been slow to penetrate these islands, and little but an accident has been responsible for awareness of a contrary view. The abrupt decision by Colonial Sugar to withdraw from Fiji, taken on the very eve of independence, has forced on Melanesians the question of their own ability to make do without foreign enterprise.

Whatever arrangements are made in Fiji, we must presume that this question will be asked about wider and wider fields of enterprise presently dominated by foreign concerns. It will be asked about timber companies that are mining Melanesian forests without replacement, of mining companies that expect to recoup enormous investments within three to five years, and of hoteliers who similarly plan to recover their capital in a like time. It will be asked of foreign-owned airlines and shipping companies, of the plantation and trading companies, of the branch-plant manufacturing concerns, and of the whole colonial economic system. And there will be a search for models elsewhere in the Third World.

In many countries new principles are being adopted in negotiations, either with new companies or with existing companies. A majority of new moves seek a local stake in the equity of the companies. Commonly, a majority share, minimally 51 per cent, is sought, offering continued participation to the foreign enterprise on terms that many of them have found reluctantly acceptable. Within Melanesia, indeed, France has already forced such a majority-control principle on the non-French partners in new nickel-mining enterprises in New Caledonia, albeit for the benefit of the metropole rather than the colony. Collectively, a number of Latin American countries have adopted new guidelines for their dealings with foreign enterprise, seeking to exclude outsiders altogether from defined fields of activity – mainly in the public utility area – and laying down conditions for progressive increase in the share of local equity.

Such moves are prompted by various motives. Though a nationalistic will may be uppermost, almost equally important is resentment of the high profit levels demanded by most foreign entrepreneurs – commonly twice the profit levels required to justify investment at home. It is believed that in such circumstances a local equity purchased generally on loan can be paid out of profits, shared between the foreign enterprise and the home government. The high profits obtained and repatriated are a source of grievous resentment. Though many companies nowadays seek to mollify their hosts by conducting local training schemes, employing as few expatriates as possible, offering aid to local enterprise and providing infrastructure, their very ability to do these things sometimes merely confirms the belief that the foreign enterprises can afford to admit local equity.

The problem of negotiation is, however, complicated for the new nations by their poor competitive position vis-à-vis the multinational corporations with which they deal. In their eagerness to gain capital investment and employment, countries with small, open economies are apt to compete against each other in offering advantageous terms to investors and buyers of primary produce, to their serious aggregate disadvantage: the external system is far more closely integrated. Realization of this weakness has prompted international cooperation, such as recently evidenced in Latin America, and most effectively over a long period now by the Organization of Petroleum Exporting Countries, who have, by collective bargaining, been able to achieve a most notable improvement in terms. International cooperation between producing countries is possible over a much wider range of fields, and it is surprising that it has not been more followed.

Such methods as these constitute a gradualist approach toward economic self-determination, cautious and pragmatic in method, probing for weaknesses in the external economic system that can be exploited by negotiation of confrontation. They seek change in favour of the developing countries, but the objective is limited to creation of a mixed economy in which there is a larger measure of local control, but which does not really change the metropole-periphery relationship. Nor is progress easy, for the external economic system has many ways in which to react. The integrative power of the expanding multinational corporations makes the achievement of bargaining strength easier for the external system than for the fragmented countries of the Third World. There are many devices to manipulate the local systems, through what is sometimes called the 'third culture' – the body of local entrepreneurs, officials and politicians who are able and willing to collaborate with the companies to their own benefit, and whose ties with their own national culture are thereby weakened. In an illuminating recent discussion on the operation of international business management, Fayerweather (1969, 96) disarmingly suggests that:

> There would seem...to be at least some hope that localized third-culture groups or an international subculture composed of international businessmen and the government officials who work with them around the globe may achieve such a sense of unity and dissociation from internal nationalism. The prospects along this line are intriguing...A key question...will be the extent to which a true community of interests exists, drawing managers of the multinational firm and officials of the host nation together.

It is perhaps not surprising that activists are emerging throughout the Third World who demand more radical solutions. A minority may even be prepared to pay the whole price. Thus in American Micronesia in 1970 were to be found advocates of independence, rather than self-government, who argued that if total separation meant the loss of the large financial and other support enjoyed, they would still prefer to go it alone. Debate between protagonists of collaboration and of wholly new economic arrangements grows more and more acrimonious. Not wholly accurately, the gradualist view is identified with capitalism and the radical with socialism in many parts of the world – though not, perhaps, in Eastern Europe. It might be more correct to say that different orders and concepts of nationalism are involved.

RADICAL ECONOMIC SOLUTIONS

The earliest and most often availed of radical solutions has been the sequestration of enterprises, nationalization either without compensation or with very small compensation. We discussed this possibility briefly in Chapter 11, and it is at first sight surprising that so seemingly simple a device, requiring no more than the stroke of a presidential pen, is not more widely adopted. But experiences with nationalization have been very variable. Only partly because they were done in such a way as to dismember integrated structures, the Indonesian nationalizations between 1957 and 1965 were an economic disaster, and had ultimately to be partially reversed, while policy was changed after 1965 to readmit foreign enterprise in mining on favourable terms. Simple sequestration invites economic reprisals, including rupture of marketing channels, boycotts by the well-integrated buyers, and refusals to supply equipment. Grave hardship has sometimes resulted, so most countries resolving on the assumption of total control adopt the milder device of nationalization with compensation for assets. But the benefits of such action can be quite limited. A nation seeking to nationalize a large company, with compensation for the sequestered property, will normally decide to pay the compensation out of profits, which are thereby sharply reduced. New costs are added, since the former company had its own channels of supply and marketing, often within its organization, and these must be contracted anew.

Then while the foreign company was a fair target for wage demands, Government must now face its organized labour as an employer, and in addition recruit, train, or divert from other areas of need the specialized personnel that the company formerly provided. There may still be benefit, but there will be cases in which the benefit is very small indeed. Under such conditions, it may be safer to seek a larger share in the equity than to nationalize.

The arguments in favour of nationalization may thus rest more on national self-respect than on simple economic considerations. The experience of Guyana with a Canadian-owned bauxite company may be cited. The company has alternative sources of supply, and it would seem that the Guyanese mine was no longer its most profitable subsidiary. Government attempted to negotiate a more favourable equity-sharing arrangement, but company conditions were unacceptable and finally a decision was taken to nationalize, with compensation. A steep increase in costs must be expected; new marketing and supply channels must be negotiated, and new specialized personnel recruited. But the Guyanese Government felt that more than money was at stake. Thus the Prime Minister, in announcing the decision to nationalize:

> We have seen in Guyana and other underdeveloped countries foreign owned extractive industries prosper while the native population remained poor and destitute. We must now get the larger share of the cake, otherwise what is the difference between Guyana and a colony? What shall we tell our children when they ask us to explain the gaping holes in the earth whence rich minerals have been won? (*Guyana Graphic*, 25 February 1971).

Fundamentally, what was at issue here was legitimate national self-respect, in conflict with a company which did not feel it worth-while to make sufficient concessions, or to meet Guyanese demands for a change in production methods which would permit greater processing before export. Guyana's case is intermediate between that of countries which opt for safety and continued investment inflow, and others where a truly revolutionary doctrine has been adopted. Nationalization may then be essential to the restructuring of the whole of society and economy, and short-term cost must be disregarded in the wider interests of such policies. Here Cuba is the outstanding example, having been to all intents and purposes a colony in the economic sense before the 1959 revolution, with a population and an economy that makes it especially appropriate as a model for the mainly small, open economies of ex-colonial countries. The Cuban problem replicated the situation of many such countries, though it was particularly severe, as Furtado (1964, 4) remarked in words written before the triumph of Castro's revolution at the end of 1958:

> Let us take Cuba as an example. Few economies have developed faster than Cuba's, thanks to her growing integration into international trade. However, few are today

facing greater difficulties in emerging from stagnation due to the nature of the relationships of external exchange. Thus foreign trade appears as both a stimulating and restrictive factor in relation to development.

The policies of the new government were certainly naive, but had a directness that clearly displayed their purpose:

The logic of most of the policies was natural and simple – to reverse what imperialism had been doing. Imperialism meant a Cuba of large plantations and idle land and labor; the thing to do was make a land reform and put the idle land and labor to work. Imperialism meant a one-crop Cuba; therefore diversify. Imperialism monopolized Cuba's foreign trade; Cuba must trade with all countries. Imperialism kept Cuba from more than token industrialization; Cuba must industrialize rapidly. Imperialism had made Cuba into an economic vassal of the United States; Cuba must try to create an independent economy (Boorstein, 1968, 182).

Mutatis mutandis, these are no more than the yearnings of all popular radical movements in Third World countries. But Cuba's early experiences have not encouraged widespread adoption of the model. Diversification failed; huge balance of payments problems appeared accompanied by a sharp fall in GNP – though perhaps not in living standards at the peasant and proletarian levels; industralization encountered grave limitations of resources and infrastructure; worst of all, Cuba's 'liberation' from United States domination has seemed to lead to no more than a change of master, the Soviet Union assuming the rôle of principal market and principal supplier of capital and technical skill. The goal of an independent polity and economy was not quickly achieved. Cuba soon turned back from diversification in agriculture to a renewed and even enhanced emphasis on sugar cane. In consequence, demands that the new east European trade partners reduce their own beet-sugar expansion programmes in Cuba's interest seemed simply to echo the pleas of Commonwealth producers of cane sugar and dairy products in the face of Britain's application to join the west European Common Market. Despite the substantial development of nickel mining, again for the east European market, a decade of revolution has not yet demonstrated conclusively that this radical, socialist model for liberation from a colonial condition is superior to pragmatic probing and opportunism within the international capitalist system.

Yet the Cuban experiment remains in being, and has preserved the power of independent economic decision to a surprising degree. The return to sugar in 1963 obscured a parallel emphasis on cattle, to replace imports of meat and lard and hopefully develop a new export capable of commanding a less restricted market. Scientific research on the integration of sugar with cattle production, increasing potential yields from resource manipulation (Preston and Willis, 1970), has already commanded interest among other countries with similar environment and economy, and it remains to be seen whether greater diversification, and greater economic independence, will result from such development, from the growth of mining, and other efforts to widen the economic base: a stage may have been reached in 1971 at which steps to diminish the dependence on export growth are becoming possible. Meanwhile, the transformation of social and economic structure retains a wide, though often discreetly quiet, audience. The emergent rôle of Cuba as a nation-scale experimental station in methods of decolonization is now more widely appreciated, and the recent formation of new radical, reformist governments in other Latin American countries both reflects this appreciation and widens the potential range of models for observation. The wishes of some Western governments notwithstanding, the Third World has not written off the Cuban model as uninteresting, and any demonstrable measure of success in the 1970s is likely greatly to encourage those who wish to adopt and adapt it to their own situations.

Though certain of its excesses have discouraged observers, the Chinese model has also proved to be of growing interest, especially in Asia. The evident success of massive reconstruction in creating the basis for industrial advance has been widely noted, and even conservative Indian observers have been constrained to compare the relative stagnation of their own country during the same period. The sheer size of China makes the model of rather limited utility to the smaller ex-colonial countries, but the methods adopted are by no means as repugnant to people with no real experience of true self-determination as they are to the people of democratic nations among the advanced countries.

One aspect of the socialist experiments is perhaps of surpassing interest. Deliberate efforts have been made to constrain or crush them by cutting off trade in essential areas, in the hope of causing economic breakdown. For reasons of world politics, especially significant in Cuba, such sanctions have never achieved completeness, any more than comparable sanctions against white-dominated states of very different polity in southern Africa. But they have had much the same effect. Forced to organize production and consumption internally to a great degree, and to develop as less-than-open economies, the affected countries have found it possible to do so. Moreover, they have found the spur to innovation and invention a positive benefit in achievement of long-range plans. Though the short-term hardships have sometimes been severe, they have tended to facilitate progress toward the creation of balanced, independent economies.

THE POLITICAL DIMENSION: THE POST-COLONIAL REVOLUTION

With comparatively few exceptions, the metropolitan authorities withdrawing from direct rule have been able to hand over power to men who have either opposed them, or cooperated with them, from within the former colonial system, and who have some degree of commitment to the maintenance of existing institutional structures. Most are Western-educated, and comparatively affluent. Such élites might even have a deeper vested interest in the *status quo* of society than the colonial administrators they replace; the latter had always their own remote society into which to withdraw.

Many and hard things are now being said about such 'national heroes' of an independence day only a few short years ago. It is alleged that such restructuring as has taken place has been mainly to the benefit of the élites, and that the leaders have deliberately diverted dissatisfaction by exploiting pluralistic or regional divisions within the new countries, or supposed conflict of interests with neighbouring states. Large expenditures under such welfare heads as primary education are interpreted as a sop to the masses, obscuring the continued cornering of power and privilege by the élites. The continued dependence on foreign aid and investment that has followed the deficit budgeting needed to finance welfare programmes is sometimes interpreted as use of foreign support to bolster the position of these already in power. These things are being said of the first-generation post-colonial leadership in countries as far apart as Nigeria, Pakistan, Ceylon and the West Indies. Such views are in no way dimmed by the deposition of truly revolutionary leaders such as Sukarno and Nkrumah, whose excesses led to a reaction in favour of more conservative men. Only some able pragmatists who have shown ability to trim their sails according to changing winds have been able to retain the veneration and support of the newly independent populations.

The post-colonial generation has already little real recollection of colonial rule in many countries. They have an image of colonialism, and the society which they see – with its privilege, foreign investment, dualism and pluralism – seems to them unpleasantly like this image. Though many embrace doctrinaire socialism, it would be more accurate of most to describe them as 'Levellers', in the precise sense of the English Levellers of the late 1640s, who felt that their revolution had failed to achieve a society fundamentally different from that which it overthrew, and that their leaders had betrayed the revolution. Again like the English Levellers, they remain ambiguous toward the men who led them in extirpating the old rulers, still venerating them for their record, but attacking them for preferring entrenched stability and parting company with the yearnings of the rank and file. Their search is for equality, and for achievement of the rights and dignity of man, of which they continue to feel deprived.

New directions in economic thinking are inextricably embedded in these political and social dissatisfactions. Opposition is directed not only at foreign investors, residents and sometimes visitors, but also at local élites who are said to 'think white'. Such terms as *peau noir–masque blanc* in the French West Indies, *Afro-Saxons* in the Commonwealth Caribbean, are used to describe these latter, and some opposition groups have adopted the name and basic ideology of the *black power* movement of the United States, different though local conditions may be from those which generated this movement. Yet the aim is perhaps better described as the achievement of meaningful indigenous self-determination, revealed sometimes in such seeming absurdities as a Trinidadian remark that 'Fidel Castro is the blackest man in the the Caribbean'.

Nationalism and class conflict are the hallmarks of the post-colonial revolution. Xenophobia toward foreigners and bitterness toward those who have 'betrayed the revolution' characterize the new wave; yet there is also utopianism, lacking – as so many utopian movements have done – any agreed body of doctrine or any integrated organization. The appeal to nation and especially to class represents a totally new element in the politics of these countries, where sectional interests – be they of pluralist groupings or of restricted common interest groups such as labour unions – characterized the politics of the late colonial era. Class conflict has also a cross-national appeal, and is a force that weakens not only ethnic pluralism, but also the startling emphasis on national and intra-national territorial loyalties which was so unexpected a feature of the early politics of ex-colonial countries.

Such movements are as yet often incoherent, and despite their revolutionary activities few have any real hope of seizing – still less holding – the power. Hence perhaps the appeal of such imported doctrines as Maoism with its model of revolutionary organization. But a highly unstable condition is created in many countries, weakening the control of established government, and sometimes leading to frequent 'revolutions' and *coups-d'état* which do nothing to eliminate the privilege of the élites. Such situations are also open to manipulation by charismatic leaders and calculating opportunists, who are able to seize power and hold it by establishing régimes supported by armed and ruthless bodies of men, who, by the fear which their excesses create, come to depend on the charismatic leaders for life itself, as well as simply livelihood.

In such conditions the national armies can play more than one rôle. As disciplined bodies, national in conception and ideology, with a well-developed structure of leadership and strongly developed emphasis on personal loyalty to officers or to their units, they stand out as firm organizations in a shifting polity. Armies have been used by the leadership to retain power, and sometimes the élite group constituted by the senior officers of the armies have first served the leadership then manipulated the political élites, and have finally taken over control 'in the national interest', though essentially to preserve the institutional structure of society. Though they have often been a conservative force in politics, the use of armies in civil affairs and control has sometimes brought them into close contact with citizen agitation, leading to erosion of notions of political neutrality among the military. The conception of armies as bodies having political utility within the State is bound to have repercussions on the soldiers' conception of their own rôle, and signs are not wanting in Third World countries that armies are themselves coming to adopt and seek to further the levelling doctrines of the post-colonial revolution.

THE STRATEGIC DIMENSION: INTERVENTIONISM BY THE POWERS

Were the economic and political trends we have discussed the only forces at work, the Third World would be a much simpler place. But the large foreign companies exert political power, and so do their governments, both on their particular behalf and also in the collective interest of the metropolitan nation as a whole. There are many ways in which such power is exercised. The provision of aid, even if notionally 'without strings', gives the donor country or company a certain leverage. The guarantees sought by companies, banks and loan agencies – even international bodies such as the World Bank – impose constraints on the freedom of political and economic experiment. Aid given through the supply of military equipment, training programmes and technical advice can yield more direct returns in the guidance of a country's foreign policy, even though refusal to supply spare parts and other military equipment to a recalcitrant former partner has by no means always been a successful form of pressure. More subtly, there may also be aid given to the political campaign funds of parties, and there are very many ways in which individuals can be bribed and coerced. Overt interventionism, with physical presence of metropolitan military and other accredited personnel, is much more rare, while direct action such as we have seen in Vietnam and the Dominican Republic, and against Cuba, is but the tip of an enormous iceberg. A little below this level, still within the depths to which light penetrates, as it were, the wide support given to local movements by the American CIA, and other foreign agencies, is a well-known feature of Third World politics.

Such interventionism is only to a limited degree the province of the former colonial powers. The post-1945 great powers – the United States, the Soviet

Union and now also China – have not even waited for the advent of political independence to commence activity: even in the 1950s the composition of governments in certain still-colonial territories reflected the wishes of the United States. After independence there is often a very sharp increase in the level of interventionist activity, and there is no doubt that the massive increase in foreign investment and aid has greatly facilitated such leverage in the 1960s.

The effect of these forces should not be underrated, for it reduces enormously the freedom of action of independent governments and of opposition groups and parties. There are both political and economic dimensions. In the commercial area the objective is to secure unimpeded operation of international business enterprise, and especially of the multinational corporations, which exert a direct and acknowledged influence on the policies of the metropolitan governments themselves. In the strategic area, the main aim is the exclusion of actively or potentially hostile influences, and the maintenance of support for the foreign policies of the intervening country, hence also of governments readily amenable to 'friendly suggestion'. A solid measure of protection for compliant groups or governments is offered in return.

By far the most prevalent of such interventionist forces are those of the United States, and since the primary objectives of American policy in this area were largely achieved by the mid-1960s, American interventionism operates mainly in support of the *status quo*. By contrast, the main thrust of Russian and Chinese interventionism, especially the latter, is toward disruption of the *status quo*, since there are so few ex-colonial countries in which governments complaisant to their wishes are in power. Third World countries have sometimes sought to play off these conflicting forces against each other, seeking sometimes or in some areas to placate the one while at other times in other fields seeming responsive to the wishes of the other. But such a dangerous game demands both strategic and tactical skill of a high order. Most governments find it safer, and more rewarding in terms of payoff, to accept interventionism from only one principal source. But some are being forced by pressure of their own public opinion to become more variable in their responses.

It is easy to be critical of interventionism, for there are many ways in which – to paraphrase a famous dictum – new interventionism is but old colonialism writ large. One most unfortunate result has been the maintenance in power of many corrupt and unpopular governments long past their term of optimal service to their own countries. Interventionist agencies have been insufficiently pliable, unwilling to take risks with new and unknown personnel and parties, grossly insensitive to changing trends in the countries affected. All the intervening countries show this same want of sensitivity, flexibility and willingness to experiment and accept the chance element involved in change. In consequence, revolutions arising from insupportable stress in the system have sometimes been unnecessarily violent, and the unsuccessful intervener has suffered greater loss of its interests than might have happened had its policy been more realistic. The almost paranoic tendency of the agents of American intervention to see communists under the bed and behind the desk of every public figure who questions the enlightened wisdom of their country would be ludicrous were not its consequences so serious. Sometimes interventionist support of 'friendly' régimes has gone far beyond the merely inflexible: it has led to tolerance of and even aid to the cruel repression of opposition, and to a callousness toward the inhabitants of affected countries that equals the worst sins perpetrated by man on man. More than any other single force, interventionism has been responsible for the death of the once-trumpeted 'century of the common man'.

Yet it is difficult to see how some form of outside interference could have been avoided in the context of the changing world power situation since 1945. World War II and its aftermath destroyed beyond recall a system of spheres of influence that had endured more than half a century. The elimination or attenuation of the regional influence of Japan, Britain, France and the Netherlands in the Third World created a space that was bound to be filled: the United States moved swiftly to occupy the space, but was quickly challenged by the Soviet Union. The competition for influence has grown more and more intense as the Soviet Union has grown more powerful, and the entry of China as a third competing force already casts a long shadow before it in many parts of the world. Nor are the older powers entirely passive. There are plentiful signs of a recrudescence of Japanese competition for economic influence in an area somewhat larger than Japan's former empire. Britain and especially France have continued to sustain some interest in interventionism, and if western Europe as a whole were ever to resolve its internal differences it would be surprising if it did not re-emerge as an effective force in the wider world. Though Orwell's prophecy of conflict around the periphery of empires between 'Oceania', 'Eurasia' and 'Eastasia' may have been misdirected in many points of detail, several elements of his world of 1984 are clearly recognizable in 1972. Competition in the Third World is an integral part of the more direct conflict for power and economic growth among the great nations; while it may be regrettable, it is also inevitable in a fluid situation.

This is not to say that there should be no blame, but a share of this blame must be laid at the doors of the Third World leaders themselves. Like tribal leaders in nineteenth-century Melanesia, but with less excuse, many of these men have sought support from one or other great power for their own internal ends, or to aid them in disputes with neighbours. It has been too easy.

Americans and Russians alike could be enticed by the prospect of excluding the other, and it was for years a relatively simple matter to gain American support by crying 'communism' each time a nationalist or levelling opposition group raised its head. There have been many successes through skilful manipulation. In the last analysis, Sukarno's Indonesia gained West Irian from the Dutch by obtaining Russian support. The United States then became prepared to desert its Dutch allies, and sacrifice the interests of 750,000 Melanesians, for the 'greater' aim of preserving its own stake in southeast Asia. Australia readily went along with this shift of policy.

At first sight it may seem that this latter instance is all that might make a discussion of great-power interventionism of relevance in Melanesia. Except for the brief interlude between 1941 and 1945 this region has been devoid of any but marginal strategic significance in world affairs, and interventionism has been conspicuous only by its absence. Today Melanesia lies deeply within a secure sphere of 'Western' influence. Yet this very fact may tempt non-Western adventure once these small, weak countries become independent, and there are reasons for supposing that the western Pacific basin could become an area of strongly conflicting great-power interests in the last quarter of the century.

Several possibilities exist which could change the strategic significance of Melanesia. America's position in Japan is less secure than it was, and it is continuously possible that simmering unrest in the Philippines could escalate into a major insurrection. The political stability of Indonesia is by no means assured. But the real key to the future lies in the imminent emergence of China as a major world power which must inevitably pay closer attention than hitherto to its sea frontiers in southeast Asia and the Pacific. In preparation for this new situation, the Soviet Union has been rapidly building up its position in the Indian Ocean and southeast Asia, while Russian research vessels of various descriptions have been regular visitors to Melanesian waters for a decade. Interventionism by the United States, the Soviet Union and China, and perhaps also Japan, is not only possible but probable, and the political fragmentation of Melanesia and other parts of the Pacific makes these small countries especially vulnerable. It is surprising that so little appreciation of this probability has yet been exhibited in discussion of the political future of Melanesia, and also rather disturbing, since the rapid modern changes in the power structure of the east and southeast Asian regions suggests that very little time remains for independent decision.

REFERENCES AND SOURCES

This chapter is a deliberate attempt to present the more revolutionary viewpoint as emerging in the post-colonial world, and it draws heavily on field experience in the Caribbean, especially in Trinidad, on extensive contact with Caribbeanists both white and black, and on a continuing seminar which I chaired in the Centre for Developing-Area Studies in 1970–2, with participants mainly from Third World countries. The West Indian periodical literature, especially from Trinidad, has also been an important source. More solid backing derives from the work of Lewis (1968) who observes at p. 389 that 'Independence, then, means a national stock-taking of heroic proportions. Literally every institution of the society comes in for close re-examination by the new nationalist ethic.' The post-independence Asian literature tells a similar story, though with less bitterness, as witness the re-interpretation of Asian colonial history by Pannikar (1953), and a similar tone is to be found in modern revolutionary literature throughout the world. There is not the slightest reason to suppose that Melanesians will fail to absorb this climate of opinion, and a reading of the periodical *New Guinea* (Sydney) or the student newspaper *Nilaidat* (Port Moresby) makes clear that much has already been absorbed. Although such periodicals as *Pacific Islands Monthly* – or its partial counterpart *Caribbean Business News* (Toronto, Canada) – might prefer to adopt the detached and critical view toward such trends preferred by most post-independence governments and colonial authorities, it would be folly to ignore such massive movements in attempting to look forward into the future.

CHAPTER 15

PERILS AND PROSPECTS

Melanesia is as yet innocent of much of the turmoil described in the last chapter, though the seeds are all present. But three-fourths of the population of Melanesia is likely to be under independent governments by the middle of the 1970s and the manner in which the new countries will be able to respond to internal and external sources of stress is being determined now. Education and the manpower problem, the formation of élites, the state of public information, the effectiveness of the apparatus of statehood, and the problems of pluralism and regionalism, among others, are all critical – at least as much so as the question of economic viability with which planners mainly concerned themselves in the 1960s. Despite this emphasis we have seen that the capacity of the Melanesian countries to develop independent economies is severely limited. What of the capacity of these people to take command of their own destinies in the very near future?

EDUCATION AND THE MANPOWER PROBLEM

Huge strides in the improvement of education have been achieved during the 1960s, so that by 1970 the education budgets of several territories had come to equal or exceed the whole national budgets of years in the 1950s. Numbers in school have improved at all levels, there has been significant growth in secondary and technical education, and a solid foundation of tertiary education has been established. Still more significant has been a widespread improvement of standards, as education has come to depend less on the voluntary and poorly supported efforts of the Christian missions and far more on the State. Yet the distance to be travelled was enormous, and even if present rates of change were to be maintained it would be more than another decade before any countries but Fiji and New Caledonia could be said to have a satisfactory system of education.

When governments finally awoke to their responsibilities in this area in the early 1960s the situation was deplorable. In Australian New Guinea there had been almost no public expenditure on the education of Melanesians until after World War II, and as late as 1963 only 220,000 pupils were in schools of all types, the overwhelming majority in the lower primary grades; fewer than a hundred had completed a full secondary education and there was not a single university graduate. Only some 30 per cent of the estimated age-cohort of primary-school age were in school, only 0.375 per cent of the age-cohort of secondary-school age. In the Solomon Islands, where the level of performance was hardly better, an un-numbered Government White Paper of 1962 described the modal mission-operated primary school in these terms:

> In a typical school there may be two to four classes housed in a church or leaf building, with few books, little equipment, and inadequate or non-existent seating and desk accommodation. The teachers are untrained and often barely literate; they are frequently unable to speak English adequately much less to teach it. Many such schools are almost wholly unsupervised. The curriculum comprises English, Arithmetic, Religious Instruction and very little else, and classes are normally held for four hours in the morning on five days a week. Most of the pupils are boarders, and in consequence much of the time is taken up by work in the school garden, since the pupils must produce the bulk of their own food.

Such a description would stand for the education received by the great majority of Melanesians at that time, and by many Melanesian children even today. Discipline in schools was often quite harsh, and rebellious children – often the brightest – were habitually expelled. Such education, though much sought after by the parents of the children, fitted its output for nothing but labouring employment, and for most victims of the high attrition rate nothing of any real value in either rural or urban life was imparted. Only in Fiji was the situation notably better at the primary level: even in wealthy New Caledonia rural schools were poor, and Melanesian children living in the reserves were often taught only by *moniteurs*.

Improvements in this condition have demanded a dual, or even triple, strategy. Expansion and reconstruction of the primary base has been a fundamental task, but its reward can only be in the long term. The more urgent task was the construction of a system or systems of secondary and tertiary education in order to form, *de novo* to all intents and purposes, a pool of potential skilled workers and professionally qualified people to constitute an educated élite. The high capital cost of the latter task had to be carried even though only very small student intakes, and still smaller output, could be anticipated; for this reason governments hesitated even after the need was clearly demonstrated to them by expert opinion. Political considerations nudged governments: Indonesia established a university at Djajapura in 1963, and though it was little more than a 'junior college' for some years, its creation forced the hand of the Australian authorities in setting up the excellent University of Papua and New Guinea in 1966. A third regional university, serving a group of territories, was founded at Suva in 1968, but this University of the South Pacific has not equalled its New Guinea counterpart in early performance, notwithstanding the far superior base in secondary education available. A fourth university was being created in Nouméa in the early 1970s, and technical colleges of high standard were also set up in New Guinea and Fiji.

The University of Papua and New Guinea awarded its first degrees in 1970 – a memorable moment for those privileged to observe it. Student numbers remain small in all the higher institutions, and in many of the secondary schools also. So intense is the demand for qualified personnel that the rate of loss from education to employment is severe at all levels, and is growing more and more serious as governments seek to localize their personnel with all possible speed at the very same time as a significant expansion is taking place in mining and industry. As in so many other countries, the demand for skilled personnel is overwhelmingly in the towns, where wages are higher than in rural areas even for unskilled workers. Not only are the rural areas being starved of trained personnel, but all forms of rural work are being devalued in popular estimation: it can hardly be otherwise. Among the people I studied in Chimbu, for example, not one young person who has been away for post-primary training has ever returned home to stay.

But the élites and quasi-élites remain a thin scatter of persons, concentrated as groups only in the main centres of government and in the institutions of higher learning themselves. They do not yet form a social class, and the élites do not yet have any group values and goals distinct from those of peasants and proletarians. Fiji represents a partial exception to this statement, but it holds among Melanesians elsewhere. But a 'new class' must be expected to develop quickly once power comes into the hands of the Melanesian élites. Despite the potential for class conflict thus created, it is perhaps desirable that stratification should occur since the élites might on present indications be national and to some degree international in outlook, and the need for more-than-local leadership is very acute in Melanesia.

THE CHANNELS OF PUBLIC INFORMATION

Much less has been done to improve the flow of public information than to expand and enhance formal education. The network of radio stations has been enlarged, and there is more broadcasting in the *lingues franches* and in some major vernacular tongues, but the very multiplicity of languages presents an acute problem, not helped by the reluctance to accept Melanesian Pidgin as a true language rather than merely a poor form of English. Yet Pidgin, in its four major dialects, is in fact a true language, spoken far more between Melanesians than in exchanges between the latter and expatriates: indeed, very few expatriates speak fluent and colloquial Pidgin. While it is true that

Pidgin is not and cannot become an international language, it is equally true that English is not and cannot become an intra-Melanesian language in any but the longest term. Pidgin, with its mainly English vocabulary, substantially Melanesian grammar and syntax, richness in idiom and facility for ready adaptation to changing needs, is the second language of well over a million Melanesians, and the first language of several thousands. English, French, Standard Fijian, Hindustani, Bahasa Indonesia, Police Motu and such oddities as the Lutheran *lingua franca*, Kotte, might collectively find more users, but individually none even approach the position of Pidgin. The language is certainly here to stay in Australian New Guinea, the New Hebrides and perhaps also the Solomon Islands, where Pidgin is greatly anglicized. English is a true *lingua franca* only in Fiji, but it does serve this rôle for the élites of all parts of Melanesia.

Linguistic problems alone, however, are not sufficient to explain the poor condition of information channels over very large parts of the region. The situation has certainly improved since the mass introduction of relatively cheap transistor radios of Japanese manufacture, and the quite spontaneous diffusion of this innovation may well be among the most important developments of the 1960s – thus far quite un-researched. But broadcasting is limited, and except in Fiji incorporates a high proportion of metropolitan programmes designed for an expatriate minority among the listeners. Local and regional news consists largely of items supplied by government information services, with limited independent reportage and even less open and critical discussion of national and sub-national affairs. The situation is better in Fiji and in New Caledonia where there is also television, but the true potential of broadcasting, in generating an informed public with an interest in its own culture and personalities, remains almost totally unexploited.

Nor is the situation much better with newspapers, though private enterprise certainly offers better service in regard to local affairs. The New Guinea newspapers, printed in the main towns, are only now becoming daily, and only in the 1960s did they begin to include any substantial Pidgin content. Fiji and New Caledonia have long had daily newspapers – but owned by an Australian company and by the Société le Nickel respectively, and there is quite a range of publications in Fijian and the main Indian languages in Fiji. The Solomon Islands and the New Hebrides still rely only on weekly or fortnightly government newsletters, or else on newspapers imported from abroad. Local journalism is emerging in New Guinea, and is tolerably viable in Fiji and New Caledonia, but truly national mass media industries have still to emerge.

Even in the towns, and most certainly throughout the rural areas of Melanesia, public opinion is thus very poorly informed. The people of different regions know little about one another, and stereotypes are readily adopted. Rural people know little of what really goes on from day to day in the towns. Potential 'personalities' of whatever kind find it hard to generate mass appeal. The local representative on a national legislature, even the representative on a district or local council, may perhaps tell his people what has been going on when he returns, but it is more probable that his constituents know little or nothing of what he does. As we saw in discussing political change, information flows still consist very largely of downward transmission of government information and instruction, through the chain of officialdom and local representatives, to the people. The people's representatives 'tell the government' what the people think, but on a very narrow range of issues, and what they bring back is simply the government's reply, if any. Loss of information through this system is enormous.

A great quantity of information, covering matters well treated in the mass media of more developed countries, is therefore carried only by word of mouth, and depends on travelling and migrating individuals for transmission. The slow changes that do occur in public opinion demonstrate that these channels are of some effect, but the scope for distortion and loss is very great, while the possibilities of truly informed discussion are limited. In countries characterized by widely dispersed populations speaking many languages, this is not a happy situation. The sort of foci for national feeling provided by popular programmes widely heard and discussed, national entertainers whose names and doings are known to all, sporting events of universal interest, even colourful political personalities to arouse adulation or fury, hardly exist as yet. Yet they would do a great deal for the creation of national ethos, and the present paucity of public information channels is a grave – and still neglected – weakness in the preparation of Melanesia for independence.

HOW TO RUN A COUNTRY

The startling events in Fiji after 1969 demonstrated the determination with which Melanesians, like other colonial peoples, can tackle the task of independent government. In Fiji there was almost a rush to dispense with expatriate officials, advisers and 'experts', but this country has a better foundation than the others. Melanesians have been involved in administration for years in Fiji, and paradoxically the only other territory with a comparable record is West Irian, where the Indonesians have been able to build on a good foundation of Melanesian officialdom left by the Dutch. In Australian New Guinea no Melanesians were to be found in responsible positions until the 1960s, and there are still few. Whole District administrations were still staffed by expatriates as late as 1970, with Melanesians employed only in clerical and ancillary grades: thus late in the day Europeans were even found replacing Melanesians as the work grew too complex for semi-literate clerical personnel to cope with the task.

The situation is little better in private enterprise, notwithstanding the very serious efforts made by certain companies to train Melanesians for executive positions. There are from none to only a few Melanesians in such occupations as company management, engineering and architecture, university and even secondary teaching, banking above clerical grades, telecommunications, the professions, entrepreneurship of any but very small businesses. The first air pilots qualified only at the end of the 1960s, and only at sea do we encounter a high proportion of Melanesians in positions of command. At the highest possible rate of output of the new educational and training institutions, it will be another decade before expatriates can be substantially replaced by Melanesians in the more highly skilled occupations over a large area of Melanesia.

There is again no difficulty in pointing a critical finger. There were many critics of inadequate policies, both government and private, even as far back as the 1950s, yet it was only in the later 1960s that serious acceleration took place, and even in 1971 the pace cannot be regarded as sufficient. Sudden crash programmes are no substitute for a proper build-up of qualified personnel, and the legacy bequeathed to countries about to become independent is unenviable.

One aspect is perhaps of especial significance. Communication is the fundamental problem of these island territories, yet the main-line communication system, alike by sea, air and telecommunications, is almost all operated or controlled by expatriates, and there is limited prospect of an early transfer of control. The tendency is still toward closer integration with metropolitan operations. In view of the overriding importance of air transport in these countries, the implications for continued dependency are serious indeed.

AN ISLAND IS NOT A WORLD

Given the situation outlined above, he would be an optimist who could contemplate the independent future of Melanesia with a feeling of quiet confidence. Fiji and New Caledonia are better equipped materially, but each has internal pluralistic problems. The three central territories – the New Hebrides, the Solomon Islands and Australian New Guinea – are approaching independence with only nascent élites, inadequate systems of education and public information, and without the ability to staff essential parts of the apparatus of statehood from local personnel resources. One might be tempted to agree with those Melanesians who have maintained that their countries are not ready for independence, if one were satisfied that continued colonialism would prepare them better. But the prolongation of a colonial political status thus far into the period of expanding economic colonialism has already seriously aggravated some of the perils that must be faced on independence.

In that concepts of supra-local nationality are a colonial creation in Melanesia, evolving within territorial units created by external forces, Melanesia is different only in degree from a great many other parts of the colonial world: the very profusion of language groups, and absence of traditional political groups of any size, may even be advantageous in facilitating such national concepts. The danger, however, is that regional loyalties will develop faster than national loyalties. Regionalism threatened the unity of the Dutch-sponsored Partai Nasional in West New Guinea during its brief existence in 1960–2; it threatens the unity of Australian New Guinea's one truly spontaneous political organization, the Pangu Pati. We have noted the strong desire of Bougainvilleans for independence, and this has prompted other regional movements in the Bismarck Archipelago and on the mainland.

Concern that the new states will have to spend much of their energy and resources on maintaining unity is being more and more freely expressed. Commenting on discussion at a seminar in Port Moresby in 1970, Crocombe (1970, 146) has presented the argument squarely:

> The possibility that the long term future of the peoples of Papua-New Guinea might be better served if the present colonial unit were divided into several separate states, has not been adequately explored. The official view, that such units would not be 'viable', seems to be fallacious. Each of the units would be considerably larger than the average self-governing unit in the South Pacific... The advantage of the undoubted economies of scale which could be achieved with a large unit would be more than offset if the chances and costs of maintaining internal stability and harmonious growth appear much less favourable than with smaller units.

As an historian, Crocombe might with reason have gone on to remark on the historically demonstrated disadvantages of balkanization, but it is clear that arguments of this sort are becoming more and more prevalent, and also effective. The Prime Minister of Australia himself suggested, a little later in 1970, that different 'regions' of Australian New Guinea might advance toward independence at different speed, in accordance with the 'expressed will of the people': at best a weak federalism could emerge from such a course, and total fragmentation is far more probable.

Just as the territories themselves are the product of political colonialism, soon to end, so the 'regions' in their present form are the product of economic colonialism, to which no end is in sight. Export-based economic growth, orientated into transport systems focusing on main ports and thence to the metropoles, compartmentalizes the larger territories and connects their separate parts more closely with the external economic system than with one another. The major expansion of economic colonialism during the 1960s has accentuated this compartmentalization. The solution seemingly advocated by Crocombe would lead straight to a situation such as that which has evolved in the Commonwealth eastern Caribbean where, in place of the federal state once hoped for, we have three independent states and seven territories separately in 'associated' status with Great Britain, four currencies (though still at par), and moves to develop four or even five 'national' airlines to the great loss of rationalization. West Indian writers unanimously attribute this deplorable situation to the want of a structural base for federation, with every territory orientated separately toward the metropole, economically and culturally, and with the minimum of common interest, notwithstanding widespread similarities in history and society.

Even given the capacity of south Pacific leaders and writers to regard their problems as 'unique' and different from those of a wider world by virtue of remoteness, it is remarkable that the dangers inherent in further weakening Melanesia's already unsound defences against commercial penetration and foreign interventionism should fail so widely to be perceived. It is a well-known principle needing no elaboration that the weaker the economy and the less the diversification of resources in a 'host country', the poorer is its bargaining strength vis-à-vis external forces, whether commercial or political. Fragmentation leads very readily to competition between small political units for foreign enterprise and aid, and hence to the acceptance of conditions which a stronger nation would be more likely to resist. This is not to say that unification is always desirable at all costs, or that there are not instances where territorial split would offer advantages of internal stability outweighing the disadvantages of smaller scale. But Melanesia is not included in such a list: the divisions are no more 'natural' or 'indigenous' than the territories themselves.

Fortunately, there are Melanesians who themselves see the advantages not only of retaining the present territories as whole states, but also of forms of *ad hoc* joint operation in certain areas. Air Pacific is a case in point, and tenuous proposals for a South Pacific Shipping Line have been bruited. The very paucity of national élites leads educated men to seek out *confrères* in other territories, and at many levels there is a growing sense of common Pacific culture, and common interest in the face of external forces. But while this is hopeful, the perils of fragmentation remain great, and have grown rather than diminished through the last years of political colonialism.

TOWARD THE NIGHT OF THE GENERALS?

At least in Australian New Guinea, the hopes of some Melanesians who wish to be rid of colonial domination and at the same time hold their country together are frankly centred on the model of military takeover. While it is distressing that this should be so, the reasoning is clear. The small, well-trained and mobile army in this territory is recruited among men of above-average educational attainment. The army is itself something of an élite group, and the soldiers might well feel superior to factional, local and often illiterate politicians. Above all, the army is a national body in recruitment, organization and indoctrination, and its training includes no small element of civilian service. Whoever wishes to hold power in the coming years of organizing a nation must have its loyalty.

There is nothing comparable with New Guinea's Pacific Islands Regiment in the other territories. Fiji has a very good small military force, with a record of service in World War II and in Malaya. But it is almost wholly Fijian in composition, and while it represents no threat to the present régime, it might well be a force to contend with if the opposition party were to obtain power in a future election. New Caledonia has only local units of the French army, multiracial in composition, but closely integrated with the national forces. The Solomon Islands have no army, but are acquiring a small, mobile force of 'riot-control' police which might in time become of greater significance. The New Hebrides have only the two national police forces, of size rigidly controlled by protocol. And in West Irian military forces recruited locally in the early 1960s were disarmed after the troubles of the middle 1960s, and the military in the territory are drawn mainly from other parts of Indonesia. Except on the land border through New Guinea, military forces have no externally-orientated function, and their significance is in aid to the civil power. But this rôle is weakened by the continued absence of all but the most minimal naval forces, or of any air force units whatever save those operated by the metropolitan powers. Sea and air mobility are essential in archipelagic states, and one must expect to see efforts made to create such facilities in the very near future.

Ultimately, the rôle played by the armed forces and police will be determined by political events within the new countries. If we can proceed by the analogy of other ex-colonial states without strong political parties, with only weakly-developed apparatus for national management and with well-marked divisive tendencies, it would seem unlikely that these national forces – however small – will escape direct involvement in the government of at least some of the Melanesian territories. Though ambition may be a factor, a sense of public service is more likely to be the impelling force. There are no

Melanesian generals, and except in Fiji no colonels – a rank notorious for its interest in political intervention in many countries. But there is a goodly number of NCOs, and a growing body of junior commissioned officers who are highly trained. An important rôle may yet fall to such men, in creating a still-nascent sense of national pride and purpose.

REFERENCES AND SOURCES

The most important sources on the question of education concern Australian New Guinea: they are the Commission on Higher Education in Papua and New Guinea (1964) and an article by one of the authors of this report, Spate (1966). There is also important material in the United Nations Development Programme (1968) on West Irian. On the wider questions discussed, there is a great body of material, analysis and comment in the successive papers given at the Waigani Seminars, especially in the last two (1970b, 1971), though the rôle of Melanesians in business is more extensively treated in earlier discussions (1967, 1970a). Throughout, there is much valuable information in the territorial *Newsletters* and in *Pacific Islands Monthly*.

EPILOGUE

TOWARD AN UNDERSTANDING OF COLONIALISM

Thus far Melanesia. We cannot conclude, because no conclusion is possible in a continuing play, and must leave the story at the open end reached in the last chapter. The rules of the game are being changed even as I write, and neither the strategies of the players, nor the outcome of the next stage, can be predicted with more than a low order of probability. But there remains a concluding question of another order: what can we add to the sum of general propositions about colonialism from our observations on the individual case of Melanesia? Though we have not set out to advance any theoretical system, or test any existing system, we have none the less generalized about reality and its organization, and in so doing have employed 'an abstract framework of presumed inter-relations', which 'constitutes theory in research' (Myrdal, 1968, I, 24–5).

It is simplest to approach this question by relating the method adopted here to another which has gained considerable popularity in my discipline in the last few years. This is the employment of multivariate methods and surface-fitting, applied to a range of quantifiable data, to yield measurement of our observations concerning the spatial diffusion of colonial change (e.g. Soja, 1968; Riddell, 1970). The basic concepts underlying this 'geography of modernization' derive from a view of colonial change as a passage from 'traditional' to 'modern' ways of life, part of the diffusion of 'a world culture based on modern science and technology and specific standards of government organization and operation' (Soja, 1968, 1). The process envisaged is one of 'social mobilization' (Deutsch, 1961), under which traditional forms of organization and behaviour are weakened, and new structures more appropriate to the creation of a modern society are substituted.

At the conceptual level there are certain elements in common between Soja's approach and mine. His basic rendering of the spatial schema is, like mine, a superimposed system of external origin overlying and modifying a complex of traditional cells. He emphasizes the rôle of communication and information flow, and gives some consideration to 'restrictions to the spread of modernity'. On the face of things, Melanesia would seem to offer an ideal testing ground for this approach, interestingly complicated by the problems of fragmentation and insularity, for in the last analysis the origins of all the forces of change in Melanesia have lain outside the region. We encounter no strong residentiary developments rising in the face of colonialism, comparable with the evolution of modern nationhood in Asia, or even with the swift emergence of nationality in Zululand and central Madagascar, so early in the initial penetration phase of colonialism that the rôle of external forces cannot be isolated with certainty. All evidence suggests that, had there been no colonialism in Melanesia, the modern region would not have differed fundamentally from that of the eighteenth century. With a possible exception only in eastern Fiji, we have no evidence to suggest that there were any strong latent forces in pre-colonial Melanesia capable independently of creating a new sort of society.

Given this situation of virtually 'pure colonial' change, one hopes that the methodology of the geography of modernization will be applied and tested in these islands; valuable insights might be gained. Yet we must also take note of complexities which modernization 'surfaces' might overlie and obscure. In examining the external system, we have found it valuable to make a clear separation between the economic, political and cultural forces in the invading system. We have noted how a commercial policy based on export growth has persisted across major variations in the political objective, but the spatial aspect has varied through time in accordance with the politically-derived weighting given to equity rather than efficiency considerations in its execution. We have also observed that the external forces do not always lead to the diffusion of innovations, or to 'social mobilization'. Empirically, we have noted that when it has been possible for the colonial economy, operating on alienated land with external capital, to import its labour, this has been done. The result is an implanted economy comparable in modern times with the historical 'pure plantation model' of Levitt and Best (1969), and the residentiary population is virtually excluded from participation. We have encountered abundant evidence of checks to diffusion created through the colonial process itself, in the form of the structural phenomena of economic dualism. Indeed, we have found grounds for leaning toward Frank's (1967) interpretation of underdevelopment as a creation of capitalist development, which in its turn is only a more forceful statement of Myrdal's 'backwash' effect, or of Friedmann's 'downward transitional' problem in the periphery. We can certainly identify, as Howlett (in press) has done, instances in which modernization and social mobilization have been halted following the creation of a peasant economy from a primitive economy, leading to an 'infinite pause' in the supposed transition to modernity.

More fundamentally, we have reason to question the underlying supposition of uni-directional transition, leading to assimilation of the colonized society in 'a world culture based on modern science'. The very concept of 'modernization' is thoroughly ethnocentric, its optimal values being those of some idealized distillation of Western, technological culture. Most certainly, this is what the people say they want – at a rather superficial level of thinking – but they also want self-determination of their future, not assimilation. It is empirically clear that few among them are willing to accept the full implications in terms of a denial of their own culture. If we doubt this, we may observe in Melanesia the phenomenon that strong resistance to 'total modernization' sometimes arises closest to the most active centres of innovation diffusion, and this resistance is emerging as a new sort of innovation, itself diffusable through the colonized society.

Explanation of colonialism must take account of both external and residentiary systems, both innovation and reaction, and hence also of interaction between the systems and the consequent modification of both. Modification of the external system may be obscured by a continual supply of new innovations and inputs, but it takes place none the less. Interaction is to some degree governed by a range of structural and institutional checks to diffusion, some of which are deliberately created while others occur unwittingly, but as part of the colonial process. Nor may it be presumed that penetration of the colonized system by the colonial leads necessarily to 'spread' effects in Myrdal's terms, a 'lift-pump effect' in Soja's. There may also be 'backwash'. Riddell (1970, 80) concludes that 'the patterns of change move like waves across the map, and cascade down the urban hierarchy as they are funnelled along the transportation system'. But the selection of inputs determines this conclusion: 'cascading' may also take place in the reverse direction, for loss of human resources, and linkage to the external system in a persistently subordinate rôle, may leave the rural areas more impoverished than before in terms of real ability to advance. Both sides of the coin need to be studied if complete explanation is to be approached.

The 'geography of modernization' belongs to a tradition of aggregative modelling of open economies, going back to Adam Smith and Ricardo, and in modern times owing much to marginal analysis and the prescriptions of Keynes. Although the superimposition of systems is recognized, there is no follow-through to analysis of the structural complexities created by interaction. Failure to disaggregate by systems imperils the power of explanation, and the result remains essentially simplistic, and descriptive of only part of the whole. The approach attempted here is more untidy and less elegant; much is unquantifiable and would be resistant to mathematical symbolism, a language which demands precise definition if its deductive power is to be availed. But it is firmly grounded in observation, and reasoning is primarily inductive. The resulting emphasis on structure and institutions derives directly from the Melanesian evidence, but it is in line with modes of explanation adopted in the tropical American context by such writers as Prebisch, Furtado, Demas, and Levitt and Best. Emphasis on the historical dimension coupled with concern for the connections between process and structure is a common element, while the weight given to disequilibrium between systems is also in line with the work of Myrdal, in a wider context.

Such an approach does not lead readily to the creation of tidy theory. Cognitive description remains its base, and generalization and comparison loom larger than deduction in the search for explanation. But it leads to one methodological conclusion that is perhaps fundamental. This is the need to consider colonialism as a process of constant interaction. The colonial system is a projection of external forces, and all kinds of controlling, transforming and restricting forces of external provenance are part of the total colonial impact. They are influenced and modified both by the nature of the interaction and by changes in their remote areas of origin. The colonized residentiary system does not merely receive innovations, adopting, adapting, resisting or rejecting inputs of external origin. Its members seek constantly to comprehend and manage a changing total system which includes both their own complex and the impinging or invasive forces. The will to sustain self-determination is always present even though the power may be lacking, and action at any stage follows from comprehension attained of opportunities and constraints within the changing system as a whole. This simple opposition of forces is complicated by the creation of neo-residentiary complexes which operate in alliance with both basic forces and which themselves seek to command events.

Once a society and economy have become open this is a continuing play. Colonialism and independence are not states occupying discrete blocks of time, but are continuously conflicting forces. Independence has meaning only in the face of colonialism. Although an 'imperialist' phase in the conflict may now have given way to a 'modernization' phase, the interplay goes on. We must strive equally to comprehend both sets of forces, and their interaction, if we are to make progress in our understanding of a constantly changing world.

REFERENCES AND SOURCES

A comprehensive discussion of the 'geography of modernization' would require reference to work in parallel fields, especially sociology and economics; only partial comment is offered here. Some of the more important published sources on this branch of work in geography are Gould (1964, 1970), Soja (1968) and Riddell (1970).

Epilogue

In a conference paper, Soja (1970) attempts to review the contribution made and makes substantial claims for its future potential. A more traditional approach to the geographical study of development and change is presented by Hodder (1968), but much the closest approach to the position adopted in this book, and earlier in Brookfield with Hart (1971), is presented in a recent paper having specific reference to the Pacific by Watters (1970). A more comprehensive discussion is offered in Brookfield (In press, 1973).

STATISTICAL APPENDIX

TABLE I. *Distribution and use of alienated land in German New Guinea, 1905* (see also Figure 2, inset, p. 59)

	Gazelle Peninsula (New Britain)			All areas		
	Area (ha)	% Planted	% Under coconuts	Area (ha)	% Planted	% Under coconuts
Imperial Government	—	—	—	461	85	100
Neu-Guinea Compagnie	43,000	5	90	67,032	9	81
All others	10,706	n.a.	n.a.	22,265	n.a.	n.a.
Total	53,706	11	84	89,758	13	84
			Number		Number	
White 'officials' resident			27		90	
'Coloured' labour			2550		5259	
	Area (ha)	% bearing		Area (ha)	% bearing	
Area under crops						
Coconuts	4846	27		10,181	18	
Coffee	192	15		202	19	
Cocoa	8	63		133*	4	
Cotton	537	71		537	71	
Kapok	52	100		72	100	
Ficus rubber	139	—		954*	—	
All crops	5774	27		12,079	19	

SOURCE: German New Guinea Reports (in translation by H. A. Thomson) in the Commonwealth National Library, Canberra.

* Mostly on the New Guinea mainland (Kaiser Wilhelms-land) on Neu-Guinea Compagnie plantations.

TABLE 2. *Population of the Melanesian territories* (rounded)

	West Irian	Australian New Guinea	Solomon Islands	New Hebrides	New Caledonia	Fiji	TOTAL
Melanesians and other indigenous	850,000+	2,540,000	158,000	70,000	55,000	230,000	3,903,000
Europeans	1,000	31,000	1,000	3,000	42,000	14,000	92,000
Indo-Fijians	—	—	—	few	—	263,000	263,000
Indonesians	20,000+	—	—	few	2,000	—	22,000+
Other Asians	—	3,000	1,000	2,000	3,000	5,000	14,000
Other (mainly mixed and Polynesian immigrants)	—	3,000	1,000	2,000	17,000	15,000	38,000
Total	871,000+	2,577,000	161,000	77,000	119,000	527,000	4,332,000
Year of data	1969	1970	1970	1967	1971	1970	—
Nature of data	Census and estimates	Estimate	Census	Census	Estimate	Estimate	

SOURCE: Census Reports and other official documents.

TABLE 3. *Sundry comparative data on economy and development*

	West Irian	Australian New Guinea	Solomon Islands	New Hebrides	New Caledonia	Fiji
Imports *per capita* ($A)	3.00	57.7	64.4	107.7	728.3	137.3
Exports *per capita* ($A)	1.00	20.9	36.3	137.6	731.3	85.9
Leading exports making up 60 % or more of total value	Oil	Coconut products Coffee Cocoa	Coconut products	Coconut products Fish	Nickel products	Sugar
First ranking source of imports	Indonesia	Australia	Australia	Australia	France	Australia
First ranking destination of exports	Japan	Australia	UK	France	France	UK
GDP from monetary sources *per capita* ($A)	n.a.	83	89.7	n.a.	n.a.	338.0
Percentage of population in urban areas (approx)	10	6	8	19	60	35
External budgetary support *per capita* ($A)	7.00	50.6	32.5	48.1	253.4	8.0
Latest year of data	1969	1967–8	1968	1967–8	1967–8	1970

SOURCE: Various government sources.

REFERENCES

The following is a list of references cited in the text. No attempt is made to list all works consulted in research and writing, and in particular, the large pamphlet literature consulted is totally ignored. Comprehensive bibliographies are available, and since 1966 an excellent listing of published work of historical or political interest is maintained in the *Journal of Pacific History* (Canberra, Australia). Some principal bibliographic studies of value include:

Taylor, C. R. H., 1965. *A Pacific Bibliography*. Oxford (2nd edition).
Australian National University, Department of Anthropology and Sociology. 1968. *An Ethnographic Bibliography of New Guinea*. Canberra (3 vols.).
Doumenge, F., 1966. *L'Homme dans le Pacifique Sud*. Publications de la Société des Océanistes 19. Paris.
Maude, H. E., 1968. Searching for sources. *J. Pac. Hist.* 3, 210–22.

The reports, papers and documents of Government departments were a major source in writing this book, but reference is made only to certain Annual Reports, as follows: TPR – Territory of Papua Reports; TNGR – Annual Report on the Administration of the Trust Territory of New Guinea; BSIPR – Annual Report, British Solomon Islands Protectorate; FR – Annual Report, Colony of Fiji; NNGR – Annual Report on Netherlands New Guinea, English version (to 1961). A few additional documents are listed below.

The following journals and periodicals were a major source of material:

Journal of the Polynesian Society (Wellington, N.Z., 1892–).
Revue du Pacifique (Paris, 1922–36).
Pacific Islands Monthly (Sydney, 1930–).
Pacific Viewpoint (Wellington, N.Z., 1959–).
Réalités du Pacifique (Paris, 1963–7?).
New Guinea and Australia, the Pacific and South-east Asia (Sydney, 1966–).
Journal of Pacific History (Canberra, 1966–).
Journal of the Papua-New Guinea Society (Port Moresby, 1967–).
BSIP Newsletter (Honiara, Solomon Islands).
Papua and New Guinea Newsletter (Canberra).
News from Fiji (Suva, Fiji).
British Newsletter (Vila, New Hebrides).
Bulletin d'Information de la Résidence de France (Port-Vila, Nouvelles-Hébrides).
Bulletin du Commerce (Nouméa, Nouvelle-Calédonie).

List of references

Allan, C. H., 1951. 'Marching rule: a nativistic cult of the British Solomon Islands'. *Corona* 3, 93–100.

Andrews, C. F., 1937. *India and the Pacific*. London.

Archbold, R., Rand, A. L. & Brass, L. J., 1942. 'Results of the Archbold Expeditions 41'. *Bull. Amer. Mus. Nat. Hist.* 79, 197–228.

Baker, J. R., 1928. 'Depopulation in Espiritu Santo, New Hebrides'. *J. Roy. Anth. Soc.* 58, 279–303.

Baldwin, R. E., 1966. *Economic Development and Export Growth: a Study of Northern Rhodesia, 1920–1960*. Cambridge.

Barateau, G., 1931. 'Le coton aux Nouvelles-Hébrides'. *L'Océanie Française* 122, 104–7.

Belshaw, C. S., 1947. 'Native politics in the Solomon Islands'. *Pacific Affairs* 20, 187–93.

Benedict, B., 1962. 'Stratification in plural societies'. *American Anthropologist* 64, 1235–46.

Benoit, F., 1892. 'Etude sur les mines de nickel de la Nouvelle-Calédonie'. *Bulletin de la Société de l'Industrie Minérale*, 3me série, 3, 753–804.

Bernard, A., 1894. *L'Archipel de la Nouvelle-Calédonie: Thèse présentée à la Faculté des Lettres de Paris*. Paris.

Best, L., 1968. 'Outlines of a model of pure plantation economy'. *Social and Economic Studies* 17, 283–326.

Bettison, D. G., Hughes, C. A. & van der Veur, P. W. (eds.), 1965. *The Papua-New Guinea Elections, 1964*. Canberra.

Biskup, P., 1970. 'Foreign coloured labour in German New Guinea: a study in economic development'. *J. Pac. Hist.* 5, 85–107.

Boeke, J. H., 1953. *Economics and Economic Policy of Dual Societies as exemplified by Indonesia*. New York.

Bolton, C. G., 1967. 'The rise of Burns Philp, 1873–1893'. *Wealth and Progress: Studies in Australian business history*, ed. A. Birch & D. S. Macmillan. Sydney.

Boorstein, E., 1968. *The Economic Transformation of Cuba*. New York.

Bridon, E., 1890. *Histoire abrégé, mais très véridique, des Mines en Nouvelle-Calédonie*. Nouméa.

Brookfield, H. C., 1961a. 'The highland peoples of New Guinea: a study in distribution and localization'. *Geogr. J.* 127, 436–48.

1961b. 'Independence for West New Guinea'. *Current Affairs Bulletin* (Sydney) 27, 179–92.

1968. 'The money that grows on trees: the consequences of an innovation within a man-environment system'. *Austr. Geog. Stud.* 6, 97–119.

In press, 1973. 'On one geography, and a Third World'. *Transactions, Inst Brit. Geogrs.* 58.

Brookfield, H. C. & Brown, Paula, 1963. *Struggle for land: agriculture and group territories among the Chimbu of the New Guinea highlands*. Melbourne.

Brookfield, H. C. with Hart, Doreen, 1971. *Melanesia: a geographical interpretation of an island world.* London.

Brown, Paula, 1966. 'Social change and social movements'. *New Guinea on the Threshold: aspects of social, political and economic development*, ed. E. K. Fisk. Canberra.

Brunet, A., 1908. *Le Régime International des Nouvelles-Hébrides.* Paris.

Burns, A., Watson, T. Y. & Peacock, A. K., 1960. Report of a Commission of Enquiry into the Natural Resources and Population Trends of the Colony of Fiji, 1959. *Legislative Council of Fiji, Council Paper* 1. Suva.

Burridge, K. O. L., 1960. *Mambu: a Melanesian Millennium.* London.

Burton, J. W., 1910. *The Fiji of Today.* London.

Caillard, E., 1924. 'Le coton aux Nouvelles-Hébrides'. *L'Océanie Française* 80, 171–8.

Campbell, P. A., 1873. *A Year in the New Hebrides, Loyalty Islands and New Caledonia.* Geelong (Victoria).

Chayanov, A., 1966. *The Theory of Peasant Economy.* Homewood (Illinois). (Translation by R. D. Irwin of Tschajanow, A., *Die Lehre von der Bauerlichen Wirtschaft: versuch einer theorie der familiewirtschaft im landbau.* Berlin, 1923.)

Chinnery, E. W. P., 1934. 'The central ranges of the Mandated Territory of New Guinea from Mount Chapman to Mount Hagen'. *Geogr. J.* 84, 398–411.

Cochrane, G., 1970. *Big Men and Cargo Cults.* Melbourne.

Colijn, A. H., 1937. *Naar de Eeuwige Sneeuw van Nederlands-Indië.* Amsterdam (6th edition, 1957).

Commission on Higher Education in Papua and New Guinea. 1964. *Report to the Hon. Minister for Territories.* Canberra (2 vols., mimeo.).

Cordeil, P., 1885. *Origines et Progrès de la Nouvelle-Calédonie.* Nouméa.

Corlette, E. A. C., n.d. (*c.* 1942). *Some Notes on the Natives of the New Hebrides, together with some of their Customs, Laws and Ceremonies.* (Ms. from the files of the British Residency, Vila, reproduced by AC of S, G–2, III Island Command.)

Corris, P., 1968. 'Blackbirding in New Guinea waters, 1883–84: an episode in the Queensland labour trade'. *J. Pac. Hist.* 3, 85–105.

1970. 'Pacific island labour migrants in Queensland'. *J. Pac. Hist.* 5, 43–64.

Couper, A. D., 1967. *The Island Trade: an analysis of the environment and operation of the seaborne trade among three island groups in the Pacific.* (Ph.D. thesis in Geography, Australian National University, ms.) Canberra.

Crocombe, R. G., 1970. 'Conference report: the politics of Melanesia'. *Pacific Viewpoint* 11, 145–9.

Davidson, J. W., 1966. 'Constitutional changes in Fiji'. *J. Pac. Hist.* 1, 165–8.

1971. 'The Decolonization of Oceania'. *Journal of Pacific History* 6, 133–50.

De Iongh, R. C., 1967. 'West Irian confrontation'. *Sukarno's Guided Indonesia*, ed. T. K. Tan. Brisbane.

Demas, W. G., 1965. *The Economics of Development in Small Countries with Special Reference to the Caribbean.* Montréal.

Derrick, R. A., 1946. *A History of Fiji, I.* Suva (revised edition, 1950).

Deutsch, K. W., 1961. 'Social mobilization and political development'. *Amer. Pol. Sci. Rev.* 40, 493–514.

Dewey, Alice G., 1964. 'The Javanese of Nouméa'. *South Pacific Bulletin* 14, 4–9.

Doumenge, F., 1966. *L'Homme dans le Pacifique Sud.* Publications de la Société des Océanistes. 19. Paris.

Dumont, R., 1966. *False Start in Africa.* New York. (Translation by Phyllis N. Ott of Dumont, R., *L'Afrique Noire est mal partie.* Paris, 1962.)

Eggleston, F. W. (ed.), 1928. *The Australian Mandate for New Guinea: record of a round table discussion.* Melbourne.

Epstein, A. L., 1969. *Matupit: land, politics and change among the Tolai of New Britain.* Canberra.

Epstein, T. Scarlett., 1968. *Capitalism, Primitive and Modern: some aspects of Tolai economic growth.* Canberra.

Faivre, J. P., Poirier, J. & Routhier, P. 1955. *Géographie de la Nouvelle-Calédonie.* Paris.

Fayerweather, J., 1969. *International Business Management: a conceptual framework.* New York.

Finney, B. R. 1970. "Partnership" in developing the New Guinea highlands, 1948–1968'. *J. Pac. Hist.* 5, 117–34.

Fisk, E. K., 1962. 'Planning in a primitive economy: special problems of Papua–New Guinea'. *Economic Record* 38, 462–78.

1964. 'Planning in a primitive economy: from pure subsistence to the production of a market surplus'. *Economic Record* 40, 156–74.

1970. *The Political Economy of Independent Fiji.* Canberra.

Fisk, E. K. & Shand, R. T., 1969. 'The early stages of development in a primitive economy: the evolution from subsistence to trade and specialization'. *Subsistence Agriculture and Economic Development*, ed. C. R. Wharton. Chicago.

France, P., 1969. *The Charter of the Land: custom and colonization in Fiji.* Melbourne.

Frank, A. G., 1967. *Capitalism and Underdevelopment in Latin America: historical studies of Chile and Brazil.* New York.

Furnivall, J. S., 1939. *Netherlands India: a study of plural economy.* London.

1945. 'Some problems of tropical economy'. *Fabian Colonial Essays*, ed. R. Hinden. London.

1948. *Colonial Policy and Practice: a comparative study of Burma and Netherlands India.* London.

Furtado, C., 1964. *Development and Underdevelopment.* Berkeley and Los Angeles. (Translation by R. W. de Aguiar and E. C. Drysdale of Furtado, C., *Desenvolvimento e Subdesenvolvimento.* Rio de Janeiro, 1961.)

Garnier, J., 1867. 'Essai sur la géologie et les ressources minérales de la Nouvelle-Calédonie, avec carte géologique'. *Annales des Mines* 6me série, 12, 1–92.

1876. *La Nouvelle-Calédonie.* Paris.

Geertz, C., 1963. *Agricultural Involution: the process of ecological change in Indonesia.* Berkeley and Los Angeles.

Geslin, Y., 1948. 'La colonisation des Nouvelles-Hébrides'. *Les Cahiers d'Outre-mer* 1, 245–74.

Giles, W. E., ed. D. Scarr, 1968. *A Cruize in a Queensland Labour Vessel to the South Seas.* Canberra.

Gillion, K., 1962. *Fiji's Indian Migrants.* Melbourne.

Gould, P. R., 1964. 'A note on research into the diffusion of development'. *J. Mod. Afr. Stud.* 2, 123–5.

1970. 'Tanzania 1920–63: the spatial impress of the modernization process'. *World Politics* 22, 149–70.

Grattan, C. H., 1963. *The Southwest Pacific to 1900: a modern history.* Ann Arbor.

Groenewegen, K. & van de Kaa, D. J., 1964. *Resultaten van het Demografisch Onderzoek Westelijk Nieuw-Guinea,* Deel I. The Hague.

Guiart, J. 1952. 'The Jon Frum movement in Tanna'. *Oceania* 22, 165–77.

1956. *Un Siècle et Demi des Contacts culturels à Tanna.* Publications de la Société des Océanistes 5. Paris.

1968. 'Le cadre traditionnel et la rébellion de 1878 dans le pays de la Foa'. *J. Soc. des Océanistes* 24, 97–119.

Guiart, J. & Worsley, P., 1958. 'La répartition des mouvements millénaristes en Mélanésie'. *Archives de la Sociologie des Réligions* 5, 38–46.

Haas, A., 1970. 'Independence movements in the south Pacific'. *Pacific Viewpoint* 11, 97–119.

Hailey, Lord, 1943. *Britain and her Dependencies.* London.

Hancock, W. K., 1962. *Smuts: the sanguine years 1870–1919.* Cambridge.

Hasluck, P., 1958. 'Present tasks and policies'. *New Guinea and Australia,* ed. J. Wilkes. Sydney.

Healy, A. M., 1967. 'Bulolo: a history of the development of the Bulolo region, New Guinea'. *New Guinea Research Bulletin* 15.

Hides, J., 1936. *Papua Wonderland.* Edinburgh.

Higgins, B., 1959. *Economic Development: problems, principles and policies.* London (2nd edition, 1968).

Hodder, B. W., 1968. *Economic Development in the Tropics.* London.

Hoselitz, B. F., 1955. 'Patterns of economic growth'. *Can. J. Econ. and Pol. Sci.* 21, 416–31.

Howlett, Diana R., 1967. *A Geography of Papua and New Guinea.* Melbourne.

In press. Terminal development: from tribalism to peasantry. *Changing Geography in the Changing Pacific,* ed. H. C. Brookfield. London (1973).

International Bank for Reconstruction and Development, 1965. *The Economic Development of the Territory of Papua and New Guinea.* Baltimore.

Jacomb, E., 1914. *France and England in the New Hebrides.* Melbourne.

Jarvie, I. C., 1963. 'Theories of cargo cults: a critical analysis'. *Oceania* 34, 1–31; 108–36.

1964. *The Revolution in Anthropology.* London.

Kindleberger, C. P., 1958. *Economic Development.* New York.

Klein, W. C. (ed.), 1953–4. *Nieuw-Guinea: die ontwikkeling op economisch, sociaal en cultureel gebeid in Nederlands en Australisch Nieuw-Guinea.* The Hague (2 vols.).

Kuper, L. & Smith, M. G. (eds.), 1969. *Pluralism in Africa.* Berkeley and L.A.

Lasaqa, I. Q., 1972. 'Melanesians' Choice: a geographical study of Tadhimboko participation in the cash economy, Guadalcanal, British Solomon Islands'. *New Guinea Research Bulletin* 43.

Lawrence, P., 1964. *Road belong Cargo: a study of the cargo movement in the southern Madang District, New Guinea*. Manchester. (Reprinted, with a postscript, 1967, Melbourne.)

Leahy, M. & Crain, M., 1937. *The Land that Time Forgot*. London.

Leaney, Caroline & Lea, D. A. M., 1967. 'Some recent changes in New Hebridean trade'. *Aust. Geogr.* 10, 286–97.

Le Borgne, J., 1964. *Géographie de la Nouvelle-Calédonie et des Iles Loyauté*. Nouméa.

Le Chartier, H., 1885. *La Nouvelle-Calédonie et les Nouvelles-Hébrides*. Paris.

Legge, J. D., 1956. *Australian Colonial Policy*. Sydney.

Lemire, C., 1884. *Voyage à Pied en Nouvelle-Calédonie, et Déscription des Nouvelles-Hébrides*. Paris.

Le Roux, C. C. F. M., 1948–50. *De Bergpapoeas van Nieuw-Guinea en hun Woongebeid*. Leiden (2 vols.).

Levitt, Kari, 1970. *Silent Surrender: the multinational corporation in Canada*. Toronto.

Levitt, Kari & Best, L., 1969. *Externally-propelled Growth and Industrialization in the Caribbean*. Montreal (4 vols., multilithed).

Lewis, G. K., 1968. *The Growth of the Modern West Indies*. London.

Lewis, W. A., Scott, M., Wright, M. & Legum, C., 1951. *Attitude to Africa*. Harmondsworth.

Leyser, C., 1965. 'Title to land in the Trust Territory of New Guinea'. *Yearbook of International Law*, 1, 105–17.

Lijphart, A., 1966. *The Trauma of Decolonization: the Dutch and West New Guinea*. New Haven.

Lindt, J. W., 1893. 'The resources and capabilities of the New Hebrides'. *Trans. Roy. Geog. Soc. Australia*, 10, 32–45.

Lowndes, A. G. (ed.), 1956. *South Pacific Enterprise: the Colonial Sugar Refining Company, Ltd*. Sydney.

Lyng, J., 1919. *Our New Possession: late German New Guinea*. Melbourne.

McArthur, Norma, 1967. *Island Populations of the Pacific*. Canberra.

McArthur, Norma & Yaxley, J. F., 1968. *Condominium of the New Hebrides: A Report on the first Census of Population, 1967*. Sydney.

McCarthy, D., 1959. *Australia in the War of 1939–45: South-west Pacific Area–First Year, Kokoda to Wau*. Canberra.

Mackenzie, S. S., 1927. *The Australians at Rabaul: the capture and administration of the German possessions in the southern Pacific*. Sydney.

Mackinder, H. J., 1907. *Britain and the British Seas*. Oxford.

Maher, R. F., 1958. 'The Tommy Kabu movement of the Purari delta'. *Oceania* 29, 75–90.

1961. *New Men of Papua: a study in culture change*. Madison.

Mair, Lucy, 1948. *Australia in New Guinea*. London.
Maisonneuve, V. F., 1872. *La Nouvelle-Calédonie et les Iles de la Déportation, avec une carte*. Paris.
Marx, K., ed. E. J. Hobsbawm, 1964. *Pre-capitalist Economic Formations*. New York.
Maude, H. E., 1968. *Of Islands and Men: studies in Pacific history*. Melbourne.
Mayer, A. C., 1961. *Peasants in the Pacific: a study of Fiji Indian rural society*. London.
1963. *Indians in Fiji*. London.
Meller, N., 1968. Papers on the Papua–New Guinea House of Assembly. *New Guinea Research Bulletin* 22.
Miller, D. H., 1928. *The Drafting of the Covenant*. New York (2 vols.).
Milner, S., 1957. *The United States Army in World War II, the War in the Pacific: Victory in Papua*. Washington.
Moorehead, A., 1966. *The Fatal Impact: an account of the invasion of the south Pacific 1767–1840*. London.
Morison, S. E., 1950. *History of United States Naval Operations in World War II. V. The Struggle for Guadalcanal, August 1942 – February 1943*. Boston.
Morton, L., 1962. *The United States Army in World War II, the War in the Pacific: Strategy and Command: the first two years*. Washington.
Myint, H., 1964. *The Economics of the Developing Countries*. London.
Myrdal, G., 1957. *Economic Theory and Underdeveloped Regions*. London.
1968. *Asian Drama*. New York (2 vols.).
Naval Intelligence Division, 1943–5. *Geographical Handbook Series: the Pacific Islands*. London (4 vols.).
Nkrumah, K., 1965. *Neo-colonialism: the last stage of imperialism*. London.
Oliver, D. L., 1951. *The Pacific Islands*. Cambridge, Mass. (2nd edition, 1961, New York).
O'Reilly, P., 1953. *Calédoniens: repertoire bio-bibliographique*. Publications de la Société des Océanistes, 3. Paris.
1957. *Hébridais: repertoire bio-bibliographique*. Publications de la Société des Océanistes, 6. Paris.
Panikkar, K. M., 1953. *Asia and Western Dominance: a survey of the Vasco da Gama epoch of Asian history, 1498–1945*. London.
Parker, R. S., 1966. 'The advance to responsible government'. *New Guinea on the Threshold: aspects of social, political and economic development*, ed. E. K. Fisk. Canberra.
Parnaby, O. W., 1956. 'The regulation of indentured labour to Fiji 1864–1888'. *J. Polynesian Soc.* 65, 55–66.
1964. *Britain and the Labor Trade in the Southwest Pacific*. Durham, N.C.
Parsons, T., 1952. *The Social System*. London.
Pelatan, E., 1892. *Les Mines de la Nouvelle-Calédonie: esquisse géologique de la colonie*. Paris.

Pelleray, E., 1922. 'La question des Nouvelles-Hébrides'. *Revue du Pacifique* 1, 56–75.

Pisier, G., 1962. *Esquisse d'un Plan de Développement Economique et Sociale de la la Nouvelle-Calédonie*. Nouméa.

Plotnicov, L. & Tuden, A. (eds.), 1970. *Essays in Comparative Social Stratification*. Pittsburgh.

Polanyi, K., Arensberg, C. M. & Pearson, H. W. (eds.), 1957. *Trade and Market in the Early Empires: economies in history and theory*. Glencoe, Ill.

Preston, T. R. & Willis, M. B., 1970. *Intensive Beef Production*. Oxford.

Redactie, TKNAG, 1940. 'Uitreksel van het algemeen verslag van de Nederlandsch-Indisch-Amerikansche expeditie naar Nieuw-Guinea'. *Tijd. Kon. Ned. Aardr. Gen.* 57, 233–48, 404–23.

Riddell, J. B., 1970. *The Spatial Dynamics of Modernization in Sierra Leone*. Evanston.

Rivers, W. H.R. (ed.), 1922. *Essays on the Depopulation of Melanesia*. Cambridge.

Rivière, H., 1881. *Souvenirs de la Nouvelle-Calédonie: l'insurrection Canaque*. Paris.

Robequain, C., 1954. *Malaya, Indonesia, Borneo and the Philippines*. London. (Translation by E. D. Laborde of *Le Monde Malais*, Paris, 1946.)

Roberts, S. H., 1927. *Population Problems of the Pacific*. London.

Robertson, C. J., 1931. 'The Fiji sugar industry'. *Econ. Geog.* 17, 400–11.

Robinson, R. & Gallagher, J. with Denny, Alice, 1961. *Africa and the Victorians: the climax of imperialism*. London.

Rocheteau, G., 1966. *Le Nord de la Nouvelle-Calédonie: région économique*. Nouméa.

Rostow, W. W., 1960. *The Stages of Economic Growth*. Cambridge.

Rowley, C. D., 1958. *The Australians in German New Guinea 1914–21*. Melbourne.

1965. *The New Guinea Villager: a retrospect from 1964*. Melbourne.

Rubin, Vera (ed.), 1960. 'Social and cultural pluralism in the Caribbean'. *Annals N.Y. Acad. Sci.* 83, Art. 5.

Sack, P. G., 1969. 'Early land acquisitions in New Guinea – the Native version'. *J. Papua–New Guinea Soc.* 3, 7–16.

1971. 'Land law and policy in German New Guinea'. *Austr. External Territories* 11, 7–19.

Sahlins, M. D., 1962. *Moala: culture and nature on a Fijian island*. Ann Arbor.

In press. 'The intensity of domestic production in primitive societies: social inflections of the Chayanov slope'.

Salisbury, R. F., 1970. *Vunamami: economic transformation in a traditional society*. Berkeley and Los Angeles.

Sautot, H., 1949. *Grandeur et Décadence du Gaullisme dans le Pacifique*. Melbourne.

Scarr, D., 1967a. *Fragments of Empire: a history of the Western Pacific High Commission 1877–1914*. Canberra.

1967b. 'Recruits and recruiters: a portrait of the Pacific islands labour trade'. *J. Pac. Hist.* 2, 5–24.

Schwartz, T., 1962. 'The Paliau movement in the Admiralty islands, 1946–1954'. *Anthrop. Papers Amer. Mus. Nat. Hist.* 49, 211–421.

Service des Affaires Economiques, 1957. *L'Economie de la Nouvelle-Calédonie en 1956*. Nouméa.
1969. *Notes sur l'Economie de la Nouvelle-Calédonie 1967*. Nouméa.
Shephard, C. Y., 1945. *The Sugar Industry of Fiji*. London.
Shineberg, Dorothy, 1966. 'The sandalwood trade in Melanesian economics 1841–65'. *J. Pac. Hist.* 1, 129–46.
1968. *They came for Sandalwood: a study of the sandalwood trade in the south-west Pacific 1830–1865*. Melbourne.
Smith, M. G., 1965. *The Plural Society of the British West Indies*. Cambridge.
Soja, E. W., 1968. *The Geography of Modernization in Kenya: a spatial analysis of social, economic and political change*. Syracuse, N.Y.
1970. 'The geography of modernization: some comments on the relevance to Latin America of recent research in Africa'. *National Conference of Latin Americanist Geographers*, ed. A. D. Bushong. Munice, Indiana.
Souter, G., 1964. *New Guinea: the last unknown*. Sydney.
Spate, O. H. K., 1959. 'The Fijian people: economic problems and prospects'. *Legislative Council of Fiji, Council Paper 13*. Suva.
1966. 'Education and its problems'. *New Guinea on the Threshold: aspects of social, political and economic development*, ed. E. K. Fisk. Canberra.
Stanner, W. E. H., 1953. *The South Seas in Transition*. Sydney.
Théry, R., 1931. 'La crise neo-Hébridaise'. *Revue du Pacifique* 10, 181–6.
United Nations Development Programme, 1968. *A Design for the Development of West Irian: Report prepared for the Government of Indonesia*. New York.
Van der Veur, P. W., 1966. *Search for New Guinea's Boundaries: from Torres Strait to the Pacific*. Canberra.
Waigani Seminars, 1967. 'New Guinea people in business and industry: papers from the first Waigani seminar'. *New Guinea Research Bulletin* 20.
1969. *The History of Melanesia: papers delivered at a seminar...held at Port Moresby from 30 May to 5 June 1968*. Port Moresby and Canberra.
1970a. 'The indigenous role in business enterprise: three papers from the third Waigani seminar, 1969'. *New Guinea Research Bulletin* 35.
1970b. *The Politics of Melanesia: papers delivered at the fourth Waigani seminar held at Port Moresby from 9–15 May 1970*. Canberra.
1971. 'Change and development in rural Melanesia'. Ms.
Ward, J. M., 1948. *British Policy in the South Pacific (1786–1893): a study in British policy toward the south Pacific islands prior to the establishment of governments by the great powers*. Sydney.
Ward, R. G., 1965. *Land Use and Population in Fiji*. London.
1969. 'Land use and land alienation in Fiji to 1885'. *J. Pac. Hist.* 4, 3–25.
Watters, R. F., 1963. 'Sugar production and culture change in Fiji'. *J. Polynesian Soc.* 4, 25–52.
1969. *Koro: Economic Development and Social Change in Fiji*. Oxford.
1970. 'The economic response of south Pacific societies'. *Pacific Viewpoint* 11, 120–44.

Wawn, W. T., 1893. *The South Sea Islander and the Queensland Labour Trade 1875–1891*. London.

Wilkes, J. (ed.), 1958. *New Guinea and Australia*. Sydney.

Wilson, C., 1954. *The History of Unilever: a study in economic growth and social change*. London (2 vols.).

Wilson, J. S. G., 1966. *Economic Survey of the New Hebrides*. London.

Wong, Judy A., 1963. *The Distribution and Role of the Chinese in Fiji*. M.A. thesis in Geography, University of Sydney.

Worsley, P., 1957. *The Trumpet shall Sound: a study of 'cargo' cults in Melanesia*. London.

INDEX

agriculture, 22
  concessions, 34
  pastoral, 37
  indigenous, 37
  settlements, 49
  European, 49
  Solomon Islands, 73
  Extension Service, 100
  investment, 130
Allan, C. H., 177
Andrews, C. F., 64
anti-colonialism, 63
Archbold, R., 87
Asians, 33, 49, 53, 64, 149–52; *see also* Fiji, Indians, New Caledonia
Australia, 23, 27, 43, 60–1, 66–9, 190
  Sydney as focus of S.W. Pacific, 20, 66–8
  New South Wales, 22
  Chinese miners, 27
  Queensland, 32
  'Kanaka' labour, 32
  as colonial power, 64
  Navigation Act, 67–8
  shipping, 68
  World War II, 90–1
Australian New Guinea, *also* Territory of Papua and New Guinea, Papua New Guinea, xv, 1, 39, 60–1, 98–109, 112, 144, 192–6
  as pace-setter in policy, 98
  rehabilitation after World War II, 98
  establishment of control, 100
  restructuring of Government, 100–1, 112, 116–17
  exports, 106
  imports, 106
  gradualism, 98–109
  administrative system, 112–13
  local government, revenue, 115–16
  effect of West Irian changes, 117
  House of Assembly, 118
  Pidgin, 118
  border with West Irian, 124–5
  Bougainville copper, 125, 132
  New Britain, 126
  Oil, gas, 131
  air transport, 133
  tourism, 134
  Chimbu, 163
  land politics, 171
  'stomach' politics, 173
  education, 192–4
  independence, 198–9
  'balkanisation', 198
  army, 200

Baker, J. R., 29
Baldwin, R. E., 7
banks, 14, 81, 128–9, 132, 138, 187
  Rothschild, 38, 81
  Banque de l'Indo-Chine, 40, 66, 69–71, 81
  Australian, 68
  trading, 128–9
Barateau, G., 76
Belshaw, C. S., 177
Benedict, B., 157
Benoit, F., 29
Bernard, A., 29
Best, L., 19
Bettison, D. G., 126, 177
Biskup, P., 47, 56
Boeke, J. H., 6, 7
Bolton, C. G., 47
Boorstein, E., 183
Brathwaite, E., 160
Bridon, E., 29
Britain, 21, 42–3, 60–2, 65, 83, 157, 189
  rule in Fiji, 42
  sphere of influence, 43
  transfer of New Guinea, 60
Brookfield, H. C., ix, 8, 19, 23, 47, 52, 87, 105, 109, 145, 158, 177, 206
Brown, Paula, 161, 177
Brunet, A., 40
Bulletin du Commerce, 109
Burns, A., 109, 158
Burns, James, *see* Burns, Philp
Burns, Philp (Company), 40, 74
  shipping services, 41, 56
  Sydney base, 66
  operations, extent of, 66
Burridge, K. O. L., 177
Burton, J. W., 47, 57, 60, 64

Index

Caillard, E., 76
Campbell, P. A., 36
capital *also* investment, 8, 12, 16, 38–42, 48, 50, 66, 70–2, 75, 98, 127–44, 179–84
  investment: in forestry, 130, 179; in mining, 131, 179; in oil search, 131; in tourism, 134, 179; in manufacturing, 136
  Melanesian investment in Australia, 138
  need for foreign investment, 179
  'aid', 187
capitalism, 7–9, 14, 62, 106–7, 181
cargo cults, 160–4, 169, 175–6
  Jon Frum, 162
Carpenter, W. R. (Company), 67–8
Chayanov, A., 10, 12
China, Chinese, 184, 189–90
  miners, 27
  labour, 33, 52
  competition for, 58
  manufacturing, 136
  traders, 151–2
Chinnery, E. W. P., 87
Cochrane, G., 177
cocoa, 52, 71, 77, 103; *see also* Solomon Islands
coconuts, *also* coconut oil, copra, 26, 40–1, 48, 50–3, 61, 70–1, 74, 77
  uneconomic spread, 51
  crop combinations, 53
  price fluctuation, 53, 77
  Unilever, 78
  see also Fiji, Solomon Islands
coffee, 49, 71, 74, 77, 100, 168; *see also* New Caledonia, New Guinea, West Irian
Colijn, A. H., 87
Colonial Sugar Refining Company (CSR), 66, 79–80, 142–3, 157
  Reports, 35
  in Fiji, 35, 38, 48, 55, 79, 157
  mills, 48, 143
  transport network, 55, 79
  Sydney base, 66
  and peasant producers, 79
  and tenant farms, 79
colonialism, 1–19, 31, 62–4, 82, 111–44, 152, 178–90, 202–5
  definition, 1
  structure, 4–5
  colonial companies, 5, 14; *see also* companies
  centralized control, 13
  multi-national process, 14
  sequence, 18
  anti-slavery, 31
  loans and subsidies, 82
  non-exploitive, 82
  completion of penetration, 87
  doctrine of uniform developmen, 99
  post-war policy, 105–6
  end of gradualism, 108
  comparison of administrative systems, 111
  commercial system, 127, 139–41, 150, 170, 175
  post-colonial issues, 176, 186
  economic colonialism, 176
  and the Third World, 178–90
  nationalization, 181–3
  interventionism, 187–90
colonization, 20–1, 30
  stages, 30
  expansion, 62
Commission on Higher Education in Papua and New Guinea, 201
companies, colonial, 5, 13–14, 38, 40, 43, 49, 55, 65–75, 78, 127, 137–8, 175, 179–81, 187–8
  mining corporations, 28, 131
  French, 66, 69–71
  shipping, 67–8, 75
  air, 68
  oil, 75
  shares, 138
  foreign interests, 142, 179
  political pressure, 187
communism, 63
contract workers, 5, 48, 51, 60, 69, 95, 149–50, 164
convicts, *see* penal colony
copper, *see* Bougainville, New Caledonia, New Guinea
copra, *see* coconuts
Cordeil, P., 29, 34, 39
Corlette, E. A. C., 24
Corris, P., 47
cotton, 26–7, 70–1; *see also* Fiji, New Hebrides
Couper, A. D., 45, 57, 76
credit, commercial, 16, 78–9; *see also* peasant
Crocombe, R. G., 198
currencies, xv, 83, 128
  collapse of, 83
  linkage with colonial currencies, 128

Davidson, J. W., 28, 119, 126
decolonization, 4, 121, 124, 176
De Iongh, R. C., 109
Demas, W. G., 140, 145
Derrick, R. A., 29, 47
Detzner, M., 84
Deutsch, K. W., 202
Deutsche Handels- und Plantagen-Gesellschaft der Sudsee Inseln (Company), 38
development, 10, 138–41, 164, 203
  uneven, 12
  uniform, 99
  growth indices, 138–9
  residentiary *v.* expatriate, 139

Index

Dewey, Alice G., 150, 158
disease, human, 20, 23–5, 86, 99
  malaria, 30, 86
  deficiency, 94
  precautions, 99
Doumenge, F., 25, 28–9, 47, 87, 109, 158
dualism, dual economy, 6–9, 16–18, 185
Dumont, R., 176

economy, 6–19, 51, 138–41, 180, 203
  mixed, 17
  equity principle, 107, 140
  dependent, 127
  'satellite' economies, 128, 142
  'closed' economies, 129
  local entrepreneurs, 136
  'enclave', 138
  national, 138–41, 170, 175, 180; nationalism, 174–6
  lack of integration, 139–42
  small, 141–4, 180
  balance of payments, 144
  European-run, 149
  motivation, Melanesian, 165, 180
  risk, minimization, 167
  economic protest, 169–70
  perception of inequality, 175
  gradualism, 180–1
  open, 204–5
education, 192–4, 197
Eggleston, F. W., 76
Epstein, A. L., 56, 177
Epstein, T. S., 56
Europeans, 148–9, 153–4, 175
exchange rates, xv, 83
exports, 48, 104–5, 141
  per capita, 104
  see also Australian New Guinea, Fiji, New Caledonia

Faivre, J. P., 87, 212
Fayerweather, J., 180
Fiji *also* Colony of, Dominion of, xi, xv, 1, 22–3, 110–14, 142–4, 193–4
  Vanua Levu, 21
  Viti Levu, 22, 35, 45, 83
  population, 24, 80, 103
  cotton, 26
  land alienation, 26
  Moala, 26
  plantations, 26, 51
  mining, 28, 83
  island labour, 31
  Indian labour, 34–5, 60
  sugar, 35, 48, 142–3; *see also* CSR
  land commission, 36
  British rule, 42, 157
  Bau, 44
  exports, 48
  Lautoka, 48
  Indian canefarmers, 48
  bananas, 48, 103
  copra, 48
  Fijian Regulations, 54, 103–4
  local government, 54, 114, 116
  ports, 54
  Suva, 54–5, 137, 141
  Levuka, 54
  roads, 55
  traders, 65
  trade through Australia, 67
  Fijians *v.* Indians, 72, 153
  education, 72, 193–4
  peasant production of sugar, 79
  tenant farms, 79
  gold, 83, 103
  independence, 104, 196
  administrative system, 112–13, 116
  constitutional change, 118–19
  air transport, 133–4
  tourism, 134
  manufacturing, 136–7
  distribution of national income, 139
  political parties, 156
Finney, B. R., 175
Fisk, E. K., 11, 109, 139, 145
forces, armed, police, 93, 200–1
  legacy of armies, 95–7
France, French interests, xv, 32, 65, 69–71, 81–2, 88–9, 155, 189
  Anglo-Australian rivalry, 70
  fall of, 88
France, P., 29, 47, 177
Frank, A. G., 8, 145, 176, 203
Furnivall, J. S., 6, 157
Furtado, C., 19, 145, 182

Garnier, J., 29
Geertz, C., 8
Germany, 61–2, 65
  sphere of influence, 43
  administration, 56
  German plantations, 61–2
  elimination of, 67
German New Guinea, *see* New Guinea, trust territory
Geslin, Y., 76
Giles, W. E., 32
Gillion, K., 35, 47, 57, 64
Godeffroy und Sohn (Company), 26, 38
gold, 28, 83–4, 98; *see also* Fiji, New Guinea, Papua
Gould, P. R., 205

Index

government
  white man's, 42–4
  local, 54, 114
  rôle, 55
  intervention in economy, 81–2
  public works, 81
  establishment of control, 100
  structure in New Guinea, 101
  maximisation of welfare, 106
  taxation, 107
  constitutional change, 117
Gratton, C. H., 47, 64, 76
Groenewegen, K., 76, 109
gross national product, 15, 139
Guiart, J., 47, 177

Haas, A., 126
Hailey, Lord, 82, 99
Hancock, W. K., 64
Hasluck, P., 98–101, 108
  policy of uniform development, 99
Hawaii, 21, 27
Healy, A. M., 29, 87
Hides, J., 87
Higgins, B., 7–8, 11, 19
Hodder, B. W., 206
Hoselitz, B. F., 127
Howlett, Diana R., 109, 203
Hughes, I. M., 85

independence, *also* self-government, 1, 18, 142, 144, 182–3, 192, 197–200, 205
  definition, 2
  objective, 96
  delay, 99–100, 172
  Fiji, 104, 119, 157, 174, 196
  West Irian, 110
  Nauru, 110
  New Hebrides, 121
  dependent economies, 127, 142
  pro-colonialism, 172
  reluctance, 174
  black nationalism, 178
  Guyana, Cuba, 182–3
  indigenous élites, 185–7
  national armies, 186–7
  interventionism, 187–90
Indians, Indo-Fijians, 34–5, 41, 48, 60, 72, 79, 139, 149–50; *see also* Asians, Fiji
Indonesia, Republic of, *also* Nederlands Indië, 1, 15, 20, 60, 63, 124, 144, 172, 190, 193
  Dutch government system, 101
  education, 193
industry, 136–7
International Bank for Reconstruction and Development, 109
interventionism, 187–90

invading system, 12, 18, 22, 166
investment, *see* capital

Jacomb, E., 44
Japan, 27, 64, 68, 88, 90–3, 96, 189–90
  occupation of New Guinea, 61, 85
  World War II, 90–6
  investment, 130–1, 137
  bauxite mine, 132
Jarvie, I. C., 177
Journal of Pacific History, 28, 126
Journal of the Polynesian Society, 28

Kindleberger, C. P., 140
Klein, W. C., 29, 57, 76
Kuper, L., 157

labour, 8, 31–5, 50–2, 165, 203
  scarcity, 8, 52, 100
  specialization, 23
  division between sexes, 23
  recruitment, 25, 31–2
  contract workers, 31–2, 35, 48, 51, 60, 70–1, 95
  for Australia, 32
  island, 32–3
  white, 32; policy, 53
  convict, 33
  Chinese, 33
  Japanese, 33
  Vietnamese, Tonkinese, 33, 49, 69–71, 95, 151
  Javanese, 33, 69–70, 95, 150
  Asian, 33, 48, 53, 64
  residentiary Melanesian, 33, 50
  Indian, 35, 41, 48
  control, 54
  Australian, 66
  New Hebrides, 69–70
  New Caledonia, 69–70
  West Irian, 75
  Fijian, 80, 170
  Highland Labour Scheme, 99
  protest, 170
  political issue, 171
land, 9, 23, 45, 164–7, 170–1
  property, 9
  poverty, 23
  borrowing, 23
  'vacant', 24, 37
  alienation, 26, 36–7, 40, 44, 51, 53, 171
  demand for, 31
  low-cost, 36
  Fiji commision, 36
  'waste' land, 37, 40, 53
  lease hold, 38, 53
  method of acquisition, 39

land (*cont*).
  loss, 45
  leased to Indians, 48
  New Hebrides, 69–70, 171
  tenure in Fiji, 79
  speculation, 135
  supply, 165–6
  social rôle, 166–7
  protest, 170–1
  Mataungan Association (Tolai), 170–1
language, 152, 194–6
Lasaqa, I. Q., 37, 41, 47, 57, 109, 158
Lawrence, P., 47, 56, 161, 177
Leahy, M., 87
Leaney, Caroline, 76
Le Borgne, J., 87
Le Chartier, H., 29
Legge, J. D., 109
Lemire, C., 32–3, 39
Le Roux, C. C. F. M., 87
Levers Pacific Plantations (Company), 41, 73, 103
Levitt, Kari, 19, 145, 203
Lewis, G. K., 145, 191
Lewis, W. A., ix
Leyser, C., 37
libérés *also* ex-convicts, 33, 39
Lijphart, A., 109
Lindt, J. W., 36
L'Océanie Française, 76
Lowndes, A. G., 47, 57, 87
Lyng, J., 56

McArthur, Norma, 24, 29
McCarthy, D., 97
Mackenzie, S. S., 56, 61, 64
Mackinder, H. J., 58
Maher, R. F., 177
Mair, Lucy, 97
Maisonneuve, V. F., 47
mandates, 63, 67
manufacturing, 136–8
Marx, K., 9
Maude, H. E., 28
Mayer, A. C., 47, 149, 158
Melanesia, xi, xv, 1, 4, 6, 20–1, 30, 44, 46, 48
  atomisation, 22, 198
  agriculture, 22
  population, 24–5
  geology, mining, 27–8
  colonization, 30
  land resources, 37
  economic set-back, 64
Meller, N., 173
mercantilism, 18, 65–75
Micronesia, 61–3
migrant workers, 25, 99; *see also* labour
Miller, D. H., 63–4
Milner, S., 97
miners, mining, 27–8, 49–50, 131–2
  investment, 131, 179
missionaries, 5, 26, 40, 65, 74, 87, 161, 192
  Australian Presbyterian Mission, 40, 69, 162
Moorehead, A., 23
Morison, S. E., 97
Morton, L., 97
Myint, H., 8, 19
Myrdal, G., 19, 202

nationalization, 17, 181–3
Naval Intelligence Division, 28, 87
networks, 4, 6, 55, 66, 95, 106, 136
  social, 166
Neu-Guinea Compagnie (Company), 39
New Caledonia *also* La Nouvelle-Calédonie et Dépendances, xi, xv, 1, 21, 42, 112, 144
  nickel industry, 1, 27, 49, 82, 88, 95, 122, 131–2, 179
  sandalwood, 21
  nineteenth-century population, 24
  land alienation, 26
  plantations, 27, 65
  coconuts, 27
  penal colony, 27, 32
  mining, minerals, 27–8, 32, 49–50, 104
  cattle, 27, 49, 104
  labour, 31–3
  naval station, 32
  Asians, 33, 95, 104; *see also* labour, Javanese, Vietnamese, Tonkinese
  agriculture, 37, 104
  Loyalty Islands, 40, 122
  rebellions, 45–6, 49
  Nouméa, 45, 49, 54, 104, 111, 115, 121, 123, 137
  exports, 48
  coffee, 49, 52, 104
  communes, 54
  local government, 54, 115
  ports, 54
  roads, 55
  traders, 65
  missionaries, 65
  relations with France, 88–9
  World War II, 88–96
  Australia, 89
  Government intervention, 104
  'le désert Calédonien', 105
  administrative system, 111–12, 116
  constitutional change, 117–22
  South Pacific Commission, 123–4
  tourism, 134
  education, 193
New Guinea, whole island, 20, 22

Index

New Guinea, trust territory, *also* German New Guinea, xi, xv, 72, 112
  population, 24
  mining, gold, 28, 83, 86
  Lae, 28, 127
  Bulolo, 28
  Bougainville, 28, 43, 84, 125, 132, 171, 199; and the Solomons, 125
  plantations, 31, 52
  Bismarck Archipelago, 31
  labour recruitment, 31, 53, 86
  Rabaul, New Britain, 43, 54–6, 61, 91, 126, 171
  Madang, 52, 54
  rubber, 52
  crop research, 52
  Tolai people, 54, 93
  local government, 54
  Kokopo, 54
  ports, 54
  roads, 55
  German surrender, 61
  traders, 65
  missionaries, 65
  strikes, 83
  copper, 84, 125, 132
  discovery of highland population, 84, 86
  Chimbu-Wahgi area, 84–5, 163, 168
  'uncontrolled areas', 85
  Sepik, 86, 91
  Japanese, 86
  World War II, 90–7
  ANGAU, 94
  agricultural Extension Service, 100
  constitutional change, 117
  manufacturing, 137
  coffee, 163, 168
New Hebrides *also* Anglo-French Condominium, xi, xv, 1, 21, 43–4, 112, 144
  population, 24
  Malekula, 24, 70
  Efaté, 27, 40
  labour, 31, 69–70
  Santo, 40, 95, 171
  plantations, 51–2, 70
  local government, 54, 116
  Vila, 54, 114, 154
  land claims, 69, 171
  employment, 69
  cotton, 70
  World War II, 89–96
  administrative system, 112–14, 120–1
  air transport, 133
  tourism, 134
  land speculation, 135
  Tanna cargo cult, 162
  S.F.N.H., 171
nickel, *see* New Caledonia
Nkrumah, K., 176

oil, 75, 131
Oliver, D. L., 97
O'Reilly, P., 40, 47, 76

Pacific, general, 20–1, 31
Pacific Islands Company, 40–1
Pacific Islands Monthly, 76, 97, 126, 149, 191, 201
Pannikar, K. M., 191
Papua, xv, 42, 51
  Port Moresby, 28, 43, 54, 137, 154
  mining, gold, 28, 50
  labour, 31, 98–9
  plantations, 51–2
  local government, 54
  ports, 54
  Samarai, 54
  shipping, 67
  copra, 67
  rubber, 67, 98
  trade, through Australia, 67
  wages, 73
  border with Queensland, 125
  oil, gas, 131
  see also Australian New Guinea
Parker, R. S., 126
Parnaby, O. W., 31, 46
Parsons, T., 157
peasant society
  motivation, 10
  risk taking, 10
  supply of effort, 11
  reciprocal relationships, 15–16
  credit, 16–17
  peasant-producers, 79
Pelatan, E., 29
Pelleray, E., 69
penal colony
  Sydney, N.S.W., 20, 22
  New Caledonia, 27, 32, 55
Pisier, G., 109
plantations, planters, 26–7, 31, 37–42, 50–1, 65, 67, 74, 77, 80, 105
  labour, 31, 50, 69, 100
  sugar, Fiji, 48, 80
  bananas, 48
  coconuts, copra, 50–1, 61, 77, 130
  rubber, 51, 77
  diversification, 52
  German, 61
  chartered shipping, 67
  aid from government, 81
  World War II, 84–5
  rehabilitation, 98

plantations (*cont*).
coffee, 100, 130
highland, 100
v. indigenous interests, 105
benefit/cost ratio, 130
investment, 179
'pure plantation model', 203
pluralism, plural society, 6–7, 146–57, 185
immigrants, 155
Polanyi, K., 15
politics, 65, 155–7
rôle of companies, 39
universal suffrage, 155
parties, 155–6, 176
and land, 171
'stomach' politics, 172–3
apathy, 176
integration, 176
Polynesia, 20, 23, 31
population,
explosion, 8
decline, 24–5
over-, 25
Fiji, 80
Melanesia, 93, 146
stratification, 146, 148
European, 148
immigrants, 155
ports, 4, 54, 93
Preston, T. R., 183

radio, 195–6
reef products, 21
residentiary system, 1–19, 22–3, 72, 203
structure, 4
new populations, 5–6
economy, 17, 139–41
labour, 50
reciprocity, 166
Riddell, J. B., 202, 204–5
Rivers, W. H. R., 29
Rivière, H., 45, 47
Robequain, C., 19
Roberts, S. H., 29
Robertson, C. J., 87
Robinson, R., 65
Rocheteau, G., 87
Rostow, W. W., 138
Rowley, C. D., 29, 56, 58, 109
rubber, 51, 77, 98

Sack, P. G., 47, 56
Sahlins, M. D., 10, 12, 26
Salisbury, R. F., 56
Samoa, 61, 68
Apia, 26
sandalwood, 20–1, 27, 44, 66
Sautot, H., 97
satisficers, 7, 9, 12
Scarr, D., 31, 39–41, 47, 57
Schumpeter, 12
Schwartz, T., 177
SFNH, Société Française des Nouvelles-Hébrides (Company), 69–71
Shephard, C. Y., 87
shipping, 40–1, 51, 54–5, 66–8, 75, 199
gunboat government, 43
German, 43, 68
Sydney-based, 66
Panama Canal, 66, 68
Messageries Maritimes, 67
Australian, 67–8
freight rates, 68
Australian Navigation Act, 67–8
Japanese, 68
war-time, 88
local, 136
Shineberg, Dorothy, 21, 29, 44
slaves, 5, 20, 31
SLN, Société le Nickel (Company), 38, 49, 55, 81–2, 131, 137, 155
Smith, M. G., 147, 157
Soja, E. W., 202, 205–6
Solomon Islands, *also* British Solomon Islands Protectorate, xi, xv, 1, 42–3, 112, 144
mining, 28, 84, 125, 132
labour, 31–2, 53
Guadalcanal, 36, 84, 90–1, 103, 171
land purchase, 36, 40
Santa Cruz islands, 43
plantations, 51
coconuts, 52, 73
Tulagi, 73, 90–1
economic development, 73, 120
wages, 73
Malaita, 74, 103
World War II, 90–6
U.S. attitude, 94
Honiara, 95, 103, 113
post-war economy, 102–3
cocoa scheme, 103
New Georgia, 103
self-help, 103
administrative system, 112–13, 120
High Commission, 113
local government, 116
Governing Council, 120
Bougainville, 125
land control, 171
education, 193
Souter, G., 29
South Pacific Commission, 102, 123–4
Soviet Union, 189–90
Spate, O. H. K., 109, 158, 201

Stanner, W. E. H., 87, 97, 109, 177
sugar, 35, 48
  milling, 48
  peasant producers, 79
  prices, 80
  cutting gangs, 80
  Imperial Preference, 81
  see also Fiji
Sydney Morning Herald, 37, 46–7

tax, 130, 137
Théry, R., 76
Third World, 2–4, 97, 178–90
Tonga, 26
tourism, 132–5, 179; *see also* transport, air
towns, 153–4
  growth of, 55
  destruction of, 95
  see also under territories
traders, trade goods, 20–1, 26–7, 31, 42, 44, 65–6, 74
  labour, 31
transport, 48, 51, 179
  facilities, 55
  roads, 55
  shipping, 66–8
  air, 68, 132–4
  CSR rail, 79
  investment in, 179

underdevelopment, 7
United Nations Development Programme, 109, 201
United States, 188–90
  colonial expansion, 62
  World War II, 90–4
  troops, 93

Van der Veur, P. W., 47, 126
villages, 22, 75, 153

wages, 35, 52, 69, 71, 73, 103, 121; *see also* labour
Waigani Seminars, 29, 46–7, 56–7, 97, 109, 124–6, 177, 201
Ward, E. W., 105
Ward, J. M., 28, 31, 46–7
Ward, R. G., 47, 57, 87
Watters, R. F., 87, 153, 158, 206
Wawn, W. T., 31, 46
Western Pacific High Commission, 42–3, 54
West Indies, 15, 24
West Irian, *also* Nederlands Nieuw Guinea, Papua Barat; West New Guinea, xv, 1, 20, 22, 42, 74, 101–2, 144, 196
  Act of Free Choice, 1, 110, 117
  Baliem, 22, 85
  subdistricts, 74
  exploration, 74, 84
  economic development, 74–5, 102
  missionaries, 74
  coffee, 74
  coconuts, 74
  Geelvink Bay, 74
  plantations, 74
  Merauke, 75
  Manokwari, 75
  Hollandia, 75, 91, 95
  oil, Shell Co., 75, 131
  Javanese labour, 75
  Vogelkop peninsula, 75, 172, 175
  World War II, 88
  Dutch colonial system, 101–2, 108
  Indonesian control, 102
  United Nations mission, 102, 117
  Nieuw-Guinea Raad, 108, 117
  administrative system, 112–13
  constitutional changes, 117
  refugees, 124
  border, 124
  Ertsberg copper, 132
  migrants, 153
  revolt, 175
Wilkes, J., 109
Wilson, C., 41–2, 47
Wilson, J. S. G., 109
Wong, Judy A., 147, 158
World War II, 4, 18, 71, 88–97, 189–90
Worsley, P., 177